HOLLYWOOD
PEOPLE

Douglas Thompson is a biographer and international journalist who was based in Los Angeles for twenty years. He has interviewed most of the world's best-known film and television stars, and is a regular contributor to major newspapers and magazines world-wide. His biographies include *Like a Virgin: Madonna Revealed*, *Clint Eastwood: Sexual Cowboy*, *Pfeiffer: Beyond the Age of Innocence*, and *Sharon Stone: Basic Ambition*. He lives with his wife and daughter in an English farmhouse near Cambridge when not 'commuting' to California.

Based on the series of programmes *Hollywood Women*, *Hollywood Kids* and *Hollywood Men*, produced by September Films for Carlton Television Ltd.

DOUGLAS THOMPSON

HOLLYWOOD PEOPLE

A no-holds-barred look at the seductive dream and brutal reality that is HOLLYWOOD

PAN BOOKS

First published 1995 by Pan Books
an imprint of Macmillan General Books
25 Eccleston Place London SW1W 9NF
and Basingstoke

Associated companies throughout the world

ISBN 0 330 34393 9

1 3 5 7 9 8 6 4 2

A CIP catalogue record for this book is available from
the British Library

Typeset by CentraCet Limited, Cambridge
Printed and bound in Great Britain

CONTENTS

HOORAY FOR HOLLYWOOD?
Chapter 1

'Hollywood is a town that has to be seen
to be disbelieved.'
Legendary American newspaper columnist Walter Winchell

Hollywood is where almost everyone wants to be a *star*
and will do *anything* – from sex to criminal acts and
sometimes both – to achieve it. It's a town of fantasies
and tragedies where fame and fortune compete with status
and power for the absolute deity.

For more than a century Hollywood People have
soared to the dizzy heights of international acclaim. And
have suffered heartbreak and horror resulting in despair,
divorce and death in frantic efforts to be a member of the
Tinseltown élite. Those drawn by the magnet of Hollywood either overcome or overdose on life in the fastest
lane of all.

Until now the ups and downs of rollercoaster Hollywood have only been imagined. Using the unique access
of the television series on which it is based and sensational
new material, *Hollywood People* lifts the lid off the town.
You will find out how Hollywood People live, what they
really think – about their bizarre lusts, addictions and
painful loneliness, about leading men and ladies, house-

hold names, who pay for sex, about the drive for power and control. About the dark secrets and dangerous liaisons in the bedrooms and boardrooms from the Hollywood Hills to Beverly Hills to surf-lapped Malibu.

For Hollywood People show*business* means billions of dollars every year. They recognize no limits. Toddlers fight for acting roles and at the age of 100, George Burns was still at work, still clinging to the spotlight. And the money.

Hollywood is an eclectic mix of people. Clint Eastwood has kept control, River Phoenix lost it and died. Winona Ryder fights for serious fame while Sharon Stone emerges as the new Monroe. Brad Pitt chases the heels of Redford and Newman, Madonna sits alone atop the Hollywood Hills, Arnold Schwarzenegger (despite a recent paternity suit) plays happy families at the beach while Tom Cruise and John Travolta rely on the Scientology cult to help them stay 'focused'. This book is about everyone from the pornographically wealthy to the dysfunctional, from the boys and girls turning tricks on Sunset Strip to pay for drugs or acting lessons, to the society queens and, of course, the biggest names at the movies on and behind the screen.

Hollywood People are everywhere: today, movies are made worldwide. The stars fly from London to Lisbon and Malibu to Milan, Scotland and Ireland are important locations for high-profile films like Liam Neeson's *Rob Roy* and Mel Gibson's *Braveheart*. But the deals are made or destroyed along with lives and careers in Hollywood itself. You *have* to be there to be a real player. And, in some cases, to believe you are a real person. Hollywood can be good, bad – and ugly.

In the past the studios set the rules. Clark Gable and Loretta Young were forced to hide their love child because discovery of their illicit affair would have ruined their careers; their baby didn't know who she really was until she was thirty-one. Today a Hollywood Couple, like Don Johnson and Melanie Griffith, can admit to drug and alcohol abuse, children out of wedlock, and be regarded as politically correct.

As an environment, Hollywood works and evolves differently for everyone who is born or makes their way there.

British doctor's daughter Jacqueline Bisset made it work for her: 'Hollywood's been really good for me in many ways. I don't think I'm understood here but I just sort of treat it like a place. I don't think you have to be caught up in anything. I didn't have the grains of what Hollywood was in me, so there was nothing to really build on. It was not one of my aspirations. It was not the cinema, American cinema – I didn't know the American cinema. I came here for a contract back in 1966 and didn't have any understanding or any knowledge about America. I was on the defensive when I came and determined not to be changed or to do anything that would be part of the image of Hollywood. You don't see as much "Hollywood behaviour" as there used to be – people living up to an image. People call it showbusiness. I feel it's a sort of a soul business. People who have instincts to become actors usually feel something inside. Some are motivated by money and fame but many are also motivated by the desire to show the emotions, the feelings, the love in themselves, whatever. They want to be part of a larger consciousness, I believe.'

Where there are stars there are also wheelers and dealers. Elaine Young, the former wife of the late, and often petulant, film star Gig Young: 'I love California. Not only because I was born here. I love the climate. My friends are here. I love houses and I love people and I put them together. I would never leave California. I haven't been mugged and I haven't lost my car. I think violence goes on everywhere. Hollywood's just getting a bum rap because it's so highly publicized. Hollywood is so visual. We lead the world in everything. Everything good. Everything bad. And people tend to talk more about the bad than the good. So you're not hearing all the wonderful things that go on here. It's the land of opportunities. I think you can do anything in Hollywood. Anything. Waiters can own restaurants in two years.'

Elaine has been one of Hollywood's most successful real estate agents for thirty-four years. You name a star – she's bought or sold them a mansion.

'For the last two years real estate has not been a wonderful thing but it used to be second to the picture business. We were all making fortunes and I had what I considered the greatest career a woman could have. The last two have been difficult because many houses are for sale that the banks have taken over. My father was one of the heads of Universal Studios for forty years so I'm working now with men who've had ten million, five million, one million, which they worked all their lives for. And now I'm selling their homes through the bank. It's been very difficult but it is picking up. Because prices are low people are finally starting to buy. The big homes are selling. I'm selling one next week for seven million to a person in films. I just sold one for three million to a doctor. It is easier to sell a five- or six-million-dollar house than a five-hundred-thousand-dollar house. So there must still be money here. It's still either coming in or the people here who had money have kept it.

'I'm working with a lot of Saudis, and Germans. People are still moving here. And I think it's gonna get better. It's still the glamour capital of the world. It sounds superficial but that's what I've grown up with. Cars, beautiful women, beautiful men, beautiful homes. Today they're even putting jacuzzis in the maids' rooms because no one wants to lose their housekeeper. Status counts here. I have a manner of living which I have to keep up because I work with these people – have to take them out in a nice car, have to have a nice home. When the market's not so great it's not easy.

'I've seen Hollywood change a lot. When the Shah of Iran fell our prices started going way up. The Persians started coming in droves. It was nothing to them to buy a five-million-dollar house because in their country, houses were four and five million. They didn't even barter so prices started going up. The Japanese finished where they left off and our prices just became so inflated that now we're paying the price for it.

'The super rich want everything. A tennis court, a

swimming pool. Most of the women won't even get their bathing suits wet, or their hair, but they have to have a swimming pool. They will buy a house that an interior designer has just finished. Then they'll bring in their own and redo it to their own taste. Everyone's trying to outdo their neighbour. It's like real important to have a gorgeous home. Here people entertain at home. So they want to show it off. My most expensive sale was an eight-million-dollar house behind the Beverly Hills Hotel, to a Saudi. I'm working right now on getting a listing of a thirty-two-million-dollar home.

'My first sale was to Tuesday Weld for twenty-nine thousand dollars. My first rental was to Warren Beatty for three hundred a month. All we do now is add zeros. I'd been in real estate four years when I met Gig Young. I showed him a house while he was married to Elizabeth Montgomery. We became good friends and he divorced her. Then I married him. I made two commissions off him because I sold him a house, and then I married him, and then I moved in and then we had a daughter and we needed a bigger house so – I sold him another house.

'I think everybody's searching for something in California. We have the most beautiful cars and homes, the most beautiful women and men. There's a surplus of everything. But to find happiness in this town is very difficult. People are answering personal ads, joining Singles clubs.'

It's hard to imagine anyone being lonely in Hollywood. It's such a hustle. All is for sale. Every petrol pump attendant is writing a screenplay, every video store assistant – as Quentin Tarantino was before he wrote and directed *Pulp Fiction* and was key player in *Reservoir Dogs* and *True Romance* – *expects* to be a HIP, a Hollywood Important Person. I've had a dozen waiters slip me screenplays in restaurants simply because I was reading film-production notes following special screenings. They shake them around like peppermills. Only the imagination can conjure up what might be on offer if you're someone who can deliver stardom. An exhilarating, sometimes dangerous game.

But it is a game which can bring rich rewards. Times change but Fantasyland remains a magical magnet. And a land of escape where everything goes every which way and millions inside and outside the fantasy factory want more. How far can Hollywood and Hollywood People go? The place and the residents spell glamour. They are fun and outrageous, crazy and lovable. Often a tease. Which is why so many want to join the Tinseltown Team.

But only a few get to play on the A-Team.

THE 'A' LIST
Chapter 2

'An extraordinary kind of temporary place.'
John Schlesinger

Superstars Burt Reynolds and Clint Eastwood were rejected on the same day by a Universal Studios 'talent' agent. Reynolds was told he couldn't act. Eastwood was warned that his Adam's apple protruded too much and he would never make it in the movies. Reynolds, who remains one of Eastwood's closest friends, walked out of the interview and turned to his friend saying: 'Well, at least I can learn to act. I don't know what you're going to do . . .'

Both men found television series: Eastwood played in *Rawhide* and Reynolds was Quinton the blacksmith in the longest running 'oater' ever, *Gunsmoke*.

On the big screen, Reynolds spent five years as the world's number one box office star. Eastwood remains, despite competition from much younger players, the action icon of the cinema. They are a fine example of anyone's tenuous hold on superstardom. While Burt Reynolds is yesterday's man, Eastwood, a multiple Oscar winner for *Unforgiven*, remains a box office champion.

What of the others? Megastars like Arnold Schwarzenegger, Paul Newman, Robert Redford, Kevin Costner and Sylvester Stallone stay at the top through hard work and dedication. Younger but established 'new boys' like Bruce Willis and Tom Cruise apply a similar work ethic. Like Cruise, Keanu Reeve paid his dues – small roles in big movies, big roles in small movies – until breaking through with *Dracula* and then the 1994 action thriller *Speed*. Brad Pitt, The Sexiest Man Alive in 1995 according to America's *People* magazine, was an instant star from his brief appearance in *Thelma and Louise* with Susan Sarandon and Geena Davis. He went on to work for director Robert Redford in the acclaimed *A River Runs Through It* and then co-starred with Cruise in *Interview With a Vampire*. In 1995 he appeared in *Legends of the Fall* and there was early talk of Oscars in March 1996.

Kim Basinger went from model to Bond girl to Batman's girlfriend to powerful Hollywood actress and producer, and wife of actor Alex Baldwin. Jodie Foster was a child star, a Disney star and then an Oscar winner for *The Accused* and *Silence of the Lambs*. Black actress Halle Berry fought the ethnic question for leading roles – and got them in films as diverse as *The Flintstones* and *Losing Isaiah*. In the latter she starred opposite double Oscar-winner (for *Tootsie* and 1995's *Blue Sky*) Jessica Lange, who overcame the jokes over her 1976 début appearance co-starring with King Kong – as the natural mother of a child Lange's social worker wants to keep. Sophia Loren, a legend, returned to acclaim in 1995 in Robert Altman's satire of the fashion business *Prêt-à-Porter*.

The young actor Val Kilmer – Doc Holliday in 1994's

Tombstone as well as legendary rocker Jim Morrison in Oliver Stone's *The Doors*, became the new Caped Crusader in *Batman Forever* in 1995, having taken over the role from Michael Keaton. He's now on the 'A' list. As is John Travolta following *Pulp Fiction* and the Oscar nomination for his portrayal of a smack-addicted hitman which pushed his asking price from nowhere to $9 million, for films like the Tinseltown-set *Get Shorty*. Even the most successful can stumble.

In the futuristic film *The Terminator*, which was released in 1984 to a box office as big as its star's pectorals, Arnie announced after walking out of a disdainful police precinct, 'I'll be back.'

He was. Seventeen seconds later. He crashed a car through the doors of the cop shop and did his one-man act of celebrated celluloid mayhem. Just how did this sixteen-stone 6ft 2ins of body-fatless beefcake, who looks a menace to everyone but MENSA, get to be Mr Hollywood? It has been said that not since Jean Harlow has a body alone been able to smash and grab such box office records as Arnold Schwarzenegger's.

For a multi-million-dollar moment, however, it appeared that he had lost all his muscle at the success game. In Hollywood terms, Arnie flopped in 1993 with *The Last Action Hero*. The film made $168 million but it didn't *do* the sort of mega-millions expected of the most unexpected film superstar of the century. The bigger they are the harder they fall and many took much glee out of Arnie (57–33–33) suddenly stalling. But the man who sounds as though he's talking through a tuba simply went on, as he says, 'living in the future'.

Writing him off was an error. This man who now gets faxes from all who matter in America – the White House, the Studios and Michael's Restaurant in Santa Monica, California. Michael's is the biggie.

And with 1993's *True Lies* he *was* back – bigger than ever before. Just as he said he would be. The movie cost $137 million to make – the most money then ever spent on a production not including advertising and marketing – and when it opened in cinemas it devastated all the competition. Every minute, someone in America was spending $7.50 to see Arnie back in action. The financial analysts predicted record takings before the film moved from America to rich and ripe Arnie territory like Britain, France and Japan. Why?

The colossal success – $25 million in the first forty-eight hours – involved a repeat of his *Terminator* teaming with writer-director James Cameron who guided him in the 1984 original and also in the special-effect extravaganza *T2* which earned more than $500 million worldwide in 1991. This was a match made in box-office heaven. But huge audiences don't pay out for a James Cameron movie. They go to see shrewd Arnie – who was forty-eight in 1995. He is the star attraction. He has that 'it' – the Lauren Bacall/Humphrey Bogart spark – which transcends RADA or Lee Strasberg's Method. Years ago he would have been travelling by vine as Tarzan, or flashing a scimitar and guarding the harem, but even before *Terminator* he was a huge success. His sport was body-building: he was a seven-time Mr Olympiad and had a hat-trick of Mr Universe titles. His aggressive humour and ambition stole the body-building documentary

Pumping Iron (1976), which led to his first movie-movie, gifted maverick Bob Rafelson's *Stay Hungry*, in which he co-starred with Jeff Bridges and Sally Field in the same year. He recalls, 'I got a taste of movies. The goal? To be the tops at the box office. That's the way my thinking goes.' His muscle power took him from Graz, Austria, to California where he pumped his brain cells as well as iron. It was little more than a stretch from Muscle Beach to Hollywood and along the way he established real-estate holdings in California and Colorado.

In his time Schwarzenegger has torn, trampled, punched, shot and fought his way through sword-and-sorcery *Conan* films as well as *Commando*, *Raw Deal*, *Predator*, *The Running Man*, *Red Heat* and *Total Recall*. He did comedy with *Twins* and was clever enough not to allow Danny DeVito to steal all the laughs.

But, like Stallone does now and Eastwood always has, he knows his mass audience. Arnie watches, listens and learns. Eastwood got his break in his first spaghetti Western which had the prophetic title *A Fistful of Dollars*. Stallone was *Rocky*, then *Rambo*, but stumbled when he attempted to play it for laughs not action. He returned in 1993 in a major way with the Italian Alps extravaganza thriller *Cliffhanger*, and in 1995 was in cinemas everywhere with the thrills and spills *The Specialist* with Sharon Stone.

This trio – like long-lasting action stars including John Wayne, Charles Bronson and Steve McQueen – is not about the mystique of acting, about the *proper* way of getting the dialogue out. Forget Barrymore and Olivier. Think more of the bending of crowbars. Of audiences rather than Oscars. Arnie is John Wayne without the horse, Rambo without the Uzi, Dirty Harry with an accent. Paul Newman was famous for his azure eyes, Clark Gable for his dimples, Cary Grant for his impeccable manner, Robert Redford, well, for being Robert Redford. They were and are actors who have managed never to be estranged from their audiences. Apart from the *Last Action Hero* hiccup so has Arnie. He has a magnificent rapport with his public. He works at it: there's not a flashbulb he won't grin at or an autograph he won't sign. You make the movie and then you market, market, market. He delivers his wisdom: 'I learned a long time ago in body-building that if you want to have a great body you have to train four hours a day, have a special diet, sleep more, make certain sacrifices. There are no breaks. Three hundred pounds on a bench press will always feel like three hundred pounds. If you want something badly enough you go through anything – no matter what it takes – and learn whatever you have to.'

He's learned a lot, and he listens to himself. When he's at his Spanish-style home in Pacific Palisades, California, where he lives with his television newswoman wife Maria Shriver (niece of Jack, Bobby and Teddy Kennedy) and their three children (Katherine, born in 1990, Christina 1992 and Patrick 1993), he's in the gym at 7.30 a.m. every day (on location the gym goes with him). Then he spends four hours working on acting (To Be or Not To Be?).

By the mid-1990s he was what the *New York Post* called 'The Mightiest Movie Star on Planet Earth'. Arnie never believed the plot would be any different: 'As a professional athlete you learn about yourself – how you operate emotionally and mentally, what makes you turn on and be more aggressive, what makes you turn off. All of that helped me in movies in the first place. It certainly wasn't my acting ability, that's for sure. The ultimate goal is to do different types of movies and have successful movies all the time.'

I sat with him in a Beverly Hills hotel suite a few days before the opening weekend of *Terminator 2* and there was much discussion about the film's budget and if it could expect to make a profit. The trade papers had been giving estimates of $40 million for the first box-office days. From his Hawaiian shirt pocket Schwarzenegger produced a neatly folded piece of paper and handed it to me. It had $52 million written on it. *T2* made $55 million in that first weekend. He knows show business.

What went wrong with *Last Action Hero* for Hollywood's Hercules? This is a man who sweats every moment of the movie-making process, from the casting to the marketing, from the script to the camera work. Arnie, like all good pass-the-buck merchants, insists: 'It had nothing to do with me.' But he points out: 'It depends how you look at it. It was number 12 in the worldwide ranking of box office in terms of dollars. To be number 12 wasn't a failure. But it was a personal failure in so far as I wanted the movie to go through the roof.'

With *True Lies*, he had a film shooting into the stratosphere. It overtook Disney's 1994 animated success *The Lion King* and that year's Oscar winner Tom Hanks's film *Forrest Gump* on opening in America. The financial potential – including worldwide cable television and video – was close to *T2*.

Like much of Hollywood material the plot was not

original. It is a remake of the 1992 French film *La Totale!* which centred on a spy (Thierry Lhermitte) whose ignored wife (Miou-Miou) believes her husband works for the telephone company. In 1992 it was a small foreign farce. Bring in Arnie and James Cameron and it became James Bond Meets the Terminator. Arnie as superspy Harry Trasker proves that tough guys dance by doing a tango with his neglected wife Helen (multi-award winner for her role, Jamie Lee Curtis) who in this version believes her secret agent husband is a computer salesman. *He* suspects *her* of having an affair. They're both wrong. That's the domestic side but, naturally, there was lots of action and explosions as Arnie faced down a stereotyped Arab terrorist played by British actor Art Malik. It was all, said the *New York Times*, great fun and 'frankly exciting – when a film-maker's idea of mind-boggling mayhem is this sensational it's quite enough'.

He was back and Arnie was a happy man. His first son Patrick was born during the filming of *True Lies* and Schwarzenegger himself was about to give birth in the Ivan *Twins* Reitman comedy *Junior*. Arnie played a man who becomes pregnant and had to play female emotions with his co-star Emma Thompson. It sounded absurd but so did Arnie and diminutive Danny DeVito as *Twins*. That worked. And *Junior* did almost as well.

There was much talk in 1995 about his next film *The Crusades*, a medieval epic with his *Total Recall* director Paul Verhoeven. The talk had been bad: the word was that the $120 million film was in jeopardy. Arnie insisted: 'It *will* be made.' No one argued: previously he'd said he would be back – and he was.

As was Kim Basinger.

She began as a pouting starlet, graduated to luscious leading lady – and then Hollywood began to talk about her as a mixed-up personality. One tale gossiped into another around her classic 36–24–36 siren of a figure, which today remains more heart-threatening than cholesterol.

Kim Basinger, who was forty-three in 1995, has kept her body and mind in shape and it's helped her survive. She's had to be sharp, for the nineties were not kind to her. At one point it looked as if this ravishing creature from America's Deep South was finished when she was sued for jilting the movie *Boxing Helena*, a film about bizarre and besotted love. When she pulled out of her role as a woman with no arms or legs who is kept in a box by an obsessed admirer she was accused of reneging on an oral agreement. A jury awarded $8.9 million dollars against her and it was revealed that her net worth was $5,387,382 and 19 cents. She filed for bankruptcy. Her husband, actor Alec Baldwin, said of the verdict: 'The jury thought they handed down a bill that surely she could pay. I guess they felt that everyone who did *Batman* got $40 million.'

But the determination that got Basinger from Athens, Georgia, to California in the first place kicked in. She kept things in the family by co-starring in 1994 with Baldwin in a remake of 1972's *The Getaway*, which had starred another real-life couple, Steve McQueen and Ali MacGraw.

Worldwide reaction to her was remarkable: 'She seems to have come to the role at a perfect point in her career,' wrote one critic adding, 'Like the character she plays she's clearly been round the block a few times, made a few bad decisions, but she's looking better than ever.'

With an almost unanimously favourable press behind her, Basinger and Baldwin seemed to have come to terms with the result of the court case, although they insisted they could never agree with it. Baldwin was determined: 'I will not stop until she gets her fair shake.' And things changed.

In a startling turn of events a California appeals court overturned the judgement against Basinger in September 1994. However, in the Lawyer Land of California the case is expected to be back in the courts again involving 'appellate specialists' and other such euphemisms, meaning that this one could run for ever. But whatever happened legally Basinger had at least escaped personality purgatory. In person she does not live up to her 'difficult' reputation. Arguably she's too eager to please. In 1992 she cropped off her trademark flowing crown of curls in what seemed an attempt to be taken seriously. At an age when most pouting starlets are normally languishing, rather than lounging, at the shallow end of some producer's swimming pool and attention span she was in demand. 'It's very difficult to be taken seriously in a town as small as Hollywood and in an entertainment business like this. There are so many beautiful girls and they're this and that and the other thing. A large percentage of people don't have the guts to stand up for what they believe in and they'll go with the crowd. It's only the few who say, "I'm going to judge for myself," before they make a choice. I had to learn this, I really did.'

Kim Basinger went from hometown beauty queen to New York model to Hollywood television series walk-on and *Playboy* centrefold. Her Bond girl in Sean Connery's misunderstood 007 return in *Never Say Never Again* (1983) began a busy big-screen acting career. Since then she's been the disquieting sexual presence in many films. She tempted Robert Redford in *The Natural* (1984), was Mickey Rourke's love slave in *9½ Weeks* (1985), gave Bruce Willis a difficult time in *Blind Date* (1987), Richard Gere the runaround in *No Mercy* (1986) and *Final Analysis* (1992) and, of course, got Batman's wings flapping as Vicki Vale in *Batman* (1991).

As she did the gossips. She was involved with the singer who once called himself Prince, who created the music for *Batman*. She also dated Jon Peters, the 1970s Streisand Svengali, who co-produced the box-office giant and turned many red-blooded men green by taking up with Pamela Anderson of *Baywatch* before *her* marriage to tattooed rock star Tommy Lee. Basinger's marriage to make-up man Ron Britton ended after eight years and she swore she was never getting married again. It was just her and her dogs and cats – she picks up strays all the time – at her home in the San Fernando Valley outside of Los Angeles. Alec Baldwin changed her view. They married four times in *The Marrying Man* and then finally for real. For them it may have been romantic but many involved in the making of the 1991 film talk of it as a nightmare and Mr and Mrs B as the principal demons.

It was said that she contractually demanded that her hair only be washed in Evian water, that she asked for filming to be stopped so she could fly to Brazil to consult a psychic. One crew member said that was 'only the tip of the iceberg'. It was, in fact, 'much, much worse'.

Basinger shrugged: 'You hear a lot of good and bad about yourself and then you hear remarks about your hair ... my father always told me to judge for myself. When I started telling the truth about the way I felt, and even made it publicly known, people didn't want that. It was never intended to cause trouble but people sometimes view saying how you feel as causing trouble.'

One such public time was at an Oscars when, while watched by one billion viewers, she scolded the voters for not nominating director Spike Lee's movie *Do The Right Thing*. 'I would do it all over again. I felt it was a shame to leave out that film. Everybody had been talking about truth and I thought it presented the biggest truth of all. I wasn't reprimanding the Academy or anything like that. It just truly came from the heart, from inside. One billion people were watching and I said: "Well, Lord, help me get through this because it's the biggest audience I'm ever going to have in my life."'

To quote another rumour, she says God is her only psychic. 'He knows everything.' About the Evian water? 'You mean the gallons and gallons I wash my hair in? I drink it. But I drink all kinds of other water as well. I'm a vegetarian. I don't eat dairy products or meat. I love to exercise – it's like brushing my teeth.'

She wasn't always so careful: 'When I came to Los Angeles I said: "I want to take everything. I want to try it all." And some friend said: "Oh, try this." That's always the way it gets started. I tried cocaine and I found that it made people sleep during the day. Every time I took it I said: "This is a joke." The next day I couldn't even ... it's a debilitating drug. I hated that it made me so physically worn out. I thank God, I really do, with all my heart. Because I saw a lot of people use cocaine every day. So many girls got hooked into it, some because they were working in the industry and wanted to stay thin. And believe me I know exactly what it does to your body. Watching these girls just completely lose everything they had and then try and get themselves back in balance – it was bad. What cocaine did for me was make me very smart in one way. It made me know that you can never use it and get by. I've always been very physical. I work out every day. I love any physical activity. I'll run with anybody, do whatever they want to do. Believe me I'm no Mother Theresa. I've done a lot of wildass things in my life. It's just that I can be wild without drugs and alcohol. And so can anybody. Cocaine doesn't break your inhibitions like you think it does. I don't think there is anybody alive who can really *handle* drugs.'

If drugs is one curse of Hollywood so is ageism. Is she scared about getting older? Of being fifty? 'I don't really have time for that. Number one, I don't know what the future is going to hold. We never know how long any of us is gonna be around. I think staying and looking and feeling young has a lot to do with your beliefs. It's only society that put twenty-four hours in a day. Twenty-four hours a day, 365 days a year – from one year old to sixty or seventy or eighty years old. The clock just rules the hell out of all of us and it's so sad.'

She wants her family to grow. She became pregnant in

1995 and said, 'Alec and I want lots of kids everywhere – a big family. I never want to give up my work – don't get me wrong. But he is my life's focus.'

Her home in Woodland Hills, a very non-celebrity area of Los Angeles, is, she says, her sanctuary. The dogs follow her around, there's a gym and an entertainment centre with a white piano – she's an accomplished singer – and a chaise-longue, a keepsake from *The Marrying Man*, to remind her of when she met Baldwin. They married on 19 August 1993 – she was working and he arranged all the details of the ceremony in East Hampton, New York.

The *Boxing Helena* saga goes on – the film was finally made starring Sherilyn *Twin Peaks* Fenn who portrayed Elizabeth Taylor in the controversial 1995 television mini-series *Destiny*. Basinger remains cynical: 'It's all become such a mad dog frenzy. Who's stabbing you in the back or doing it in front of your face. A lot of that goes on. Once again it is about trust. I truly love this business between "Action" and "Cut" but I think now there's something that I never faced. There's an element of "Let's find something out on that somebody so we can bring them down". It's not about the truth – it's about seeing people squirm. That's very sad. It makes you slow to trust again . . . but I will. There's not much trust in the world – but I trust Alec. He trusts me. Together we will overcome all the obstacles.'

Clint Eastwood certainly overcame his share of obstacles. *A Fistful of Dollars* was the foundation of a career, which has been steady box office and, in the 1990s, Oscar heavyweight: a creditable achievement built on a razor-challenged character in a poncho munching cigarillos. He was not just The Man With No Name but The Man With No Dialogue.

Eastwood, an actor who has established himself as a major Hollywood power-broker by spilling other people's blood and guts on screen and who made his name and millions in the gunslinger genre, went mushy on his audiences in 1995 as the director and co-star with Meryl Streep of *The Bridges of Madison County*. The story was so sentimental and romantic that the clever should have been buying Kleenex shares. The film, based on Robert James Waller's novel, one of the biggest international hardback sellers of all time, was an instant Tinseltown titbit. Superstar producer/director Steven Spielberg won the auction for the rights and from the moment his Amblin Entertainment announced production plans the guessing game began over who would play the sensitive, under-standing, rugged-individualist *National Geographic* pho-tographer, who has a brief but passionate affair with a lonely Iowa farmwoman in the 1960s. The cinema audi-ence was guaranteed. It was over-the-rainbow gold-dust material and, of course, everyone wanted their fingers in this particular pot. Robert Redford, Michael Douglas and Harrison Ford were the first names mentioned for the role of photographer Robert Kincaid. Choices for the woman who mists his lens, the Italian-born war bride Francesca Johnson, ran riot: Anjelica Huston, Lena Olin, Sonia Braga, Peralla August, Mary McDonnell, Annette Bening, Isabella Rossellini, Cher, Susan Sarandon, Michelle Pfeiffer, Mercedes Ruehl and Kate Capshaw (a.k.a. Mrs Steven Spielberg).

The casting took longer than the novel's four days of loving – which results in twenty-four years of wondering and yearning. With hindsight Eastwood and Streep seem a perfect match. But Clint as sensitive man?

'It was not a stretch,' he said, in that confident and comfortable drawl. 'I can understand the emotions of the piece. After a time people perceive you as a one-dimensional sort of character but we grow, we change. He had changed. He is a grandfather and had become a father again in 1994 when his partner, the actress Frances Fisher, gave birth to a daughter whom they named Francesca after the character from *The Bridges of Madison County*. He has two grown-up children, Alison, a European supermodel, and Kyle, a musician and actor, from his first wife Maggie. He also has an illegitimate daughter, Kimber, from his affair with actress Rowan Tunis who worked with him on the 1958–65 television series *Rawhide*. This was only revealed in 1992 when Kimber said who her father was. He had a thirteen-year relationship with the actress Sondra Locke but that ended in acrimony and the Californian courts in 1989. She alleged that Eastwood had forced her to have abortions and be sterilized. The mess appeared to have been concluded with a multi-million dollar settlement.

But just as the romantic *Bridges of Madison County* concluded filming in 1995, Ms Locke, who was then forty-seven, interrupted Eastwood's life again. She claimed in a lawsuit filed in January 1995 in Los Angeles Superior Court that Warner Brothers film studios, Eastwood's long-time 'home', were involved in fraud and breach of contract over the financial arrangements agreed after she and the film star separated. Her new lawsuit, in which she claimed £25 million, maintains that she was the victim of a 'sweetheart deal'.

Instead of receiving £16 million in her original settlement she says it was reduced to a token sum and that her three-year acting and production contract with Warners came to nothing. Every project she put forward was rejected. The millions she was widely reported to have received in fact amounted to £250,000 and £70,000 in legal fees. The gravy was the Warner Studios contract, which she insisted had added up to nothing.

Eastwood will not now be drawn on the Sondra Locke issue. When she first tangled him in that spaghetti of paperwork in Los Angeles Superior Court he offered: 'I felt so disappointed – and the disappointment was with myself. How could I spend so many years with Sondra? How could I have been such a bad judge of character? At some point a person has to make up their mind whether they want to be a film director or an ex-girlfriend. I gather the people who advised her thought I would be brought to my knees by some public humiliation. Well, they misread me by thinking that making false statements would flush me into some giveaway programme.'

Eastwood has never given away anything. He's worked hard and long for his success but he's always been willing to take a risk. And, because of his phenomenal success with action/adventure films Warner Brothers have been happy to indulge him in projects like 1988's *Bird* in which he told the story of jazzman Charlie Parker. Or with 1990's *White Hunter, Black Heart*, which was a thinly veiled look at John Huston's making of *The African Queen* (1952). But Eastwood always paid his dues. For every *Bird* there was a *Dirty Harry* or Westerns like 1985's *Pale Rider* or the already classic *Unforgiven*, which collected seven Oscars in 1993.

The Bridges of Madison County is essentially a character piece with the two main roles, the fortysomething woman and the handsome fiftysomething stranger, providing a showcase for the talent involved. Meryl Streep was the co-star but not an easy catch: 'I didn't like the book but the script for the film was wonderful.'

She dyed her blonde hair brown with reddish highlights for the role of Francesca. Eastwood just had to be himself. He was sixty-four but as the novel's fifty-two-year-old Kincaid he was easily acceptable – as was the production in the rural town of Wintriest, Iowa (pop. 4,029) where many of the locals earned pocket money as extras. 'Everyone was helpful and wanted to enjoy the idea of the film,' said Eastwood. 'When you get out of the Hollywood environment it's a pleasant surprise just how co-operative people can be. I felt very comfortable with the movie. There is love and conflict, the basic emotions in real and movie life. This was a *warm* movie for me – and, yes, maybe it was the time and the circumstances which meant me to work with that kind of material.'

Eastwood had to wield a camera rather than a Magnum in the film and was trained by veteran American photographer Ken Regan. 'In teaching Clint how to use a camera [Nikon F, circa 1964] I was surprised how quickly he adapted. He has a natural mechanical ability, a defined visual sense, a sharp eye, and he notices things others might miss. After editing his first photos I gave him a B plus.'

Streep commented: 'As a director he is frugal but will indulge you until you feel you have done your absolute best. He is a man who doesn't have to prove anything to anybody. Except, possibly, to himself. He will always want to excel, to do and be the best. It's a great tribute to him.'

Eastwood would like Halle Berry. Not just because she looks terrific but because she has beaten the odds. When all the Hollywood Women were trying out for the main sex role in *The Flintstones* – and this is a kids'-fig sex role – she had what would be construed in Tinseltown as the disadvantage of being black. Nevertheless . . .

With John Goodman and Elizabeth Perkins were Fred and Wilma Flintstone, Rick Moranis and Rosie O'Donnell as Barney and Betty Rubble, and the legendary Hollywood Woman Elizabeth Taylor as Fred's mother-in-law Pearl Slaghoople; Halle Berry introduced us to Rosetta Stone who vamped it up like, well . . . Sharon Stone. When Fred was promoted at the Slate and Company quarry he was given Rosetta as his secretary. Before you could whisper prehistoric sexual harassment she put the make on Fred – and everything else in a loincloth – for most of the movie. Berry boasted with a laugh: 'He was putty in my hands.'

Most men would be. Berry was twenty-six in 1995, a knock-you-down gorgeous, former beauty queen but now a most determined and ambitious Hollywood actess – a fresh front-runner to become one of the world's major stars by the end of the century. Hollywood knows it, and so does she, but she's seen the hurdles of the beauty game – she was Miss Teen All American in 1985 and a year later first runner-up for Miss USA – and knows that long careers aren't created overnight but built through work and time. Her progress has been exceptional. Throughout Hollywood history black actors have only occasionally established a major presence in the movies. And there have been fewer black actresses who played roles unrelated to their colour.

Dorothy Dandridge was arguably Hollywood's first black leading lady but she ended her life desperately waiting for another movie role. After successful films such as *Carmen Jones* and *Island in the Sun*, her death in 1965 made the cover of *Life* magazine. By then, she had no family, no career ... no life. Friends said she succumbed to a broken heart.

Janet Jackson, who took the lead in John Singleton's *Poetic Justice*, wants to play Dandridge in a film based on her autiobiography *Everything and Nothing*, and it does seem that the best parts for young actesses are historical or biographical. Angela Bassett starred as Tina Turner in *What's Love Got To Do With It* and as Betty, the wife of Denzel Washington's *Malcolm X*.

Hollywood manager Dolores Robinson sees it this way: 'I used to say that if you're black and you're fat you can be a mother. If you're black and ugly you can be a nurse. If you're black and pretty you can be a prostitute. It was almost like that. Now the options have improved but not broadened. You've got twelve beautiful young actresses trying to be Wesley Snipe's girlfriend, Eddie Murphy's girlfriend or Denzel Washington's girlfriend. Those are the three roles.'

Or, rather, were the three roles. Whoopi Goldberg – an Oscar winner in 1990 for *Ghost* who was paid $7 million for *Sister Act 2* – is playing roles that are not about being black but about economics. Whoopi can 'open' a movie at the box office. In that way she is also opening doors. And Halle Berry is on track to match her success. But there are still battles, sometimes topsy-turvy ones as she explains: 'I was cast for *Strictly Business* then fired because I was "too light". I call it in-house discrimination.'

It's clear why *The Flintstones* was a landmark for her. 'To be a black woman and to be the object of everybody's desire in this movie was such a coup. The fact that these executives at the studio, who are all white males, took the risk to have a black woman as this character said a lot as to where we were going. No, we didn't want to be just sex objects or be just beautiful. We were starting to be seen a little differently.'

She's been 'named' in some rap songs – in a lusty way. Now, Berry's no prude but ... 'I have a real problem with all these songs that refer to women as bitches or in other derogatory terms. I don't listen to them nor do I buy them, nor do I encourage others to. People I know say: "Well, I don't listen to the words. I like the beat." They don't realize that subconsciously they're hearing the words. It's degrading. As women we're fighting so hard to be viewed in another way. 'I don't like my name associated with it. I know they think they are giving me a compliment but I don't see it that way.'

She slipped through the obstacle course of typecasting

and another breakthrough followed when she appeared in the drama *Fatherhood* in which she co-starred with Patrick Swayze playing an investigative reporter, a role originally written for a man. She says some of her peers put her down for taking on the sexy, fluffy Rosetta Stone in *The Flintstones* but she regarded it as part of the portfolio. Her more serio-snob colleagues, presumably, were happier with *Losing Isaiah*. In that 1995 film Berry and Jessica Lange documented the complexities of interracial adoption.

But Berry says: 'Not everything is going to be *Malcolm X* or *Losing Isaiah*. The important thing is to do your best possible work no matter what film you are in or what the subject is. If you accept a role doing it the best you can is simply being professional. It's what should be expected.' She certainly provided that in the six-hour television series *Queen* ('I gave my blood, sweat and tears for that role') which brought her strong international notices. She was a dopehead in Spike Lee's *Jungle Fever* and the good girl with Eddie Murphy in *Boomerang* (Robin Givens, the former Mrs Mike Tyson, was the bad girl). For the critics life imitated art or vice versa: 'People thought I played myself and she played herself. Robin got such a bad press because of what she did to Mike Tyson. So many people in this business think she's bitchy. People won't feel sympathetic towards her until she starts doing nice things in her personal life and people start writing about it.'

His office is full of road maps of Cuba but so is his face which is pure Havana, a matador mix of sleepy machismo and haunting burnt sienna eyes. 'Have a cigar?' asks

Andy Garcia pushing back a brown pork pie hat as he settles into a seat in what was once his back garden. He puffs on his torpedo of tobacco and grins with the confidence of an actor who knows he is one of the most sought after leading men in the world. His assistant provides what appears to be a thimble of mud with sugar. As he sips his coffee Garcia admits he adores his heritage. And, of course, like all exiles, what he can't have the more he wants it.

The 'office' is a rambling house on the outskirts of Los Angeles which, before *Godfather 3, Black Rain, 8 Million Ways to Die* and a string of other films including last year's *When A Man Loves A Woman* with Meg Ryan, was the full-time home for Garcia and his wife and three daughters. It still bustles with activity.

Today, though, it's not babies crying but power players wanting his time for this film deal or that charity concert or personal appearance. He's made and is making his dreams come true. He has a bigger family home in Los Angeles, a $1.1 million beachfront property in Key Biscayne, Florida, and, more important than the trinkets of Hollywood success, he can call the tune. And how.

He made his début as a director with a documentary about Israel Lopez better known as Cachao (pronounced ka-chow) the bassist, composer and bandleader who recorded the first mambo in 1939 as well as being responsible for the Cuban musical form known as the *danzon* and a strong influence behind the *descarga* – jam sessions. The highly praised film led to Garcia producing more of Cachao's work and *Master Sessions, Volume One* was a major success last summer in America and went on sale in Britain in

December 1994. Now, Cachao is writing the music for Garcia's next film.

Cachao was born in Havana in 1918 and left Cuba in 1961 with a couple of suitcases and more than 3000 songs. Garcia was born in Havana in April 1956, and was five when his family fled Castro to settle in Miami. Both refugees from the Communist regime Garcia and Cachao finally connected in San Francisco, by which time Garcia was a star and no longer the swaggering teenager who had hung around the music clubs on Collins Avenue in Miami Beach. 'Back then we'd drink coffee at the Royal Castle on 71st Street. The ocean was right there. We'd wait for the American girls to come around and try and pick us up. They wanted to have a good time. We were there to cater for their needs.'

He also hung around the back door of one of the music clubs where the mambo kings of the day played. 'The manager was a nice guy. He knew we kids loved the music but we were too young to go in. He kept the back door open when he could and we heard the music. You find solace in the music and that is really true of Cuban exiles because music is such an important part of our lives. That's how you carry your culture with you and the nostalgia for your country. It's something to ease the pain. I'll always miss not having grown up in Havana. I'm developing a film set in Cuba (*The Lost City*) and at least I can re-create the childhood I didn't have. I'm very passionate about my culture and the tragedy that fell upon it. My father, who died in 1993, told me that the last straw for him was when you had to turn the rights of your children over to the State, and the State determined the indoctrination of your children, their schooling, where they serve in the military. We have no relatives there. We are a small family. They all ran with us.'

He and his friends, like Zoom Zoom Zami, would go hunting for music: 'I discovered Cachao in a music store in Miami. I didn't know who he was but the owner of the store said it was a classic. I picked up the album and I was hooked. Part of the fun of it was finding out that he truly was the mambo king.' Here, Garcia marches off to his office and returns with the original LP. The cover is a little tattered but it's where the dream began. 'One night he was playing at the club where we all hung out at the back door. That night the manager unscrewed the light-bulb above one of the set-up of chairs and let us come in. It was timeless music, beautiful music which is compelling and will never go out of style.'

Without Garcia's documentary, *Cachao: Like His Rhythm There Is No Other*, and passionate interest the mambo magician would probably have continued playing at weddings and birthday parties in Miami – Cubans in Florida's Little Havana suppose he would have been 'discovered' after his death – but Garcia has created a new life for him. 'He is my second son,' says Cachao, through a translator. 'He knew all about Cuban music and I was very impressed when we met in San Francisco.' Also impressed was Cuban-born writer Guillermo Cabrere Infante, who takes part in the Cachao documentary. So much so that Garcia is now working on *The Lost City*, based on Cabrere Infante's writings about the caba-ret world of Havana in the mid to late fifties.

In his office, Garcia is surrounded by reminders of his

heritage. There are bongo drums and maps of Cuba on the wall. 'It is just in preparation for the movie,' he says. But it seems more a case of you can take the boy out of the country but not the ... 'I don't dispute that. But I'm also aware that you need to make films and recordings that are available and likeable by many different sorts of people. I am not naïve in that. But if I can do a commercial venture which allows me to indulge in something from my past then why not?

'I've worked more for British directors than any other – Ridley Scott (*Black Rain*), Ken Branagh (*Dead Again*), Mike Figgis (*Internal Affairs*) and Bruce Robinson (*Jennifer Eight*). I seem to get on with the British – must be my heritage!'

Garcia and his wife Marivi – short for Maria Victoria – met in college in Miami and married in 1982. She and their daughters, Dominik, eleven, Daniela, six, and three-year-old Alessandra, are, he says, his life. In Cuba the family is everything, and, for Garcia, part of his present and his past. Like the Mambo Kings. Like Cachao. And *The Lost City*, which opened in cinemas in late 1995. There was also talk of another movie with Sean Connery – they worked together on *The Untouchables* – while in the office the phones keep ringing with more and more offers.

Andy Garcia leans back in his green garden chair and grins. 'Like a cigar?' A Havana, of course.

Deeply delicious Dana Delany was glorified as the good girl-next-door for her award-winning performances as a well-scrubbed Vietnam war nurse in the American drama series *China Beach*. She was a saint not a sexpot. But even those drab Army fatigues could not disguise that there was something, well, Captain Crumpet-ish underneath that uniform.

John Goodman collected an award for *Roseanne* the same evening Delany won her TV Oscar for *China Beach*, and the big man ended his acceptance speech blurting out: 'I'd just like to thank Dana Delany for wearing that dress!'

Dana says demurely, 'I think what John said was great. But it was ironic. The dress I was wearing covered every inch of skin from my neck to my wrists to my ankles.' But she knows she put the va-va-voom in voluptuous. She makes faded jeans and a white T-shirt into catwalk candidates – a helpful attribute when she starred as the sexual 'mistress' of a Caribbean resort devoted to sexual kinks. Delany moved on from tender loving care and bandages to bondage, chains, cracking whips and a totally different uplifting look on life.

In *Exit to Eden* she played Lisa the darling dominatrix. So what was a nice girl-next-door like her doing in a film like that? Delany, who also appeared in 1994's Western hit *Tombstone*, is frank: 'It was the lead role which was a chance for me. Also I wanted to work with Garry Marshall and I knew it would make it OK.'

Marshall is one of American television's most successful producer-directors who moved on to the big screen with Julia Roberts's star-making *Pretty Woman* and Michelle Pfeiffer's *Frankie and Johnny*. Delany, thirty-nine in 1995, could see the potential: 'Garry told me: "I'm the man who brought you *Happy Days*." The films says it's fine to be in control and call the shots in your sex life. But, once in a while, you have to be vulnerable and let love in because love is the best.' She's an Irish (father) Yankee (mother), and, not surprisingly, has been in love a lot. But she has never married. She was involved with actors Treat Williams and Bruce Willis – she played his girlfriend who turned out to be a killer on a landmark episode of *Moonlighting* – and had a three-year relationship with John Sacret Young, the executive producer of *China Beach*. She says they are still friends. 'I've always been the younger woman. Now I'm aware of age.'

She adores the freedom to do what she wants with her life. She is a modern woman, brains and beauty, B cup and BSc, nice but naughty, but also wary of marital commitment. Her parents were divorced when she was nineteen and when Dana realized that Mary and Jack Delany weren't going to be a double act any more she recalls: 'I wasn't shocked. I wondered what took them so long.' Her father, now dead, remarried but her mother never did. 'I think men have to remarry because they don't know how to live by themselves. I think the older you get the more you appreciate your mother. My mother had a lot of energy and style and talent and I think marriage and motherhood were frustrating in a way. It was important to be *House and Garden* perfect. It was the only place to put your energy.' Which might explain her lifestyle: 'I've never lived with anybody. I like it that way. Because I saw my mother have to repress herself in such a conventional home the minute I realized I could do what I wanted and leave clothes on the floor and go to sleep in the middle of the afternoon I felt a sense of freedom. I don't think I want to lose that. Women are not supposed to like to be alone, but I need my time alone.'

She's a sassy character. Her grandfather patented a flush valve used mostly in industrial toilets although she remembers: 'When I was growing up we had a toilet you flushed by pushing a button in the wall. All the kids used to come over and flush. It was the big excitement in the neighbourhood.' It was a plush Connecticut community where she grew up. She went to the right university and then to New York for acting work on daytime soaps. She was promoted to be Tom Selleck's girlfriend on *Magnum P.I.*, did her guest shot *Moonlighting* and a decade of jobbing acting until her star shone on *China Beach*. But all along no one – especially casting directors – quite understood Dana Delany: 'I have a very wholesome face. Because of that I get away with murder – both in my real life and in my work. I have a funny side to me, a flirty side, a naughty side. The older I get the more unconventional I realize I am. I always thought I was too normal to be an actress, that I had to have more *Angst* in my life, and I now realize I have as much *Angst* as anybody. This has always been a great dichotomy to me: to be a *good* actor you have to be vulnerable, and yet to be a *successful* actor you have to be in control.

'People my age have gone on to very conventional lives and I haven't. I have never had the desire to get married – I am financially self-sufficient.'

Delany lives on Venice Beach out on the Pacific Coast from Los Angeles and loves romance and wine. 'Wine – I love to drink. I'm not giving it up, no matter what anybody says.' Sex also stays on the agenda. What was the most interesting place she ever made love? 'In a six-seater plane over the Grand Canyon with Sinatra singing "Come Fly With Me".'

What about the pilot?

'He was the pilot.'

She will not reveal the most naughty thing she has ever done but admits: 'I had sex in a public pool when I was twenty-two. When I was young I wanted to try everything. My Bible in high school was *The Sensuous Woman* by J. I memorized it. I wanted to be the perfect lover.'

She's been a lover on television and on film. There has been much girl talk in Hollywood about the assets of certain actors, and Delany has worked with several of them: 'If you put Willem Dafoe and Liam Neeson and Jimmy Woods in a room together there wouldn't be room for anyone else. It's true. We did a nude scene.' She made *Light Sleeper* with Willem Dafoe and tackled arousal in sex scenes with actors: 'Erections? Yeah, sometimes, if they're into the scene. It's sort of a compliment, isn't it? I told Willem I'd be insulted if he didn't get an erection.'

But *Exit to Eden* held a different allure for Delany: 'I like to do things that scare me. Being naked on film wasn't one of them, though. If I'm in character and I'm naked that makes sense to me if it is necessary to the scene or the plot. I'm tired of seeing hard bodies in movies because all I can think about is the actor's vanity. I, myself, think it's a little sexier if a woman has a roundness to her. *Exit to Eden* made me aware of accepting what I look like and there's a certain amount of freedom to it.'

STAYIN' ALIVE
Chapter 3

'In Hollywood you can be forgotten when you are out of
the room going to the toilet.'
Overheard disenchanted starlet

There is, of course, much freedom in worldwide success.
But even the greatest stars never lose the chains of having
to prove themselves again and again. There is nothing
more challenging than the next project's first weekend's
'take', the cinema box-office or television rating, which
spells doom or delirium – in certain cases probably both.

Fame is like a see-saw. Following major hits like *When
Harry Met Sally*, *Sleepless in Seattle* and 1995's big hit *French
Kiss*, Meg Ryan is now a producer as well as one of
Hollywood's leading ladies. She is married to actor
Dennis Quaid. When they met he was the star. Their
roles are reversed and she says, 'Dennis and I have a
theory about success. It comes in waves. It's easy to be in
a marriage with someone who does what you do if you
respect him a great deal and Dennis is an amazing actor.'

Quaid *has* been an established if not major commercial
star since the early 1980s. With every film, critics and
producers predict his 'breakthrough'. It can take time.

But it can pay off.

At the tender age of 33, Jodie Foster has been around longer than many in Hollywood. A major female player in Hollywood, by 1995 she had two Best Actress Oscars, a $100 million film production contract with PolyGram Entertainment, and her own production company, Egg Pictures. When she lost her third Best Actress chance (for *Nell*) to Jessica Lange (*Blue Sky*) in March 1995, she did so with confident dignity.

Jodie Foster has always been in charge. She is brisk, efficient, crisp and has been on display since her screen début as a three-year-old toddling through a Coppertone television suntan commercial. One of her directors dubbed her 'BLT', Bossy Little Thing. Smaller and slighter than her screen image suggests, she's always had a giant following, from playing the child prostitute in Martin Scorsese's *Taxi Driver* in 1976 to her Oscar-winning role as the rape victim in *The Accused* in 1988 and memorably as FBI rookie Clarice Starling – and another Oscar – in *Silence of the Lambs* in 1992.

There was the ugly moment when John Hinkley attempted to assassinate President Reagan to impress her – an episode on which she has not commented publicly and says she never will – but otherwise the sun has always seemed to shine on Foster.

Jodie Foster is not a glamour-puss-gossip-column-Armani-clad-blonde. She wears the designer stuff when it's part of work but increasingly she's attempted to project a more sexy image, more cleavage than trousers. There has been persistent Hollywood gossip about her sexuality and the London *Sunday Times* film critic Julie Burchill said in print of Foster's love scenes with Richard

Gere in 1993's *Sommersby* that the actress probably 'lay back and thought of Cindy Crawford'. But it's another subject she has been unwilling to discuss. At a champagne reception following a Hollywood awards ceremony she celebrated by dancing the hours away with several young men and I suggested to a film studio executive that her behaviour answered all the questions. He replied: 'Nothing is ever as it seems around her.' The girl with the startling blue eyes remains a sexual enigma.

She has a house in the San Fernando Valley – the family rather than trendy suburb of Los Angeles – but also rents the late Bette Davis's apartment near her Egg Pictures offices in Hollywood. She certainly feels a champion of film feminism: 'The thing about prodigies is that you're necessarily all by yourself because you're changing things. A lot of powerful women are feeling that – and certainly older actresses – because they have to stand outside the system and say: "I'm standing on this ground and I'm moving forward." You're the herald of the new age. We need role models desperately.'

There is no doubt that Jodie Foster *is* one. She always has an Everest of film scripts to choose from but says: 'Yes, I'm picky. Unless I know where a movie is going I can't be good. But look at how few real roles there are for women.'

She won her Oscars and made her début as a director with *Little Man Tate* before she was thirty. 'After the Oscars and directing I'm sure I'll find new goals, but they won't be the big looming neon kind that can hang over your head. I would never want to be in my twenties again.

I was very unhappy. The feeling of not knowing everything you don't know . . . it was awful. All that panic.'

Indeed there has been a change in Jodie Foster. Her co-chief of production at Egg Pictures is Stuart Kleinman and he said: 'If you read old stories about her she would always say things like: "I could leave acting any time – I could always teach." But in the last few years I think she's entered a new phase of her life. She's looking at her career in the long term. And she's passionately, completely committed to the film business.'

Foster says: 'It's hard not to give 130 per cent – that's why I don't work a lot. You can make a good movie but why bother when you can make an *excellent* movie that changes people's lives, the way movies have changed mine? If I say yes to a picture it's because I want to die for it.'

Until Foster was sixteen, however, her mother, Evelyn 'Brandy' Foster, picked her projects. She and her daughter had always been close: the day Evelyn Foster first appeared in the divorce court in May of 1962 she found she was pregnant with her fourth child. She had been married for ten years to former Air Force officer and Yale graduate Lucius Foster. The divorce was finalized, he left and that 19 November Alicia Christian Foster was born. From almost the moment she arrived at what was then the Cedars-of-Lebanon Hospital in the centre of Hollywood she was known as Jodie.

She's made a movie for almost every year of her life since her début opposite Michael Douglas in 1972's *Napoleon and Samantha*, during which she suffered lion bites on the back and stomach during a stunt sequence, scars she still carries today. Make-up hides them on screen when necessary – and she also disguises the emotional scars she carries from her days as a child star on episodic television and in Disney TV movies.

Foster was the family's breadwinner from the age of three. There were times of 'family financial strain', a euphemism for times when she wasn't working. Her mother, quite fairly, warned her that, just like Shirley Temple, by the time she was in her teens she would have lost the 'cutes' and would simply be discarded by the-bottom-line-is-the-dollar Hollywood.

Of her early days Foster says: 'To me, eight months of my life every year was spent getting up at the crack of dawn, eating shitty food, drinking shitty coffee and making things work – getting tired and dirty just doing it. I guess I grew up with that ethic.' Everything, including the coffee, is better. She believes she is, too. She thinks directing *Little Man Tate* started that: 'It was the beginning. I trusted myself as a director so I knew that I could be as open as I wanted to. I don't think it's a new me. I think it's just the old me that I didn't choose in my earlier years to show anybody. I didn't want to be a vulnerable bimbo for some director to take advantage of.

'When I was younger my mom picked everything I did, and what she wanted me to be is very revealing. She wanted me to be taken seriously. If I was going to be an actor I was going to be a real dramatic actor. Playing women who survived crises intact.'

'Brandy' Foster's role in her daughter's life is no longer

clear but her daughter said: 'She's less involved. She was my manager but now I don't have a manager. She's really valuable to me. She's really smart and has really interesting opinions about things. I don't want to devalue that at all. She's not really involved professionally now.' But for a long time they were a mother and daughter team.

Brandy's doubts about the future have always haunted Foster: 'I never thought I'd be an actor when I grew up. I spent my life in the film industry with prop men and other people saying: "So, what will you do when you grow up? Are you going to be a lawyer or a doctor?" People tried to teach me about camera operating so maybe I would have the opportunity to do something else in the film industry. The reason, of course, is that most child actors don't grow up to be actors and you might as well offer them the opportunity of thinking about other careers.

'I don't think I realized that I had a chance of being an actor when I grew up until I did *The Accused* in 1988. I was twenty-three or twenty-four then. It was late.' It was her twenty-six film. It was difficult, horrible and unexplored territory, and the rape scene took five days to film. But now she understands: 'That's when the veil was finally lifted and I said: "That's what I am. It's what I do."'

But when did she realize she had conquered Hollywood?

'The first Academy Award. But, actually, I'm not focused on the fact that I've "arrived", I'm focused on doing things right so that I can stay here. I'm not interested in the power of it all.'

The clogs and jeans have gone and she now looks as sleek as her clothes. From the age of seven she attended Le Lycée Français in Los Angeles, then left acting for Yale and graduated *cum laude* with a BA in American literature in 1985. She admits that all the academics made her 'ashamed to be an actor – I thought it was a stupid profession. I thought if I was really smart I'd want to be something else.' Now, she has changed her mind. The child star who went to Yale and read Derrida is not one with whom you would want to trade William Faulkner trivia but she doesn't carry her cleverness like a baton; it's there to help her progress. 'I was raised the way you'd be raised if you were going to be the ambassador to China where there are things you do and things you don't do. When you work you always pick up your clothes and put them on hangers at the end of the day. You always take off your make-up immediately, as soon as you finish work, because what if you have pimples the next day? All that stuff was about being responsible to the rest of the people around you. I think my mother wanted to give me this idea – myth or fiction – that acting was important and I had a responsibility to what I was doing, which, in the long run, was healthy for me.

'As kids we all had jobs and because me and my brother were always working [in commercials] my sister's job was to take care of the house. Everything was about keeping the family going, surviving.

'I don't make movies for flashy performances. I have to find something in the story that's part of my progress, part of this little train I'm on . . .'

It's been an express train for a long time. And now Jodie Foster is *the* driver.

Val Kilmer is also at the wheel of his carrer and he took even more control. In 1995 when he became *Batman*. Following Michael Keaton, who had played the Caped Crusader in the first two films (which, by the summer of 1995, had earned $700 million) was a major challenge. Director Joel Schumacher was in a similar position, taking over the reins from Tim Burton. He never lost confidence: 'Val made the movie fresher and younger. And sexier.'

Schumacher redesigned the Batmobile and Gotham City. He also introduced Robin, played by Chris O'Donnell, who co-starred memorably with Al Pacino in *Scent of a Woman*, and *Two-Face* (half of his face is acid-stained, the other half is normal), played by 1993 Oscar winner Tommy Lee Jones (Best Supporting Actor for *The Fugitive*). The role of the evil Riddler was taken on by *Mask* star Jim Carrey. The crime-busting duo's outfits were sculpted to emphasize their masculinity, so you could tell Kilmer's Batman was *really* interested in Nicole Kidman – Mrs Tom Cruise – who co-starred as a criminal psychologist in *Batman Forever*.

Kilmer has the confidence of a herd of stallions in a one-way street and there's little doubt that he will become an Oscar-winning superstar. He's already been a one-time Cher toyboy like his friend and *Top Gun* co-star Tom Cruise, an eerie Jim Morrison in Oliver Stone's *The Doors*, *Billy The Kid* and *The Man Who Broke One Thousand Chains*.

In 1988 he turned Britain's Stockport-born Joanne Whalley into Mrs Joanne Whalley-Kilmer – they met on the set of the fantasy adventure film *Willow* – he as a swashbuckling rogue, she the Princess Sorsha.

Whalley-Kilmer ('That will *always* be my professional name') took the title role in the television mini-series *Scarlet*, based on the sequel to Margaret Mitchell's *Gone With The Wind*, with Timothy Dalton as her co-star. While his wife emoted in the make-believe Deep South the ruggedly handsome Kilmer, who was thirty-six in 1995, was offering us Doc Holliday in *Tombstone*, a Southern gentleman complete with accent and a rakish wardrobe. It was a performance far removed from previous Doc Hollidays, such as those of Kirk Douglas, Victor Mature, and Jason Robards who, with their respective Wyatt Earps – Burt Lancaster, Henry Fonda and James Garner – took on the Clanton gang in Tombstone, Arizona, in 1881 at the OK Corral.

Kilmer's Wyatt Earp was played by a heavily moustachioed Kurt Russell, who is also the long-time lover of actress Goldie Hawn. The Juilliard-trained Kilmer is serious about his work and did not regard *Tombstone* as some shoot-'em-up for Saturday morning kids' cinema clubs. This was psychological stuff. 'Every film version of the relationship of these men that I'd seen ended up removing the real story to dramatize the dynamics of these characters. Doc values and respects Wyatt because he's a very solid character. Doc points out that Wyatt is the only human being that ever gave him hope.'

Despite a lavish cast, including Charlton Heston, Jason Priestly, Sam Elliott, Powers Boothe, Michael

'Terminator' Biehn, and Dana Delany, Kilmer ran away with the show. Kurt Russell raved: 'Val went into the heart of the real Doc Holliday. Nobody had attempted the refined Southern quality mixed with the psychotic look at life that he revealed.'

Off-screen, Kilmer is an expert horseman and a good rodeo rider. He, his wife and their young daughter live in Billy the Kid territory on the outskirts of Santa Fe, New Mexico. They are protective of their private life. What attracted Kilmer to his wife? 'She's a very honest person and she likes to work very hard. She's enlightened. And her toes! Nice toes.'

Kilmer is, surprisingly, a born and bred Los Angeles lad (San Fernando Valley), which may explain why he is even more serious than his intense peers about his work: 'Most of my initial training was classical theatre and it's hard to improve on that. In general I prefer theatre. It's more immediate. I started acting professionally when I was twenty. I grew up in the late sixties, early seventies – developing impressions in a cynical time when to believe in God – to believe in *anything* – wasn't cool. All the heroes died.'

Cher who is fourteen years older than Kilmer certainly thought he was a hero in the bedroom. Her recommendation was: 'He's sensitive, artistic, humorous and a great kisser. My rule of thumb – and it's never failed me – is if a man's a good kisser he's a great fuck.'

Kilmer has written plays, which have been produced, and poetry, which has been published, as well as scripts, music and songs. Acting, however, is still number one. As he talked he played a rodeo rope through his hands: 'I've been invited to a little rodeo and I don't want to look foolish. The rope is stiff but not too stiff. Ropes are just like actors – either too stiff or too soft. And if they get wet they won't work.'

Batman Forever worked for Val Kilmer, as did *Pulp Fiction* for John Travolta.

Travolta established himself in America on the funky TV sitcom *Welcome Back, Kotter*, and then internationally in *Grease* (1977) and *Saturday Night Fever* (1978). In 1995 aged forty-one he enjoyed a professional rebirth with *Pulp Fiction*. But he's wary about it.

Pulp Fiction was the film that brought Travolta back as an actor and in which he delivered a career performance. The hair is thinning at the front, there's a Prince Charles patch expanding towards the back of the neck, there are a couple of chins that weren't previously in evidence but Travolta was still a man who wanted to twist and shout. In *Pulp Fiction* he did just that in one of the movie's big moments: as the long-haired hit man, with Thurman, his evil employer's statuesque, cocaine-addicted wife, he twisted to the Chuck Berry song 'You Never Can Tell'.

And, of course, you never can. Before he made *Pulp Fiction* in 1994 Travolta thought his career was over: 'There were hints about this film or that film but there were never any serious offers. I have strong beliefs but even they could not help me from feeling that things were finished. This was a revival for me.'

In the spring of 1995 he began filming *Get Shorty*, an adaptation of best-selling novelist Elmore Leonard's hilarious tale of a Florida hoodlum who chases a bad bet in Hollywood and suddenly believes Tinseltown might deliver more. And Travolta still remains the first choice of James Cagney and his estate to portray the legendary star in a film biography. Cagney met Travolta after seeing him dance in *Grease* and *Saturday Night Fever* and offered: 'You're my man.' The now always cautious Travolta says: 'It was one of the great compliments of my life and it is a project I intend to complete.'

He was rather awkward in talking about the revival. Money has never been a problem: he and his wife, the actress Kelly Preston, have homes in California and Florida, private jets, send their son Jett, born in 1992, to a private school and their lavish lifestyle would have run and run on Travolta's past achievements. *Pulp Fiction* disrupted his 'retirement'. He let loose that shy smile: 'I thought I'd had my twenty years ... and I was pleased with it and, to be honest, I was happy to go with it until this something special happened. There had always been little things to keep me in the business, but it seemed my style was never going to be in fashion again. *Pulp Fiction* brought me back but I didn't want to be overwhelmed by it. I remain a strong member of the Scientology Church and this helps me keep things in perspective. We're all human and sometimes the compliments do get me carried away but I'd been here before and I could handle it.'

Other Scientology members, like Tom Cruise and Priscilla Presley, supported him in the difficult years. Travolta joined the cult in 1975 and says his belief helped him deal with his fall from stardom. *Pulp Fiction* is macabre comedy – there are gallons of blood, director/writer

Quentin Tarantino's trademark. How did Travolta resolve his beliefs with such gleeful sadism? 'I worried about it for several weeks and then fought through the concept and accepted it. I am the least violent person in the world – well, I think I am – but I saw it more as a cartoon than anything that could be regarded as reality. It gave me a strong part to play. It was enormous fun to do a film like that because it was an ensemble piece and I was able to concentrate on my particular role. It had been a long time since I had worked on a film that had so many scenes. My life seems to have been on a rollercoaster but I was very lucky playing Vincent Vega.'

Until *Pulp Fiction* Travolta was stuck in the memory as the flared-trousered piece of kitsch dancing along to the Bee Gees. There were moments, such as his role in Brian De Palma's *Blow Out* but they were just that – moments. The *Look Who's Talking* films made money but didn't do much for his reputation. Tarantino – an admitted couch potato and fan of *Welcome Back, Kotter* – says Travolta always attracted him as a performer and that he saw him as Vincent, the sleek-haired somewhat goofy hitman. 'John brought a whole life to the movie. I didn't need a young punk – I needed someone who would understand the depths of what was required. He provided that with no problem.'

It's always difficult to deal with fame, and Travolta commented, 'One moment you're the flavour that everyone wants, then you become yesterday's boy. I'm not bitter about what happened to me, only grateful that I was given another chance. I think it made a new life for me, made me regarded as a grown-up. For years many people perceived me as simply this guy from a long time ago who danced around in movies. What happened for me was a change in attitude. In the early 1990s I felt as low as I've ever done. I really thought that things were never going to happen for me again but it changed. Things change. Life changes – and that's what we've all got to believe.'

Sophia Loren would endorse that thought. The face, the enormous almond-shaped eyes, aquiline nose, chiselled chin and neck, is legendary, and the wide, Italian hips flagrantly emphasize a figure that has created millions of fantasies and made as many movie dollars. Sophia Loren still projects a powerful sexual mystique. She is a star survivor, a woman who has stared age in the face until time blinked. She is positive and erudite, an hourglass of wisdom. She is also the only European celebrity who has maintained an international appeal over almost four decades. Brigitte Bardot – who celebrated her sixtieth birthday in 1994 along with Loren, whom she loathes over Loren's decision to accept a multi-million-dollar contract to advertise fur coats – Claudia Cardinale, Monica Vitti, Gina Lollobrigida have, to be kind, faded.

Loren continued to flourish especially in *Prêt-à-Porter* (a.k.a. *Ready to Wear*) which is maverick director Robert *M.A.S.H.* Altman's 1995 irreverent look at the fashion business. The movie reunited Loren with her long-time co-star Marcello Mastroianni. It was very much an ensemble piece but many, including Meryl Streep who called Loren's performance 'a revelation', believed the 'old lady' stole the show. The Italian icon remains radiant. She is the wife and mother caught, rather than trapped, in the body of a sex symbol. Somehow all the wrong bits – the large mouth, weak chin and those hips that got an alphabet of men from Cary Grant to Peter Sellers into trouble – add up to one of life's more magnificent accidents.

She and her husband, the octogenarian film producer Carlo Ponti, have homes in Switzerland, Florida and the American West Coast – they spend most of their time in a leafy, suburban corner of California on the east side of Los Angeles – powerful connections, a worldwide following and enormous wealth, but Loren's most beloved treasures are her sons Edoardo, twenty-two, and Carlo Junior, twenty-six.

She is as pragmatic as she is graceful about growing old: 'The difficult time for a woman isn't reaching sixty or seventy but turning thirty. Women are children until they are thirty. Only then do they become adults. I've never hidden my age from the world because I don't care. We can't hide time. I'm not frightened of it. I'm finding my second youth. Actually, I rather like birthdays. It is a good reason to talk to yourself, to ask yourself what you have been doing, what you are doing and what you will do. Women who can't take stock turn to drink, take pills or worse. If I ever feel depressed I consider what I have done and what I have accomplished – starting from nothing and arriving now with so much happiness. It is not luck. I don't believe in luck. It is wanting that counts. I have always wanted. That is the secret of me. Even as a child from a poor family whose mother was not married to my father I wanted and I got. I did not want – ever –

for others to get for me. I pay, not just in money, but in suffering and pain and anxiety for what I have achieved.'

Loren's mother Romilda Villani lived in Pozzuoli, near Naples, and wanted to be a film star. She won a Greta Garbo lookalike contest when she was seventeen but her mother stopped her taking the prize of a first-class ticket to California and a Hollywood screen test. Villani rebelled and ran away to Rome where she met Riccardo Scicolone. He was the father Loren met for the first time when she was five. 'I always felt I had no father. Even when you're young you get accustomed to the negative things in life. You say to yourself, "Maybe it has to be like this." But, at the same time, you don't consider yourself to be like other children because they have a father and a mother. I don't talk like this about my father because I have feelings of hatred. Hatred is something I don't know. Besides, I had a lot of love around me. My grandmother and my grandfather loved my sister and me very much.'

Her sister Maria, to whom Loren is very close, is four years younger. She, too, was the illegitimate daughter of Scicolone, but it was only years later when Loren was a star that she was given his name. 'Maria suffered so much. She didn't want to go to school. We supported each other.' Loren's sons are also four years apart and she says: 'I always tell Edoardo, "You should love your brother." I say the same thing to Carlo because I like it when brothers are close to each other. For, after all, what else do we have in life but family?'

The world found her quickly. Sofia Scicolone, as she was then, suffered from mites and lice as a child. She was

so thin other children called her Sofia Stuzzicadente –
Sofia Toothpick. When she blossomed at fourteen, Loren,
like her mother, won a beauty contest, which sent her on
her way to Rome. Her mother, always regretful about her
own missed opportunity, was a supportive and often
pushy stage mother. The young Loren won her first film
role as an extra in *Quo Vadis*, the spectacular Robert
Taylor vehicle in 1951. She appeared in a string of films
including *Era lui, sì, sì!*, an Italian romp in which she went
topless, and has made nearly a hundred, including her
1961 Oscar Best Actress performance in *Two Women*. She
is not precious about her early career, joking, 'I'm not
ashamed of my bare-bottom beginnings.' She was first
seen as a voluptuous sex symbol with *Boy on a Dolphin* in
1957, but does not regret it: 'I liked it because I was doing
it in a joking kind of way. And I knew that it was a
preparation for what I would do later on. It's impossible
to be a sex symbol all your life. You have to be terribly
young and then your career is very short, so at some point
you have to choose roles that you can go further with.
That's what I did when I made *Two Women*. I was twenty-
five and I played the mother of a fifteen-year-old girl. I
really established myself as an actress with that and then
I had wonderful roles.'

Her most spectacular and often controversial one has
been her off-screen marriage to producer Carlo Ponti.
They've been together more than forty years. He is
twenty-one years older than her and there have always
been stories of other men in her life. He was married
when they met and, as Italy did not recognize divorce, his
marriage was dissolved in Mexico. He and Loren married

by proxy in 1957. They were branded in Italy as 'public sinners' and threatened with arrest for bigamy. Only when Ponti became a French citizen and secured a French divorce in 1966 was the marriage officially pronounced legal.

Nineteen fifty-seven also saw the release of *The Pride and the Passion* in which Loren co-starred with Cary Grant and Frank Sinatra. During filming – and before her marriage – Loren had an affair with Cary Grant. He was fifty-two. 'When I met Cary I was twenty-three. He had been my dream since I was a little girl – tall, handsome, charming, funny, gentle. Of course, Carlo and Cary had nothing in common but I loved them both.' She turned down Grant's marriage proposal because Ponti's divorce came through. If circumstances had been different? 'Yes, I would have married Cary Grant.'

Of her other supposed high-profile romance with Peter Sellers, who co-starred with her in *The Millionairess* in 1961, she says: 'We were never lovers. I have made pictures with Marcello Mastroianni, Clark Gable, William Holden, Alan Ladd – lots of fascinating men – but they can't all be lovers. It's gossip. Peter Sellers was a great personality and I adored him but lovers – no.'

She's philosophical about what could be seen as public attempts to wreck her marriage: the gossip columns, the sleazy stories: 'I don't resent it. I don't even like to talk about it. It seems to me so natural to be married and to stay married. I think if you find the right person to be with you have to stick to it even though sometimes you may have moments of depression and unhappiness. But that all passes. What stays is the affection you have. I think you have to try to swallow the bitter things. Most of the time I don't forget but I forgive. I am quite a fatalist. I am Neapolitan and I look at life with an optimistic eye.'

Her sons are living evidence of her optimism. She suffered two miscarriages before doctors told her she would never have children. 'I was convinced that it was not true because I believe if I really put my energies into something it happens. When I became pregnant I spent the whole nine months – both times – in bed. Maybe that's my strength – I really go all the way. The lowest point in my life was when I lost my two unborn children – I didn't want that again. As a mother I feel very vulnerable. We live in a dangerous world but I try to keep my fears to myself. You have to give your children confidence in life, people, society, and in the world today.

'Sex without love is ridiculous, like washing your face – something you do because you have to. Love starts when you like the way a man is, the way he looks at you, not simply what he does in bed. What Carlo was able to bring me was a sense of equilibrium, a balance, in a way that a younger man would never have been able to do. To keep on living the way you want to you have to fight every day. I learned to fight early. And I haven't stopped.'

Sophia's choice: 'The best year of my life? When I turned fifty. I had dreaded that birthday for a long time and when it finally came I realized something: every age has its satisfactions. I had achieved a certain harmony in my life, a summing-up. I'd been down a long road and had become reflective about my personal and professional lives. It was like a red light at which I stopped and looked back. I'd come through it all and I was proud. I still am.'

Shortly after he first broke through he became known as the 'new' Gary Cooper or the 'new' Steve McQueen but Kevin Costner seemed *different*. Whatever demons lurked he appeared to have overcome them although he frankly admitted to having 'a dark side'. That, however, sounded like public relations spice – maybe he was in need of some Tinseltown gossip-pages character-building. In Hollywood if they're not talking about you it's time to plan your memorial service – that way, at least, *someone* comes to see you.

When I first met Costner he had just completed *No Way Out*, which boasted a strong cast, a complex plot with a clever twist and a raunchy sex scene involving Kev and co-star Sean Young in the back seat of a limousine driving round and round the historic sights of Washington, DC. It was an exotic trip. But the limousine-lover image was not him, he said. The love scenes were difficult, embarrassing. Sean Young, more experienced in such brief celluloid encounters, helped him.

Since then, Costner has helped himself to the handsome pickings of Hollywood, the rainbow of fame, money and Oscars. In 1995, certainly privately and possibly professionally, it all went wrong. The man who had seemed to be above the temptations of celebrity, while having an uncanny knack at the box office, had stumbled. Hollywood people were talking about his 1995/1996 film

Waterworld – the most expensive movie ever made – as his Waterloo. His wife Cindy, who had paid her way through college by appearing as Snow White at California's Disneyland, had filed for divorce after sixteen years of marriage. There had been much gossip of Costner's serial philandering. It was a bitter battle, in the middle of which were their children, Annie, Lily and Joe, aged ten, seven and six.

Costner found himself in a corner. It was a surprise to most, for he had appeared always to be in control and to be his own man. No better example of this was his Oscar bonanza *Dances With Wolves* which the film industry had predicted would be his demise. With his wife's support he thumbed his nose at the doomwatchers and, against the odds, turned an overlong film into a box-office and critical success.

Costner will talk until the cowboys come home – or until his PR minders tap their Rolexes – when you get him on the subject of the epic Western that brought him everything Hollywood dreams of: money, power, status and the sort of sensational, life-changing superstardom that some live to regret. He was always aware of the pitfalls but says he wouldn't change a minute of his experience in bringing *Dances With Wolves* to the screen. It was simply 'the one film in my life I knew I had to make even if it meant I could never make another'.

He turned down some of the best leading-man roles on offer – *Presumed Innocent* (which went to Harrison Ford), *The Hunt for Red October* (Alec Baldwin), *Bonfire of the Vanities* (Tom Hanks) – which turned out to be a lucky miss – and *Prince of Tides* (Nick Nolte) – and spent two years trying to convince Hollywood to give him $18 million and let him produce, direct and star in a three-hour Western about peace, love, racial injustice and Sioux Indians. While gossip talked of a stupendous 'Kevingate' flop, first-time director Costner kept his cool and his faith in his vision, the film he still describes as 'my love letter to the past'. On Oscar night 1991 he was vindicated: *Dances* won him seven Oscars including Best Picture and Best Director. He also won the prestigious Directors' Guild Director of the Year and an armful of Golden Globes.

Before *Dances* Costner had been little more than a Hollywood pretty boy, as witness the sexy stud to Susan Sarandon in *Bull Durham* and to the smouldering Sean Young in *No Way Out*. She called him 'shy, puritanical and such a private guy' and worried that she'd embarrassed him during their electrifying sex scene. He'd made a lot of people, notably Sean Connery, dance on their toes in the brilliant *The Untouchables* and the word was out, at last, that he was a star in the making when he took his all-or-nothing gamble on *Dances*

Afterwards he was as famous as Madonna was infamous. The two icons met backstage after her show: he, polite, earnest, strictly brought-up Californian working-class boy, told her the show was 'neat'. She stuck her fingers down her throat as he left, a gesture captured on her no-frames-banned video that signalled 'square' to the world. The incident seemed to sum up the essential Costner. He was 'nice', polite and honest, a man of his word, a loving family man out of place in back-stabbing Hollywood. He also talked the image: 'You like to think you do the right thing. It's the way we were brought up.' His father Bill, a former railwayman, says: 'All the Costners are good men.'

Whenever possible Cindy and the children would travel on location with him. They were on the set of *Dances* in South Dakota, appearing as pioneers in the opening scene, and Cindy helped release tensions by organizing parties, including a Hawaiian luau and a 1950s' prom.

The couple were just like 1950s prom sweethearts when they met in 1978. She was shy, he was shyer; she was Snow White while he, he says, was 'a bit like Goofy, a late developer'. He's made up for it, but until the divorce action he maintained that Cindy and the children were the most important thing in his life.

He knew of the danger his superstardom had brought to his marriage: twenty-four-hour-days living and breathing work, twenty-four-hour-days of women throwing themselves at him at work, camping outside his homes in Pasadena and Malibu and wherever he might go. The possibility of dangerous liaisons was, he said, 'the coolest thing. Are you kidding? To undress somebody? To be undressed. To be physically, somehow, just taken.'

Before the divorce he said his marriage 'isn't perfect' and his brother-in-law David Silva agreed: 'It wasn't easy when he first became so famous. But Cindy grew with it real well.' Costner's brother Danny, his financial adviser, said: 'It got to be tough on Cindy. This business is such an emotional rollercoaster. It's bigger than life and the stakes are high.' Whatever the gamble, it had seemed to pay off for Costner. Until 1995.

Not only was his domestic situation nasty, there were

breakers ahead for *Waterworld*. The film was given the go-ahead by Universal Studios with a budget of $100 million. By the spring of 1995 the cost was estimated at more than $200 million once the price for marketing and prints of the film were included. All involved were so nervous that a giant water-tank on a Hollywood lot was hidden behind blue sheeting and scaffolding to shield it from prying eyes. Security guards patrolled the perimeter round the clock. At the time, 'Everyone is very paranoid at this point' was the unofficial word from the set.

Universal Studios were concerned that their star's personal problems and the endless gossip about turmoil during filming, of sackings and overspending, would jinx the film. They were just as nervy down at the City of Commerce where a replica of a huge supertanker, a great, rusting hulk, was also being used to complete some of the action sequences of *Waterworld*.

It had all the hallmarks of Arnold Schwarzenegger's box-office belly-flop, *Last Action Hero*. But, of course, no one had seen the film. Costner had been written off with *Dances* and the snipers are still keen to knock him off his pedestal. Financially, they had got a clear shot. *Jurassic Park* cost $57 million to make and, in America and Canada alone, returned $357 million. What does a 200-million-dollar film have to make to become a blockbuster? An awful lot.

Waterworld is a strong adventure film (a Mad Max on the water story). The director was Costner's friend Kevin Reynolds (*Robin Hood: Prince of Thieves*). Costner played Mariner who sounded like something out of *Star Trek*, part human, part amphibian. The co-stars include Dennis Hopper as chief nasty and Jeanne Tripplehorn who in the sex stakes made mincemeat of Sharon Stone in *Basic Instinct*. She also played Tom Cruise's wife in *The Firm*. The screenplay was action packed and was conceived by writers including those involved with Harrison Ford's *The Fugitive* and Keanu Reeves's *Speed*. However, Costner's input was all over the script. And although Kevin Reynolds was the director this was Costner's project. That was made abundantly clear when Reynolds left the film after a row with Costner over final editing. The omens were bad. And Costner *needed* a hit. Even with Clint Eastwood as his co-star *A Perfect World* only managed a little more than $30 million in America. The US domestic take for *Wyatt Earp* was $25 million and *The War* made $16.5 million. This is in an economic climate where earning $100 million is around a B minus.

Whether *Waterworld* could ever make the production costs back was in question. Filming began on 27 June 1994, on the big island of Hawaii and did not end until March 1995. Normal production of a full-scale action film would be three or, at the most, four months.

Kevin Costner was in the Sink or Swim business.

But Costner remained cooler than anyone else involved in *Waterworld* and by the summer of 1995 it was the most talked and written about movie in years. On release in America at the end of July it soared to number one at the box office. Audiences wanted to know what all the fuss was about and as July turned into August it continued to do blockbuster business. Universal Studios, relieved and happy, predicted a repeat performance throughout the world.

Nevertheless, *Waterworld* because of the vast amounts

of money involved in the enterprise, faced a tremendous economic challenge if it was ever to rise above the choppy financial waters. But Costner had certainly not sunk. He was more sought after than ever. He decided to spend some time on the golf course – making *Tin Cup*, a movie set in the world of golf. It was produced and directed by Ron Shelton with whom he made *Bull Durham*. The budget was a fraction of the cost of *Waterworld*. Costner said through that crooked grin of his that that he welcomed the change of pace.

Other stars have also dived in at the deep end. Tom Hanks began with a *Splash*.

There's a scene well into *Joe Versus the Volcano* where Tom Hanks, as the average guy of the title, is all but lost at sea floating atop some Vuitton-style luggage. The love of his life may or may not have been wiped out. She lies unconscious near by. Hanks's Joe Banks fiddles with his short-wave radio and something bouncy from around Motown bursts out. Joe, in his designer and over-long shorts, begins to boogie. Disney wouldn't try it with cartoons. But, for a moment, you believe it. And that is the magic of Tom Hanks. No other actor could pull off that one. Or being in love with a mermaid (*Splash*, 1984) or being a thirteen-year-old boy in a thirty-five-year-old man's body (*Big*, 1988). His vulnerability works wonders.

It brought him his second Oscar in 1995, for *Forrest Gump*, the unlikely tale of an *idiot savant* with an IQ of 75 who, by accident and happenstance, leads a charmed life. Computer graphics allowed us to see Gump dance with Elvis, appear on a talk show with John Lennon and meet three former American presidents during director Robert

Zemeckis's (another Oscar winner) compact capsule of forty years of American history.

Hanks also won Best Actor in 1994 for his often moving performance as a lawyer dying of Aids in *Philadelphia*. That film had a television movie disease-of-the-week feel about it, with none of the rancour that devastating disease brings out in those touched by it.

Hanks triumphed, and it's because he believes in what he does. Of *Gump* he said: 'It's incredibly sentimental – but it's not cheap sentiment. I'm perplexed by the success. It's a good movie. It's a very effective movie. But this bizarre kind of success doesn't make sense. When it first came out we were all hoping – from a box-office point of view – that it would clear $100 million. It passed $250 million in the first ten weeks, making it Paramount Pictures' most successful film ever.'

He is passport picture perfect. At six feet tall with dark hair and no distinguishing marks he calls himself 'a neutral point of view' for any project. Well, this 'neutral' person's agents were asking $15 million a film before his 1995 Oscar win.

Hanks insists: 'I'm not a chameleon. I don't disappear. I don't think I'm ugly but I don't have those chiselled good looks. That makes me something of a blank canvas for whatever the texture of the movie. I'm lucky. I've been labelled this Everyman. So, I guess I am appropriate for Everything. No one fears me when my face appears on camera. I don't carry any sort of agenda with me. I used to be a wiseass but I'm not so much of a wiseass any more. And because of all that I think the audience may be willing to go down whatever road my movies take. I don't threaten any man's sense of virility or any woman's sense of security or decorum. We're always toying with being caught in the big lie. Some movie-goers may say: "These people are faking it." Well, exactly. We're paid to pretend. It's very scary but great fun.'

Growing up wasn't, though. Hanks was born on 9 July 1956, and his parents divorced five years later. He and his brother and sister lived with their father, Amos, an itinerant cook; their baby sister stayed with his mother. Hanks's father remarried twice, his mother three times. At one time he had eleven assorted siblings: 'There were always about fifty people in the house. I didn't exactly feel like an outsider but I was sort of one. We were total strangers, all thrust together. I remember in school we had to draw a picture of our house and family and I ran out of places to put people. I put them on the roof. I had three mothers, five grammar schools and ten houses by the time I was ten.'

He suffered his own marital problems. He was twenty when he married actress/producer Samantha Lewes ('I think there should be a law against anyone under thirty-five getting married') but it failed, leaving son Colin and daughter Elizabeth coping with a family separation. 'We tried to make it work but it was a college affair – we were way, way too young.'

A year after the 1987 divorce he married again. He met dark-haired and dynamic actress Rita Wilson on his 1985 film *Volunteers*. By the time she appeared with him and Meg Ryan in *Sleepless in Seattle* they had a son, Chester, and what Hanks calls a quiet family life in a Spanish-style house a forty-five-minute drive towards the

Pacific Ocean from Hollywood. He uses a Dodge van to commute. Around Los Angeles on the car-pool circuit that's a 'Mommy Van'.

He says his biggest regret is that his two older children – they live in San Francisco with their mother – are far away. 'But I still have a lot of contact with them, certainly much more than I had with my parents when I was little.' He has now resolved all conflicts with his parents. For years he could not understand why they broke up the family but now he says: 'They had to do what they had to do.'

As had astronaut Jim Lovell. Two days into the Apollo 13 mission in April 1970, which was to have been the third moon-walking voyage, one of two oxygen tanks blew and the main rocket engine was destroyed. The explosion caused a complete loss of oxygen and electrical power, which forced the three astronauts aboard to evacuate the command module and use the lunar module – which had a separate engine – as a Star Trek-style lifeboat. The lunar module, which was designed for two people, had enough oxygen for forty-five hours. It had to be stretched to ninety hours before the module could be ferried back to Earth. For four days the world watched as Mission Control in Houston, Texas, struggled to get men and craft back alive. The astronauts did not know if they would suffocate from their own carbon dioxide, freeze or burn up on re-entry into the Earth's atmosphere. Lovell returned safely to his family.

In director Ron Howard's 1995 film *Apollo 13* Hanks, the year's Best Actor Oscar winner, put on a NASA spacesuit as Jim Lovell. It is a $52 million investment for Universal Studios but they are gambling that the combination of drama, space and Hanks will achieve lift-off. Hanks has been a space exploration freak since Stanley Kubrick's *2001*, which he has seen countless times: 'It was the first time I saw a film that used light and image and sound to tell a story.' Hanks says Rita Wilson saved him from a life lost in emotional space, a life of loneliness. Of *Forrest Gump* he comments that it is a movie without a message. Except, maybe: 'That it is better to be with a family than alone.' Hollywood saccharin, perhaps, but Tom Hanks, the man who established that nice guys can finish first, gets away with it.

Another 1985 Oscar winner was Jessica Lange. She is an off-beat beauty: a tall natural blonde with an equally natural flat nose so unlike these pert little upturned things that sniff around Beverly Hills. She was a model before she jumped into the arms of Jeff Bridges and *King Kong* in 1976. 'Successful model? I doubt that anybody could find a published photograph of me. The year I modelled was the most painful year of my life. Editors would always talk to you as though you were a piece of merchandise. You get to a point where you are tired of worrying about how people are going to judge you. I'm not pretty. I am pretty. Am I talented? I'm smart, maybe? Forget it.'

Nearly two decades later, aged forty-six, Ms Lange collected her second Oscar, as Best Actress for *Blue Sky* in which she co-starred with Tommy Lee Jones – and she will be a likely contender again in 1996, for *Losing Isaiah*. Like Lange, it is a formidable piece of work. The film, directed by Stephen Gyllenhaal, was the *Kramer vs. Kramer* of the late 1990s. It dealt with the complex situation of interracial adoption. Lange is a social worker who adopts a black child. Then, Halle Berry as the boy's natural mother, a former crack cocaine addict, wants the child back. It doesn't take much to imagine the drama and emotions involved. And the politically correct lobby stalking the corridors of the movie. 'Black babies belong with black mothers,' says the lawyer representing Halle Berry's character. But, in the movie – as often now in real life – the adoptive parents fight back.

'It was a film with a strong theme and a message,' says Lange, who felt 'compelled' to make it. She believes it is an issue which has side-stepped most people. No longer. She and Halle Berry deliver stunning performances. Which is what Lange has been doing since she got out of the clutches of King Kong. After starring as Kong's handmaiden, she became a trivia joke on the Hollywood glitz circuit. Her later pursuits proved them all wrong.

Lange is happier in the backwoods than the Polo Lounge. She lives in the Virginia countryside with Pulitzer-prizewinning writer/actor Sam Shephard, their son and daughter and her daughter by ballet maestro Mikhail Baryshnikov, cats, dogs and any bird that flies by and wants a meal. Before, they were in Santa Fe, New Mexico, and before that in her home countryside of Minnesota, where she retains her custom-built log cabin (no phone, no television) and where she chops wood and watches the trout bite. There are good fishing streams and the bites are as many as the offers she gets every day from Hollywood. Many must choke on that. This was the model/bimbo who got a little lucky so long ago. Now, like Fonda and Streisand, she's the dealmaker.

But Lange is not some snappy tyrant. She just doesn't

play by Rodeo Drive rules. That, she finds, diverts the uninteresting traffic. Her attitude deflects projects she would not consider. Movies like *Losing Isaiah* are a choice made through many years of playing the Hollywood game. 'In a sense I think I was lucky because some people take off – they're flying – and then something hits them in mid-career. Suddenly, the bottom falls out. I got over all this disappointment and rejection and self-doubt and all of those things there were imposed on me for those first couple of years. It was great, for now I know none of that will ever affect me again – or as strongly as it did.'

That uncertain period ended with Bob Fosse's *All That Jazz* in 1979. But Lange believes it was in 1980 when she and Jack Nicholson famously took over the kitchen table in the remake of *The Postman Always Rings Twice* that her career took off. The film did not do as well as the 1946 John Garfield/Lana Turner teaming but it proved something to the critics, to Lange and to Hollywood. She had that indefinable 'it'.

She rang the bells again as the hauntingly troubled actress Frances Farmer in *Frances*, and as the space-cadet soap-opera star adored by Dustin Hoffman in *Tootsie*. Those two 1982 films won her double Oscar nominations as Best Actress (*Frances*) and Best Supporting Actress (*Tootsie*). She jogged off with Best Supporting, and then received nominations for Best Actress for *Country* (1984) and for portraying country-and-western singer Patsy Cline in *Sweet Dreams* (1985). She followed that with *Crimes of the Heart* with Diane Keaton and Sissy Spacek.

Lange, soft spoken, direct as black-coffee-no-sugar-but-I-would-like-the-doughnut, possibly tries more than most to compensate. 'The hardest thing is the kids. It just kills me. The other stuff isn't hard – working long hours, doing the whole emotional thing. But being away from the kids gets worse rather than better. The thing is you get seduced by a great part. I've always felt that each one comes at a particular time in your life to give you the means to explore areas that are important to delve into. But I can look back to when I really considered myself an actress – with *Postman* – and I never felt like I was wasting time playing any of these roles.

'If I didn't have children I'd be a much better actress. I wouldn't be so distracted. I could pour 100 per cent of my energies into it, to promote the investigation which acting is. But I can't do that so I have to pick and choose really deliberately. I must say there has been a lot of suffering along the way with misjudgements. But I've got the children, work I enjoy, and the enchanted land.'

She grew up in the sixties, travelled to Europe and got caught up in the excitements of the time. She returned to America with confused emotions: 'I'd feel a cold hand grabbing my heart and starting to squeeze. That was the fear of not getting out again. Others in the family, who couldn't wait to get away, are retreating further and further into the woods. I think it's a family trait. It's something about the land – it's that mysterious, inexplicable connection to the land.'

On her family land around Cloquet (pop. 8,000), Minnesota, as a child she imagined herself as Melanie from *Gone With The Wind* one day and Scarlett O'Hara the next. Her father, Al, was a wanderer – the family moved eighteen times before settling in Minnesota – and was as much a dreamer as his daughter. Her mother, Dorothy, wanted to be a dancer. The four children followed their own dreams: Ann, three years older, is a Minneapolis art director, Jane, a year older, has a schooner and sails the seas on charter, George, six years younger, is another wanderer, an airline pilot. Their sister has settled down as one of the great actresses of the century.

During her seven-year relationship with Baryshnikov, she flew constantly between Los Angeles, New York, Minnesota, Milan, anywhere he happened to be dancing or she filming. It sounds romantic and exciting but such a lifestyle can jet-lag relationships. And it did. When she began her affair with Baryshnikov Lange was still married to Spanish photographer Pasco Grande whom she met at Minnesota University. After their divorce in 1982 she was left with $3,479 in the bank. Grande had settled for a lump pay-off. 'It was a lot,' she says, without giving the full arithmetic.

Lange is no Scrooge but she's careful, say her family, who recall that her first words when she was three were 'Charge it!' No money was involved when she and Baryshnikov separated. She and Shephard flash neither their cash nor their credit cards.

What they both push for is strong, controversial work. She says she identified so much with *Losing Isaiah* because she feels the importance of family. It contradicts her instincts: 'In my mind's eye I always see myself as settling down but I can't stand to be in the same place all the time. I love arriving in a town I know nothing about and setting up house. It's like life in a gypsy camp. But I think it's inevitable now that we'll stay in one spot. Sam and me and the kids. I've never believed much in marriage. I've never believed that someone like a preacher or a judge should determine how you live. I think I would get married if it was in the best interests of my family. It used to seem like legalese but now, with Sam, I really think I have something that is going to last a lifetime. Before it was hopefulness on my part rather than an absolute knowing in your heart. 'Before it was a dream. This is reality. No more dreaming.'

Robert Evans's mind tumbles like a dryer. He admits he's no angel but he is a Hollywood legend and, if you like characters on the racy side, a naughty delight. He has no illusions and his life has been punctuated with a Damon Runyon confection of guys and dolls, but mostly dolls. A valley of them. Pills, cocaine and girls. Lots of girls. And wives. The snag was he confused the girls and the wives. In 1996 this devil will create *The Saint* for the big screen.

Like the lawns surrounding Beverly Hills, Robert Evans has always been a perfect-looking specimen. The demons have been kept hidden. He is the pretty boy who proved terrific as a Hollywood mogul only to be professionally mugged by cocaine and personally sabotaged by an overcharged lust for life. And women.

His autobiography, *The Kid Stays in The Picture*, was a worldwide best-seller in 1994/1995 and HBO cable television bought the rights in 1995 for a mini-series. It is a brutally frank tale of being to Hollywood, hell and back. But the man who produced *Love Story* and *The Godfather*, the one-time head of Paramount Studios, former husband of actresses Sharon Huegeney, Camilla Spaarv, Miss America Phyliss George and Ali MacGraw – who left him for Steve McQueen – encourages you to believe he is in heaven. He has style. There is an English butler to greet you with an icy lager on a hot afternoon before you wander around the swimming pool with its twenty-seven separate jets of water which make a fountain out of the centrepiece. The garden is overlooked by a Wimbledon-modelled tennis court – Evans is a tennis fanatic – and the house itself, which Evans has hung on to only through the financial help of friends like Jack Nicholson, Warren Beatty and Roman Polanski (who directed his classic movies *Chinatown* and *Rosemary's Baby*), is the equivalent of a National Trust contender.

Robert Evans became a Hollywood player again in the 1990s. He produced the Sharon Stone movie *Silver* which, despite disappointing cinema box office, did financial wonders on video. It was the Evans chat that convinced Stone to make the movie so soon after establishing herself in a similar erotic role in *Basic Instinct*. It was a coup, she admits, that few could have achieved. In 1996 this tarnished Hollywood star is bringing back *The Saint*. He owns the rights to a franchise which has 007 stamped all over it. On television the likeable rogue – a *Lovejoy* adventurer but with money in the bank – has been portrayed by Roger Moore and, more recently, Ian Ogilvy. In 1940s movies suave characters like George Sanders and Louis Hayward played the role. Evans is looking for a new-century *Saint*: 'Of course, the lead is the most important aspect. I feel he has to be a certain type – a Hugh Grant or maybe Daniel Day-Lewis.'

But the favourite British star for the role of Leslie Charteris's halo-hero was Ralph Fiennes. 'I think he would be wonderful,' said Evans. Of course, the Hollywood moneymen might have demanded home-grown talent and the two names Evans has on his notepad are dimpled Oscar-winner Michael Douglas, and Ray Liotta, who was so wonderful in Martin Scorsese's *Good Fellas*. Evans adds, 'This is a business and you have to look at all the options – the end result is to get the movie made.'

He has had great experience in this. Around the table where Marlon Brando signed to make *The Godfather* he produced books and magazines that catalogue his roller-coaster life. 'I made millions for other people but I was never a businessman.' He shouts for his driver and asks him: 'Do you think I can make the payroll this week?' The man, who is clearly fond of Evans, shakes his head. 'Probably not.'

'My movies have made billions but you have more in the bank than I have,' Evans says quite happily.

You glance around at the surroundings, at the Hockney and Picasso on the walls near posters for the actor Robert Evans's films like 1958's *The Fiend Who Walked The West*, in which he played the title role, and *The Sun Also Rises* when he was a handsome matador. (It was on that 1957 picture which starred Ava Gardner that producer Darryl Zanuck vetoed his director and said of Evans: 'The kid stays in the picture.') This is grade A Hollywood living – and Evans smiles: 'Thankfully I have friends. Throughout the 1980s I earned about ten thousand dollars and that was from a photograph of me that was used for an advertising campaign. But I picked myself up and got back in business again. That was what my book was all about, reversing problems rather than immersing in them. God, if I can do it so can everyone else. We can come back even when all around us think we're dead.'

Robert Evans wasn't just dead. He was buried. Alive. He couldn't even get a coffee at the commissary at Paramount Studios, which he had turned into the number one studio in the world. As its boss he produced a remarkable series of films including classics like *The Odd Couple*, and breakthrough movies like *Goodbye Columbus* as well as *Love Story* and *The Godfather*. 'It was hell. For a decade, for the eighties, I had nothing. I have all this energy and for a whole ten years there was nothing – except the loyalty of my friends. They helped me survive. Warren and Jack and people like that helped me. Dustin Hoffman didn't – and I'd helped him through difficult times in the seventies.' Hoffman had worked for Evans in 1976's *Marathon Man*, which also starred Laurence Olivier. Evans flew to Britain to get friends of the ailing Olivier to convince Lloyds to insure him for the role of an evil Nazi tormentor and dentist. 'It was a big moment in my life. Olivier lived with me while we were filming and although the doctors were saying he hadn't long to go he lived for another dozen years or so. It was quite something.'

Soon Evans could have used another miracle. The actor-producer who was 'discovered' by the legendary Norma Shearer as he sat by the phone by the swimming pool of the Beverly Hills Hotel was known as the 'golden boy' as much for his Acapulco tan as his movie hits. By the late seventies, though, he had suffered a string of failures including *Popeye*, with Robin Williams in the title role, and the tennis romance/drama *Players*, filmed at Wimbledon with Ali MacGraw and the late Dino Martin.

He says his real mistress has always been the movies. He lost Ali MacGraw, who now lives in his guest house since her Malibu home was destroyed in a firestorm, because of his dedication to *The Godfather*, and believes that his other marriages also failed because of his work addiction. What about philandering? 'Well, that might also have had something to do with it,' he concedes. 'I love everything about women. I was never faithful to any of my wives.'

When Hollywood discovered cocaine so did Evans. In 1980 he was convicted of narcotics possession and suddenly he was bad news. The headlines got nastier. He bought the rights to a non-fiction book titled *The Cotton Club*, about 1920s jazz-age New York. It involved him in a dangerous world, from the corridors of government in Puerto Rico to the drug fields of Colombia to the good life of Miami and Manhattan and the fast lane of Beverly Hills. It also involved him with Roy Radin who was a big man with a big mouth. When they struggled with Radin's coffin in 1989 and finally got him in the ground there were more sighs of relief than tears in Hollywood. But though the corpse was buried, the rumours that he was shot to silence were not. Along with others, Karen De Layne Greenberger, also known as Lanie Jacobs, the Black Widow, the Bimbo from Hell and the Coke Whore, was charged with Radin's killing, in which Evans was falsely implicated. But the gossip and controversy stuck. He shrugs now: 'Everything about *The Cotton Club*, which starred Richard Gere, Diane Lane and Bob Hoskins, went wrong. Al Pacino had turned down the lead, Sylvester Stallone took it and then dropped out and it was eventually a critical and commercial belly-dive flop. It was one of those projects where nothing would go right. I went to people I had made millions for and asked for financial help and these people turned me down. Women I knew offered to write cheques just to get me through from Friday to Monday on the payroll. Women are much more loyal. It was an evil and difficult time for me. I thought I could never turn it around. But something makes you go on and I did it, with help from some friends. I wrote my book myself because I wanted it to be all truth. I didn't see any point in producing something that wasn't the truth. That's why I've sold the film rights to HBO Cable. Disney and all the other studios wanted it but they would have had to censor my life, which is not a mainstream movie. On cable you can use explicit scenes and language. I wanted to tell the total story not an edited version.

'That's why *The Kid Stays in The Movie* is a sensation. I have not tried to apologize for my life but simply tell it as it happened.' He buzzes off to find some old photographs.

You skip through them and he was the matinée idol Norma Shearer spotted by the swimming pool, a classic good-looking boy. Indeed, he could have played *The Saint*. It's just that the halo wouldn't have fitted.

Elizabeth Taylor Hilton Wilding Todd Fisher Burton Burton Warner Fortensky is *the* star of *The Liz Show*. The walk-on players, like the husbands, flit in and out. The

1995 instalment had Liz in a tizz over a television series, *Destiny*, based on her life. She didn't like the idea. It was not because they were calling it a mini-series – at times that seemed an absurd misnomer – but because she objected to what she regarded as an 'intrusion' into her life.

Kitty Kelley's infamous but wonderfully researched book on Taylor's life was titled *The Last Star* and was reasonably accurate. When she was twelve Taylor was stealing scenes from Lassie. That sort of celluloid felony became somewhat more difficult as she grew older and started to work with people but, nevertheless, she has always been a star. And one who has been celebrated as much for her bourbon capacity and marital record as her talent. Her life has been a tabloid headline. It wasn't the husbands, even Burton, who made the ink run so frenetically but this short, often dumpy, woman with a three-hourglass figure. She and Burton co-starred in *The Taming of the Shrew* – and Taylor had been miscast many times before that – but that, as they say in her adopted Mexican village of Puerto Vallerta, was the big *tamale*. Shrew? Tamed? Not at the last encounter. She is sixtysomething on firecrackers. Her drink of choice is now ginger ale.

On 6 October 1991 she married former construction worker and double-divorcé Larry Fortensky, whom she met in 1988 when they were both recovering from addictions at the Betty Ford Center near Palm Springs in the California desert. He is twenty years younger. It was like Cleopatra marrying Stanley Kowalski on the set of *Peter Pan*. The wedding, at Michael Jackson's Santa Ynez Valley estate near Santa Barbara – the Neverland Valley

– had the bride, sixty-three in 1995, in Valentino, the groom in Versace, and Bubbles the chimp, the ring-bearer, looking for something backless.

What sort of encore did we expect from a woman who can make earrings from the diamonds in her old engagement rings? America saw *Destiny* in May 1995. The mini-series was part of the NBC network's ratings 'sweeps' when all the big players compete for top advertising dollars. NBC believed Liz would deliver and she did. But she had shot herself in her size four shoe. She attempted to have *Destiny* banned and lost. So it became *The TV Film Liz Doesn't Want You To See*. She had the same problem with C. David Heymann who wrote a best-selling biography of Jackie Onassis and was the author of *Liz* on which *Destiny* was based. His was *The Book Liz Wanted Banned*.

What was curious – after all the headlines and horrors, the stories of near death and tragedy, of friends like Rock Hudson dying of Aids (a cause for which she is an admirable fund raiser), of friends from James Dean to Michael Jackson, and the husbands – was that 'intrusion' would be a concern. Nevertheless Taylor ('I don't pretend to be an ordinary housewife') was seriously upset by *Destiny* and hired her Armani-clad legal birds of prey. Lawyer Neil Papiano gave an instant critique of *Destiny* with: 'This is ridiculous. You don't have a right to protect yourself from these vultures?'

The said vultures – the TV producers – however, went pecking after Taylor's legal process was chucked out of court. Naughtily, they began filming in January 1995, and the first scenes were at the mansion where Taylor and Michael Wilding once lived. All Taylor's husbands were portrayed. As was her 'best friend' Debbie Reynolds from whom she stole Eddie Fisher before she dumped him for Burton.

Destiny starred Sherilyn Fenn, who was nothing for Taylor to complain about. In one sequence update for the TV film from Taylor's movie *Ivanhoe* the contrast between the two stars was quite evident.

Fenn, aptly and amply one of the stars of David Lynch's *Twin Peaks*, more than did justice to the medieval costumes. She's also quite a ringer for Taylor in a scene with Rock Hudson (another good lookalike actor in Dan McVicar) where he threatened to throw her in a swimming pool. Throughout, in the weddings, the movies and the marriages, Sherilyn Fenn made Taylor look good. What bruised the project was C. David Heymann's book, in which he alleged that Taylor was abused by three of her husbands. Hotel heir Nicky Hilton is said to have beaten her on their honeymoon. Burton is also said to have got into fisticuffs. And of Mike Todd, the extravagant entrepreneur who died tragically in 1958 in an air crash, it is said that he 'went for her'.

Lawyers again. Taylor's Neil Papiano said: 'The abuse charges are totally false.' He says such allegations could cost her millions. She is selling an image. If that is tarnished so are the gold credit cards. Her name,' he says, 'is all she really has.' And that may be it.

Why should a subject of late-night TV comics and commentators, of the tabloid tease, a British-born wartime evacuee – to Hollywood – object to the TV treatment? If you take it from a professional point she wasn't getting paid. Sherilyn Fenn was. The reason for the Taylor movie, and many like it, is shortage of subjects. The airwaves are packed with time and there is an increasing need for material. Famous names help to fill the slots.

However, many of the subjects are living: in 1995 there were films on *Mia Farrow* (Patsy Kensit played her), *Madonna* (Terumi Matthews starred), *O.J. Simpson* (Bobby Hosea and Jessica Tuck played O.J. and his murdered wife Nicole), *Tyson* (Miachel Jai White and Kristen Wilson were Tyson and former wife actress Robin Givens) and there were two TV shots at *Roseanne*. In one Patrikaa Darbo and Stephen Lee were Roseanne and Tom Arnold; David Graff and Denny Dillon did the honours on another network. Roseanne got upset about some of the casting: she thought Denny Dillon was 'a freaky little thing . . . a midget woman'.

It was bizarre. Hollywood People playing Hollywood People.

HOLLYWOOD REBELS
Chapter 4

'What are you rebelling against?' 'What have you got?'
Marlon Brando, in *The Wild One*

James Dean was the ultimate rebel. He had the glory of
youth with the hype of his early death in 1955. River
Phoenix, a supposedly 'clean' boy, died from drugs outside
the Viper Club in Hollywood – an establishment part-
owned by another Hollywood rebel, Johnny Depp. Drew
Barrymore – the cute little thing in Spielberg's *ET* and
ongoing member of the acting dynasty – went through
drink and drugs before cleaning up and finding excitement by flashing her breasts on television talk shows. She
came from the Barrymore clan, a wild, often wayward,
fabulously talented family.

Debra Winger didn't have a heritage to compete with.
But she had hurdles to jump. Her performance helped
make John Travolta a 'name' and in doing so performed
the same magic trick for herself in *Urban Cowboy* (1980),
winning better notices than her co-star. She literally
allowed Richard Gere to sweep her off her feet in *An
Officer and a Gentleman* (1982) and won a Best Actress
Oscar nomination. As Shirley MacLaine's tragic daughter

in *Terms of Endearment* (1983) she joined the Oscar race again and won the admiration of Jack Nicholson and the now classic line from her co-star and Oscar rival Ms MacLaine: 'Dear, brilliant, turbulent Debra marches to a different drummer than the rest of us.' The irony of that remark from mystical MacLaine, who says she has lived at least half a dozen times before and has led her life to a different orchestra than the majority, was not lost on Debra Winger.

In 1993 she was again in the running for an Academy Award (she lost to Hollly Hunter for *The Piano*) for her moving performance opposite Anthony Hopkins in *Shadowlands* but, typically, it was not something she dwelled on: 'I really don't think about awards very much, thank God. I think about them when I have to answer questions about them – it's great to have your peers say "good work" but I wish we could just go home and make more movies.'

She should have been grinning like a cat that got the cream from her Oscar nomination and all the acclaim, but down-to-earth Debra, who has intimidated Hollywood and most of its men for nearly two decades, just lets a smile play around her face. Jack Nicholson claims he's the only male not frightened of her, insisting that they are twin rebel souls. 'I think he meant that as a compliment,' said Winger, whose favourite film review is one that called her 'a fetching little slut'.

This unpredictable superstar is fetching and elfin as she sits in a reception room of the Raleigh Studios in North Hollywood. She's a clever chameleon who maintains that her greatest asset is the power to say no. Her role in *A Dangerous Woman* as disturbed Martha who cannot tell a lie (no future for *her* in Hollywood) won as much praise as her portrayal of New York writer Joy Gresham who, in *Shadowlands*, disrupts writer C. S. Lewis's comfortable life and then marries him. Although both she and Hopkins were remarkable in that film, it was her outing as misfit Martha, lost in a world that disregards and disdains her, of which she seems most proud. It is difficult to imagine the strange woman with milk-bottle-lens glasses Winger created as the work of the same actress who turned on a Texas bar as she mounted a mechanical bull and turned it into an erotic display as, fast and slow, in skintight red pants, a sheer top and high heels, she rode the bull in *Urban Cowboy* (1980). Or who tempted Nick Nolte in *Cannery Row* (1982) or Robert Redford in *Legal Eagles* (1985). Martha was weird, walked in an off-balance, awkward manner which somehow was threatening.

But Winger, who was forty in 1995, says it wasn't what wardrobe or the make-up department presented that helped her create Martha but rather what she stripped away from herself: 'It was more taking away the extraneous things that I've acquired in my personality that didn't fit. I believe there's Martha in all of us. You know, we become socialized, we have contacts with people and love from our families and we acquire tools to function in society. For me this part was more of a relaxation into her than a striving for something outside of myself. You get those glasses on your face and you see the world in a different way. I've spent time feeling alienated and I know people who have struggled their way out of it. We're not talking about any sort of syndrome – Martha's situation is sociological rather than psychological.

'Deep down I never felt like I fitted in. I fixated on some of the things Martha does. The truth was important to me to the point where I alienated people around me because I couldn't put soft edges on it. I became compulsive about the truth and that hasn't left. It gets me into a lot of trouble.'

Hollywood regards her as eccentric because she chases her feelings rather than the almighty dollar. She rejected Steven Spielberg's offer to be in the original *Raiders of the Lost Ark*, turned down the Kathleen Turner temptress role in *Body Heat* ('I thought they were going to use this second-rate actor in the lead' – it was first choice and Oscar-winner William Hurt) and absolutely believes in freedom to make *her* choices. Often they are original, and often they are not commercial. 'I figure I'm old enough. I get to do that now. I was lucky early on in my career to have big successes and I like some of the movies as well. But I chose what I did because of where I was in my personal life. It never has been for my career – I've always chosen a film because I wanted to explore that part of humanity. But I'm definitely not part of the machine.'

Because she's too honest?

'Because I'm too ugly,' she barks back, with that deep throaty laugh which is the trademark of the brilliant if temperamental and unconventional Winger.

She is, of course, a seductive beauty who was called 'the sexiest tough cookie in Hollywood since Barbara Stanwyck' after *Urban Cowboy*. She started off playing Lynda Carter's younger sister in the 1970s camp television series *Wonder Woman* ('I had my chest pushed up and had to say, "Wow!" all the time') and then went to run the gauntlet with some of Hollywood's major leading men.

Now, the man in her life is son Noah, born in 1989, by former husband and Oscar winner Timothy Hutton. They live in upstate New York where she's a member of the school car-pool and does lots of other 'mussy' things. Each week she travels to Manhattan to talk business. Los Angeles she loathes – or maybe it's the people rather than the city. She certainly has no plans to raise Noah there. 'I'm always very honest with my son. Sometimes I'll say that I'm not ready to talk about something; that he has to be older and he accepts it. He's a pretty honest child.'

Winger has had a colourful love life including her affair with former Nebraska governor Bob Kerrey. Recent stories suggest they are back together again but she laughs: 'I'm so busy with my kid I don't have time to philander.' She's also eased herself away from other wild ways – she allows herself two cigarettes a day now – but one thing she admits she can't control is giving her point of view. Which is anti-feminist. She disdains those who bitch on about the lack of *big* roles for women: 'I'm just so tired of that rap because it's sort of a feminist approach and the fact of the matter is that there are very few good scripts around. Period. That means less good roles for women *and* men. Original material is being encouraged despite the studios – who wants to see the same movie again and again. It's so boring.'

She found *Shadowlands* anything but. It was stimulating she said to go up with Hopkins. 'Anthony is truly from the English school. You could be stymied by the fact that he's had this enormous machine behind him for so many years, the training, the atmosphere that he has been in. But once we got on set there was a communication that went beyond that. I used to spend a lot of time feeling sort of inadequate because I didn't have that kind of training but in the end the work of characters in the movies is quite the same. It might change with theatre but when you come into film it's a world and school all of its own and so we had sort of equal ground to meet on. But what I liked most was that he was really a gentleman which you don't always find with American actors.'

There is a Helmut Newton photograph of Winger, a close, tight shot of her face showing the bump on her nose, the slight scar on her right cheek and the protruding lower lip with an unfiltered, half-smoked Camel with an inch of ash riding on it. It screams defiant Debra. Did she get fed up rebelling and start running?

'I was just living my life.'

Debra Winger is a sort of female Steve McQueen in attitude. A giant among Hollywood People, the legend of McQueen goes on. Even after his death in 1980 he still has an agent – for his estate – on Wilshire Boulevard in Beverly Hills, California. For him the supercool image was everything. Clean-cut with cropped hair and startling blue eyes, he was the original movie macho-man. Steve McQueen was always quick on the draw – he could steal a scene or a girl before anyone else had thought of an opening gambit. He was *The Cincinnati Kid* (1965), seducing Tuesday Weld and Ann-Margret with that big grin.

And the motorbike ace outwitting the Nazis in *The Great Escape* (1963). He was the detective Jackie Bisset couldn't resist in *Bullitt* (1968). The actor who put sex into chess out-manoeuvring Faye Dunaway in *The Thomas Crown Affair* (1968). The star who stole and married his screen lover Ali MacGraw, who co-starred in *The Getaway* (1972).

He was the Magnificent One.

And, even dead, he was voted in 1995 number one of the world's women's all-time top hundred favourite fantasies. After a tragic battle against cancer McQueen died with dignity, at fifty, in 1980. He remains, like James Dean and Marilyn Monroe, a cult figure. And a controversial one.

Tinseltown was bemused by McQueen's rating as number one hunk in the magazine survey – dead Nirvana singer Kurt Cobain was placed two and Sean Connery was three – because there have always been rumours that he was a homosexual. McQueen was a mystery man of the movies. He was reclusive and he was difficult. It made him more of man's man. He became a compulsive womanizer and lost his first wife, the dancer Neile McQueen, because of it. She says he slept with all but two of his female co-stars, who included Natalie Wood, Suzanne Pleshette, Candice Bergen, Linda Evans and Britain's Shirley Ann Field.

McQueen's great friend in Hollywood was Elmer Valentine, who owned nightclubs on Sunset Boulevard including the Roxy where in later years McQueen's bad-boy successors, like Jack Nicholson and Warren Beatty, would live their Lothario lives. 'I treated him nice, gave him the best booth, introduced him to all the girls,' said Valentine adding: 'Steve liked me for three reasons: he never had to pick up a check, I was a bachelor and available to him any time and put no pressure on him. I was kinda like his old lady, except I didn't bug him and he wasn't screwing me.'

Valentine was much more than a nightclub host for McQueen. He had the keys to the bedroom. When the married actor met a girl he would take her off to Valentine's home: 'I'd give him the keys to the burglar alarm but somehow the dumb bastard always managed to set it off. One night we picked up two girls who had just arrived in Los Angeles from some hick town. It's their first day here and already they're screwing *Steve McQueen*. They were thrilled. He comes out of the bedroom with his arms around them and says: "Well, girls ... this is Hollywood."'

McQueen's biographer, Penina Spiegel, says he liked women who shared drugs with him and would indulge in sexual practices that his wife would not tolerate. He was keen on marijuana, cocaine and amyl nitrate, which is used to heighten sexual climax. She wrote:

'Steve was a highly physical man, gifted by nature with the grace of a born athlete. His sexual drive had always been strong. With stardom his sphere of opportunity widened and his appetite intensified.

'Having one woman at a time was no longer enough. Private, personal lovemaking, a one-on-one experience with a woman, was not nearly as titillating as sex with an audience. Steve liked groups. He liked showing off his body and his peepee. The first guy to take off his shirt was Steve; the first guy to drop his pants was Steve.'

Spiegel quotes a lady she describes as 'a blonde, buxom starlet' as telling her about the time she and her equally amply endowed sister spent with the superstar.

'Steve made his sexual wants and needs real clear. He had real simple tastes, like meat and potatoes. Real simple, no courtship like: "Are you ready? C'mere. Fuck me or out I go." My sister and I had a great affair with Steve. Steve wanted to bring in another girl but we objected. "Just to watch," he said. "Really I love you. Our love is beautiful and I just want another girl to see it." We knew right away that this was not right. But Steve was a real lover, filled with thrills and chills. Such a boy! He sure could take you on some fast rides. He liked to take you out on the motorcycle, get you ready till you could hardly wait yourself. He never had any money. We had to buy him coffee and cigarettes. Steve liked that. He liked having women pay for him, who were almost certainly paid for by other men.'

A good friend of McQueen who became a major celebrity, stealing scenes from the rest of *The Magnificent Seven* in 1961, recalled group-sex sessions involving the star and several other men. 'We had some good times together, he and I. We did some funny things with ladies ... two or three girls at a time.' Another friend said: 'Steve liked switching. He enjoyed making love to a woman who was still warm, as it were, from sex with his buddies.'

McQueen's other sexual preferences with women led to the rumours that he was a repressed homosexual but Elmer Valentine said: 'When people say Steve was homosexual he absolutely was not. Absolutely. I personally know because there were times Steve and I fucked in the same room with different girls. He liked to switch girls but there was never a sign of homosexuality. I'm an ex-cop. I know when someone's a homo. I'd been all over the world with Steve. I've been with him for months at a time. I know how he dug women. He never left me to go cruising. I *know* a cruiser. I know the excuses. He never wanted not to be with me. He never tried to get rid of me or duck me in any way. I would have seen that. If he was gay then it was the best performance I've ever seen and he was the greatest actor – and I always told him he wasn't a very good actor. Steve loved women! He loved a nicely shaped ass on a woman – he called them "bubble asses". He wasn't even kinky. He liked being in bed with two girls. All he could think about was getting a chick. But even if Steve *were* gay he wouldn't have let himself be. He was such a macho bastard that if he had that tendency he wouldn't have done it.'

McQueen was anti-gay. He did not like working with homosexual actors and the kiss-kiss luvvie behaviour in Hollywood frightened him. He wanted motorcycles, Mexican beer drunk from the bottle and women. It was his one-track mind in the chase for 'chicks' which made him so magnetic to them. He was always in heat, always interested. At his death he regretted the failure of his marriage to Neile but by then he was married to model-actress Barbara Minty. His roustabout marriage to Ali MacGraw had also ended in divorce. Divorce seems another peril, part of the parcel, for being a Hollywood rebel.

Sean Penn has always played his own game. Once, he was 50 per cent of one of the most famous showbusiness couples ever. Mr Madonna.

By late 1995 he was like a saint with a shoulder holster, a contradiction, a slowly spoken man who walks into a room as though at any moment he will have to circle the wagons against the ambush. The eyes have always been dark and brooding but now, at thirty-six in 1995, all the boyishness has been creased from his face. The eighties brat packer with the best punch, the actor critically applauded as the best of his generation, was a father in the 1990s and a member of that precious Hollywood Trinity society as an actor, writer and director. His antics had always detracted from his work. (A good screenplay gets a mention in the Hollywood trades while a good punch makes for rather more hectic headlines – world-wide.) All around him said he had mellowed, that he had finally grown up, that in transition an antidote had been found for the Poisoned Penn. He still chain-smoked. He is equally abandoned when he indulges in amber fluid or, in his frequent visits to Ireland, in a darker brew he fell for when actress Robin Wright, the mother of his son Dylan Francis, aged five, was filming on location with Albert Finney in 1991. It was around then that Sean Penn was telling me he was no longer interested in acting. Writing and directing were the way to go.

He re-emerged as that actor of so much promise in 1993's *Carlito's Way*, which starred Best Actor Oscar winner Al Pacino. Sean Penn's hero was Robert DeNiro but there was no better movie mentor than Pacino who had himself undergone a renaissance of craft and confidence. The $40 million film directed by Brian de Palma, for whom Penn appeared in the underrated *Casualties of War*, was set in the barrios of 1970s New York. Pacino was Carlito Brigante, a Puerto Rican born in Harlem, a hood who, in stepping out of jail, wants to forget the pen and the past. The movie was adapted from two novels by New York Supreme Court Judge Edwin Torres, who understands Pacino/Carlito's difficulties over redemption: 'When you've been in the money, with fast cars and a fast lifestyle, it's hard to throttle down to a pedestrian speed.'

Tough-guy Penn had his hair dyed red and permed for the role. His scalp was shaved to give him a vanishing hairline: Art Garfunkel via the Twilight Zone. But there was trouble when he saw the original trailers for *Carlito's Way*. They focused only on Al Pacino. The advertisements were made during filming and Penn walked off the set. He said he would stay away. New ones were filmed – at a cost of $400,000 – and Penn was back at work. Despite all this Pacino and Penn stayed very much in harmony during the making of the film. 'They're not that different,' said producer Michael Bregman, a long-time Pacino partner, adding: 'They're both very intense. It's Method to them and Sean may be the master. Al is Al but Sean would come to the set early, go to his dressing room, and come out completely in character. This was definitely not the time to ask whether he wanted veal or pasta for lunch.'

When he was preparing for *Bad Boys* (1983), in which he played a teenaged gangster, he grew his hair shoulder-length, ignored the make-up department and got a real tattoo (a wolf's head). He gave in on having his teeth filed down only when his mother objected. He went out on a Chicago police raid. Director Richard Rosenthal recalled: 'We were filming when some police arrived, thought we were criminals and told us to raise our hands. Sean thought this was an opportunity to find out what it's like for a gang member to take on a cop. So he turned to the cop, who was the size of an apartment building, and said, 'FUCK YOU.' The cop picked him up and threw him into a wall. His nose was almost broken but later he told me it was at that moment that he finally made the transition to becoming the character.'

Centre stage to Penn's co-star Reni Santoni: 'I thought the kid was watching too many Brando movies.' Which, of course, they all did, the Pacinos and DeNiros and Sean Penns and Andy Garcias . . .

Pacino talked to me while he was filming *Carlito's Way* and said that after *Scent of a Woman* it was time for him to get back to action and the mob movie. He enjoyed the cut and thrust of it. 'And with Sean Penn you have to be on your mettle. He wants the scene from you. He fights you for it. And that's a terrific encouragement to do the job,' he said with a giant grin.

Michael Bregman knows his stars and his product. *Carlito's Way* was an attempt at the *Godfather* of the nineties. Penn is multi-talented. A former fledgling at that hard Hollywood game of mixing artistic endeavour and dollar bills, he appears to know the score in the mid-1990s: you do one for the studio and one for yourself. If you're good. And lucky.

Right now it's all in Penn's grasp. He's the son of noted television director Leo Penn and former actress Eileen Ryann and shares his birthday, 17 August, with legendary backwoodsman Davy Crockett and the equally renowned but more up to date Robert DeNiro.

In the star sense Penn returned to the movies with *Carlito's Way* but he had never been away. He had been writing and directing on screen and stage in Los Angeles. His own personality and power seemed to get lost during the marriage Madonna dominated. His 'alimony', if you like, was his film *Indian Runner* in which he persuaded that other legendary bad man Charles Bronson to star following the death of his wife Jill Ireland.

Penn says that *Carlito's Way* is about the day-to-day fights of America today. 'In America today there is no need to go out and hunt for food or kill the guy from the other tribe. But we've hung on to the concept and almost every guy in America has some need to live up to that tribal rite. There is nothing of value that men can do that women can't so we are in a position of transition – trying to accept what has happened. A mature life requires responsibilities and that means cutting your losses, the art of compromise. I'm supposed to have gone from boy to man but I don't know if I buy that. I think human beings grow in some ways and regress in others and that in terms of living a mature rational existence, I was probably more on the ball when I was five years old than I am now. The biggest change I see in myself over the past few years is that I gain weight a lot easier.'

He's always been at fighting weight. Already in trouble because of a fight, his quick temper once landed him in jail for a month when he broke probation by punching out an extra during the filming of *Colors*. He says he can never escape the days when he was labelled a 'punch-aholic' but tries to explain: 'I've always been fuelled by some degree of anger and I think I've always channelled my anger constructively. I never hit anybody who didn't damn well deserve to get smacked and I don't have a single regret. Obviously, if slugging someone can be avoided it's certainly preferable but there are times when it's appropriate action to take. With Madonna I was in the eye of a media hurricane, which is a kind of no-win situation. I also learned what a precious thing anonymity is and, though I have it in certain situations, people approach me fairly often – probably out of curiosity. Am I going to grunt at them or give them an autograph? Nine out of ten people who come up to me are just as willing to tell me I'm an asshole as they are to say, "Nice to meet you." Once I was in a public phone box and somebody walked up to me and said: "Are you really as big an asshole as they say?" And I said: "Yeah." It's a longer conversation if you say no.'

Of the Madonna marriage he is surprisingly open and philosophical: 'She was an up-and-coming star. She was not a superstar, she was not an icon. She hadn't even gone on tour yet. But soon she became public property and her husband-to-be was treated likewise. I knew a lot of people who were bigger stars but who had much more peaceful lives. My understanding of the direction Madonna was choosing was a misunderstanding. And the degree to which she would be choosing such an intense spotlight was not something I had seen in the cards. So that was a big surprise.'

Another surprise was the ease with which he settled down with Robin Wright, with whom he co-starred in another gangster movie, *State of Grace*. He says: 'When I met her my list of expectations had been put in the shredder. I wouldn't have had a child with Robin if I hadn't thought her resources as a human being were limitless. Not only for myself but for the child's sake.'

HOLLYWOOD COUPLES
Chapter 5

'In Hollywood the eternal triangle consists of an actor,
his wife and himself.'
Anon.

On a quiet evening you can hear the clash of egos in the
Hollywood Hills. In a town where you can't be too thin
or too rich you *can* be too famous to make marriages and
relationships last long-term. Tinseltown divorce actions
and separations fly around as fast and as furiously as
tennis balls. At times it would appear that everyone in
town is either in therapy or in their lawyer's office.
Probably both.

Break-ups are not a new phenomenon in a town in
which every waking moment is spent dealing with status
and power. And they are a double threat to any relationship. There are rows over what one partner is wearing or
looks like, where they eat breakfast, what table they get
for dinner at Morton's or Spago, whom the maitre d'
fawns over most, what premières they are invited to. They
have their entourages and hangers-on to deal with. Who
gets the most fan mail? One couple who share the same
management agent call her separately each day to check

on the amount of fan mail and film offers they have each received in the past twenty-four hours.

The pressure to be a 'perfect' couple is immense. And the egos involved are not fragile. They're brittle. Also, Hollywood remains the most male chauvinistic town in the world. Men dominate. And they like to show off their wealth and power. There is always something to prove, someone to impress, which is why you have the 'trophy' wives who emerge when the previous model has too many miles on the clock. This has turned Los Angeles into the plastic surgery capital of the world. Extra-marital affairs contribute to many break-ups but the most persistent factor is ego.

Lauren Bacall, who turned seventy-one in 1995, admits she blossomed as much on the back of Humphrey Bogart as through her own talent. Bogie died of cancer in 1957, but you still can't talk to or about Bacall without his image creeping in. The couple had been married a little short of a dozen years. Bacall was thirty-three: a lifetime loomed before her but so did a legend. Bacall has accepted it but can still be irritated that the man she fell in love with when she was nineteen still dominates her life today. She'll say: 'There's no getting away from Bogie – damn it, let's deal with what I've done for years without him.' More mellow it comes out this way: 'It was only because I was married to Bogie that there was a myth of the movie star about me. I don't think I've done anything to produce such a feeling. Bogie is the big legend. He is a bigger star now than he ever was. He will live for ever.' So, things won't change? 'I'll be fighting the battle until they close the coffin. I'll be in there shouting, "Just a minute . . ."'

Her autobiography *By Myself* was published in 1978 and was a runaway bestseller. She wrote what could loosely be described as a sequel, *Now*, in 1995. It is about her three children, her dogs (several past and present), homes (a ten-room apartment in Manhattan's landmark Dakota building where John Lennon was living when he was shot), loneliness in old age – and the wrinkles.

She *talks* positively. In *Now* the feelings were more ambivalent. At one point she wrote: 'I wonder if I will ever love anyone again or if anyone will ever love me. I know how lucky I have been to once have had in my life a man who loved me without reservation and whom I loved in the same way. But that was long ago. Can it happen again? Will it? I hope so.' Off page she's not as sentimental: 'Marriage again? Forget it! I'd simply like to find somebody I could go out to dinner with but I don't meet anyone I can have a *conversation* with. There are very few eligible men around and those I might be interested in either have no self-confidence or they want twelve-year-old girls as lovers and I have no interest in that.'

'Steel with curves' doesn't sound all that tough when it comes to personal relationships in later life. 'People have always had the wrong impression of me. If I didn't have a sense of humour I would probably have killed myself over some of the things that people have said and written about me. They hear my deep voice and think I'm tough. They think I'm always in control and can handle any situation. Well, they're *wrong*. Listen, I'm alone in the world and have been for a long time and in order to survive I say what I want to say and do what I want to do. That's always gotten me in trouble and I know it grates on those people who wish I would just shut up. Why, sometimes, *I* wish I would shut up. But I can't analyse what people think of me. I can't change anything now – it's too late.'

She met Bogart on the set of *To Have and Have Not*, the 1944 film of Hemingway's story. She wasn't twenty, he was twenty-five years older, but the magic, the charisma, the whatever 'it' is that makes a movie or a love affair or memorable Hollywood People sparked spectacularly both on and off director Howard Hawks's film set. On screen Bacall kisses Bogart and tells him: 'It's even better when you help.' Then, she says: 'You don't have to act with me, Steve. You don't have to say anything, you don't have to do anything. Not a thing. Oh, maybe just whistle. You know how to whistle, don't you, Steve? Just put your lips together and blow.' She walks out of shot and Bogart purses his lips, blows a low whistle, and smiles. Bogart called her 'Slim' in their landmark movie and she always has been. Of course, she's aged – but only in real life. On the video shelves she'll always be Slim, asking Bogie if he can whistle.

She says – and she's used to the questions – that her memories are not painful. 'Bogie was an extraordinary, sensational man and I always had tremendous admiration for him. God knows, those were wonderful years – I have no complaints. But our life together was so many years ago. I'm not sure I'm the same person now that I was back then. Why should I live in the past? It's funny but I don't think of "missing" Bogie because he is still alive in all the wonderful things he said to me and the moments and events we shared. When I want a real special memory

I reread his love letters – I've kept them all. Bogie was a very romantic man. I only wish I'd kept his trenchcoat – getting rid of that was the stupidest thing I've ever done.

'Bogie and I didn't have a perfect marriage. We argued. He drank. When I married him I was a baby – I was mindless – and since I knew nothing about marriage I was bound to get out of line. And I did. But Bogie and I had a relationship. We had love. If he hadn't died I would still be married to him. I would *always* have been married to him.'

Four years after Bogart's death she married the award-winning actor Jason Robards. It followed a torrid affair with Frank Sinatra, although she recalls now: 'I liked what I had of him. He was interesting.' With Bogart she had two children (Stephen, born in 1949, now a TV producer in New York whose biography of his father was published in 1995, and daughter Leslie, born in 1952, a yoga instructor). Her marriage to Robards produced son Sam in 1961. He's an actor based in Manhattan. Like Bogart, Jason Robards drank. He doesn't any more but he didn't stop in time to save the marriage, which ended in 1969.

The clock ticked on. Bacall finds it a strange new world: 'Maybe I should have paid more attention to my career. I made a lot of mistakes in my life and I'm not foolish enough to think I will never make another one. I've lived well but I'm not going to sit around. I'm going to keep moving. If I fall on my ass I'll pick myself up, dust myself off and go on.'

✷　✷　✷

The *Star is Born* syndrome, in which one partner's career fades while the other's blossoms, is pure Hollywood. The classic example was Frank Sinatra and Ava Gardner. Cheryl Ladd was a struggling actress when she was first married to producer David Ladd. Then she replaced Farrah Fawcett in *Charlie's Angels* and their marriage fell apart. She was a star. He was nobody.

Goldie Hawn's marriage to film production man Gus Trikonis broke up when she moved on from *Laugh-in* to film stardom. He sued for alimony – and got it. She became the first actress to have to pay out.

Burt Reynolds and Loni Anderson's marriage got into public trouble when she won a new television series and his career was on the skids.

Jack Nicholson and Rebecca Broussard separated when she announced she was going back to work after two babies. Nicholson wanted her to stay at home. His long-time relationship with Anjelica Huston ended when her career began to take off after she won an Oscar for *Prizzi's Honour*. Huston was no longer content to remain in Nicholson's reflected glory. She didn't need to. She had her own.

The *Star is Born* syndrome clearly played a major part in the dismantling of Don Johnson and Melanie Griffith's second marriage to each other. They married young, divorced, then he became an international star through *Miami Vice*. They met and married again in 1989 and had daughter Dakota a year later, his television series went off the air and she soared with movies like *Working Girl*, for which she received an Oscar nomination.

Johnson, it turned out, was more of a celebrity than a

movie star. Granted, he tried hard but a string of films scored no hits. Meanwhile, Griffith was regarded as one of the town's top leading ladies. Johnson felt sorry for himself. Ten years after quitting booze he started drinking again. For Griffith, who is a reformed alcoholic, it was the sign to take positive action and she filed for divorce.

With Melanie Griffith you look in vain for the vodka lines around her face. And what about the effects of such a dissolute life from the neck down? She's fit, tanned and wearing blonde, tousled power-hair. Aged thirty-seven in 1995, she is a survivor. It surprises even her.

Paul Newman, as private eye Lew Archer, spurned her precociously sultry offer to help her put on some suntan lotion. He told her, as bikini-babe Lolita: 'Wouldn't help, honey. You're going to be burned out by the time you're thirty.' Archer wasn't just reading the lines from the script of 1975's *The Drowning Pool*. He was echoing what most of Hollywood thought about the sexy, self-willed, self-destructive seventeen-year-old wayward daughter of beautiful film star Tippi Hedren (*The Birds*), who had a bizarre upbringing on a ranch full of wild animals ('I got my first lion when I was thirteen'). Her stepfather, whom she disliked, was Noel Marshall who produced *The Exorcist*. Griffith was expelled from school, dropped out of college, took startling, scantily clad movie roles as nymphets and seductresses, and a graduate course in recreational chemicals. She was a big, bad, spiky-haired blonde party girl with a woman's body, a baby's voice, living a bleary life of sex, drugs and booze. She still has the squeaky voice. Chain-smoking Benson and Hedges menthols, she says, is her only vice.

But that was never quite true. She's been on and off the booze and drugs for most of her life – in February 1995 she had been 'clean' for more than a year – but there was one habit she can't kick – *Miami Vice* man Don Johnson. She is addicted to the maverick actor with whom she fell in love at fourteen. She wore her Catholic school uniform on their first date. He was twenty-two and her mother's co-star. She moved in with him when she was fifteen and after four tempestuous years playing house – their super-market shopping sprees comprised beer, vodka, cham-pagne, cognac, cocaine and cigarettes – they thought marriage might solve their communication problems. It didn't. Four weeks later they decided to divorce. The wedding cake, she recalls, lasted longer than the marriage.

She called him 'Pear' and has a ripe pear tattooed on her left buttock. He called her lots of things as the years blurred by. She drank and took cocaine, won some roles, was fired from others. She was mauled by a lion, run over by a car, and received physical scars to add to the mental ones. She remarried, joined and rejoined Alcoholics Anonymous, had a baby boy (Alexander, ten in 1995, by her marriage to actor Steven Bauer), divorced, found religion, took acting lessons, smartened up, held Holly-wood agog with her Oscar-nominated performance in *Working Girl*, rediscovered Don Johnson and married him again in 1989.

It seemed like fairy-tale time. They had their daughter Dakota and homes in Miami and Beverly Hills and a sprawling Colorado ranch near Aspen in which to play Happy Families.

In 1994 it all became ugly. Johnson, an admitted

alcoholic and substance abuser, had begun drinking again after nearly a decade of sobriety. Griffith also drank for five months until a blackout frightened her into stopping once more. 'I knew I couldn't do it any more, I'm so scared of it and so off it. The other thing that was truly my drug of choice was cocaine. Loved it. And it's terrible I didn't do it with anybody except my husband.'

She says that one alcoholic partner can corrupt another: 'You want to relate – you want to be there too. After nine years of sobriety Don felt that he could have a glass of wine. And you can't. It just escalated from there. It's not his fault. That's the disease. I'm not blaming him for anything but it certainly brought out the worst in us. When I saw him take a drink an alarm went off but nobody can do anything but that person.'

Again, that's not quite true. Feeling trapped in a relationship in which she could not 'flourish' Griffith filed for divorce in March 1994. She took off the four-carat diamond engagement ring Johnson had given her and that was that. Supposedly. She did not follow through with the divorce. Then, with Johnson still boozing and behaving badly, she announced the divorce was on again.

While separated from his wife Johnson booked into the Betty Ford Clinic in the Californian desert in June 1994, and a year later was sober again. She had sworn never to return to their twenty-acre Woody Creek ranch outside Aspen but by Christmas of 1994 they were there together again.

In early 1995, she was working with Anjelica Huston on the television Western series *Buffalo Girls* in Santa Fe, New Mexico, and Johnson would take the commuter plane-hop from Denver to visit. 'I can always tell when Don's here because Melanie is so happy,' said Rod Hardy, who was directing the TV mini-series. When she had first remarried Johnson she said: 'It's better because of all we've been through. There was always this connection with Don. I can't explain it. It's almost like soulmates and it always was. I didn't want it to be like that sometimes and sometimes I wanted not to love him. But maybe it was karma. And you have to get through all that to get to where we are. Now it's different. It's like it was in the very beginning but there is so much more.'

By 1995 she didn't want to remember the words. Too much pain. In interviews she tended to cry or sniffle and then giggle. But she would not be pressed on the issue. It was as if it might jinx their latest attempt at keeping it together: 'I don't want to talk about it.' For the record? 'Yes, we are back together but we're trying to keep our life private because it became so much of an open book.'

And what a book. Life even imitates art. In the 1995 film *Nobody's Fool* she co-starred alongside Paul Newman for the first time since their sun-tan oil discussion. She played the disenchanted wife of Bruce Willis. 'We have our problems and my character decides to leave him. It helped me leave Don at the time. It made it clearer that you can only put up with so much for so long. He's a good dad. I'll love him for all the days of my life but just because you love somebody doesn't mean you can live with them. I am in charge of my life. And I can make my own choices.'

She chose to be back with her husband and the family life they have with Dakota, Alexander, and Johnson's son

Jesse, born in 1982 from his relationship with actress Patti D'Arbanville. Johnson was happy and could even joke: 'Some people fall off the wagon. I fell off a building.'

He *is* cool and charming and his wife admitted: 'I'm still very much under the influence of Don. I think when you give yourself completely to somebody you lose yourself. And he can still push buttons in me very easily. And I have to stay really strong in order not to get hurt.' Griffith leans on her close friends like Liza Minnelli and Demi Moore, a.k.a. Mrs Bruce Willis. 'It's like having friends who know that all the stuff is not really serious, that that's all part of the business and what really matters is friendship, not where you went last night or what movie you just did.'

In 1995 Demi Moore was producing *The Gaslight Addition* and appears briefly with her stars Rosie O'Donnell, Rita Wilson and Melanie Griffith, who now takes her acting very seriously. Newman told her twenty years ago: 'Study, study, study.' The impertinent seventeen-year-old wondered: 'Study what?'

'But I did go study after that. He encouraged me to learn my craft. He's just so special. He's so unpretentious and so much fun.'

In *Nobody's Fool* she exposed her bountiful breasts at Newman who was, in the circumstances, pleasantly surprised. Was this a belated, generous ad-libbed thank-you for that advice given so long ago? She laughs: 'Yeah, it was like: "Watch this guys." The only way to upstage Paul Newman! Flash your tits!' Many yesterdays ago that might have been true of Melanie Griffith but she admits: 'It *was* in the script.'

Griffith remained a busy lady. Following her strong reviews in *Nobody's Fool* she was seen in the comedy *Milk Money*, in which her voice and frame complement her role as a prostitute with a heart of gold, of course. She enjoyed it: 'It was a way to forget my domestic situation. I could concentrate on the character and I worked with a lot of nice people. I didn't feel pressure.'

One of the 'nice' people was her co-star Ed Harris, like Tommy Lee Jones a man paying his dues before bursting through to the big time, and there were scores of reports that they were having an affair. Harris, a non-gossip-column man, shrugged it off. But the publicity did not help Griffith in her relationship with Don Johnson. Did she have an affair with Harris? With a deep sigh she says: 'They've linked me with everybody I've made a movie with.' With deep sarcasm she adds: 'It's really *nice*.'

Richard Benjamin directed her in *Milk Money* and is a fan: 'She's like Marilyn Monroe but there's no self-destructive thing there. Melanie doesn't pretend to be a hidden person. She's very smart on an intuitive level – a better actor than people who show you they're acting.'

Even reunited in 1995 with Don Johnson she continued to work. When she completed *The Gaslight Addition* she moved straight on to *Too Much*, a romantic comedy directed by Fernando Trueba who made *Belle Epoque*.

But friends feared for her marriage. As her star soared her husband's remained dormant.

More bizarre is the tangled world of Roseanne Barr, who sued former husband Tom Arnold for divorce because –

she said – of his affair with Kim Silva, who was twenty-four in 1995, a member of their film and TV production company. Arnold who co-starred with Big Arnold (Schwarzenegger) in *True Lies* in 1994 said they split because he feared for his life during her 'power rages'.

Barr used the huge American ratings of *Roseanne* to get the giant ABC TV network to give Tom Arnold his own series. But while *Roseanne* remained the most popular television show in America audiences turned on her husband. The couple rowed in public, and when she discovered his affair with Kim Silva they announced that they were in a 'three-way marriage' and they were all blissfully happy.

It went wrong from there. By February 1995, Roseanne was marrying her beefy bodyguard Ben Thomas. She went through with the ceremony although she had been confined to bed by doctors after she lost two of the three triplets she was carrying. 'The wedding was nearly cancelled. It was only Roseanne's determination to keep going that led her down the aisle,' said the bridegroom.

Roseanne, then forty-two, wore a $25,000 red and white velvet gown created by designer Richard Tyler. Her sixteen-stone husband wore traditional tuxedo with an extra-large red waistcoat. Despite the triplets – Roseanne got pregnant after her eggs were extracted and fertilized with her bodyguard's sperm – the couple keep separate bedrooms. But, they said, it was because of his snoring.

✵　✵　✵

One of the great pressures on Hollywood couples is time. This did not help the complex partnership of Richard Gere and supermodel Cindy Crawford. Many mornings she was up at 5 a.m. to go through the long process of getting ready – hair, make-up and fittings – for photo shoots. On most assignments she would simply grab a simple lunch and work on until early evening. She and Gere would eat early – usually at a restaurant near their Malibu home – so that Cindy could be home literally to get her 'beauty sleep'. Her bedtime is often 10 p.m.

When did they see each other? Rarely, it would seem.

Cindy Crawford and Richard Gere's marriage has been plagued by rumours of infidelity on each side. Also, their sexual preferences have been questioned in magazine articles worldwide. The pressure got so much that the couple wrote an 'open' letter to the London *Times* – the advertisement space cost them £12,000 – to declare their heterosexuality and love for each other. But still they were linked with other partners. Gere was photographed with a string of attractive women. Crawford posed for a controversial *Vanity Fair* magazine cover with the lesbian singer kd lang.

Ironically, one marriage that was still working in the mid-1990s was that of legendary Lothario Warren Beatty. All his relationships, from Julie Christie to Madonna, have ended, not just because of his philandering but due to his obsessive work habits. With Annette Bening, who in 1995 helped Sir Ian McKellen make a film revival of *Richard III*, that's all changed. After films like *The Grifters*, for which she won an Oscar nomination, and *Bugsy*, in which she co-starred with Beatty, she put her career on hold for a short time.

Bruce Willis is fond of a saying his mother taught him. He doesn't phrase it quite the way she used to when he was a cantankerous kid in Penns Grove, New Jersey – Mr Willis has a colourful way with words, particularly the bluer ones – but the gist is: 'Sticks and stones will break my bones but names will never hurt me.'

Ma Willis's words perfectly sum up her son's attitude to Hollywood, the town that loves to hate him. Critics delight in counting his flop films, backstabbers thrill to industry talk that his wife, Demi Moore, is a bigger star than he'll ever be, rumour-mongers relish gossip about his marriage, his money and even his hair loss. Whatever did he do to upset so many people in such a short time? His fame, he says, came with a *whoosh*. One minute he was one of the world's most popular television actors with his smash series *Moonlighting*, the next he was the half-a-dozen-million-dollars-a-time movie star following the colossal box office of the original *Die Hard*. The money flowed, just like the drinks he was paid $12 million to advertise. Willis was a wild boy.

But then he met and married actress Demi Moore and his personal life settled into love and babies – his third daughter, Tallulah Belle, was born in February 1993, joining Rumer (born in 1990), and Scout LaRue (born in 1992) – but professionally he tried to escape the singlets and shotguns of his *Die Hard* image. He wanted to make more sensitive, meaningful movies. It made him yesterday's man.

He explained himself: 'Success is being in charge. And I only want to do films I want to do because the only thing left for me to do is to challenge myself, to do things I wouldn't have done before, do things that aren't safe.'

Flop followed flop until *Die Hard 2*, which once again had Willis in full-throttle action. In the summer of 1994 he filmed *Die Hard 3* in New York, and reports from the set said that not only is the movie bombastic but that Willis was a pussycat personality. Finally, he is understanding that to be indulged by Hollywood you have to have hits. Even icons like Clint Eastwood have to make their *Dirty Harry* films to be given the green light for projects like *Bird*. Sylvester Stallone – one of Willis's partners in the Planet Hollywood restaurant chain – has given up comedy for a return to action in movies like 1993's *Cliffhanger* and the corny *The Specialist*, which includes sizzling sex scenes with Sharon Stone.

Willis wonders why he has had such a rough time: 'I'm not a devious man. I don't cheat, lie or go out of my way to mess people over, but I'm still amazed at the garbage that goes on in this town. People lie about you. People want to see you fall. It's so competitive here you can *see* how much they want to see you fail.' He cannot believe the attitude – or his success. 'If anyone said this career was going to happen, if anyone said I was going to make more money on one picture than anyone in my county in New Jersey made in their entire lives, if anyone said I'd have people trying to take pictures of me when I walk outside and wackos following me, I would have said: "Hey, you're out of your mind."'

He turned forty in 1995 and was looking forward to ageing into different roles, but he's bright enough to know that there is no secret formula for Hollywood success: 'If you can find out why any film does any good I'll give you all the money I have. No one knows. You see dogs, idiotic films make $150 million. And you see terrific films that die. Nobody knows the answer. Maybe it's because people like me are in these films.'

When his wife, the disquieting Demi Moore, found international fame in the out-of-this-world fantasy romance *Ghost* in 1990 her image was white T-shirt-girl-next-door, cropped hair, neat smile and big eyes on a fresh face and not much evidence of hips or waist. She was demure. And unthreatening. By the mid 1990s she was Wonderbra woman. Coy is not in her vocabulary. In Hollywood she *is* The Body. And the boss. *She's* the manipulator. Few stars have worked so hard – and successfully – to present the image they want. Ms Moore would make public appearances squeezed into gowns which emphasized that all the bits are in all the right places. Her look, her attitude set off fire alarms. It brought her attention and an asking price of $8 million a film. This was Nicholson/Cruise/Costner financial country. The wily, one-time wide-eyed innocent-looking brat packer was as totally in control. She was also the screen's queen predator of 1995.

The actress has an off-camera reputation for being 'assertive' and going after everything she wants with a passion. She doesn't regard that as a criticism but much more a compliment. It is her nature to shoot for the bull's-eye. She admitted she does not hold back. It won her showy roles in *A Few Good Men* (as a tough Navy legal officer opposite Tom Cruise and Jack Nicholson) and *Indecent Proposal* (as the wife of Woody Hareleson to whom Robert Redford offers $1 million to spend the night with her). Her mantra is the secular if-you-don't-ask-you-don't-get. Which is somewhat ironic because in *Disclosure*, which became a box-office giant in 1995, she didn't so much ask as grab. And that, surprisingly, still did not work on real life sex addict Michael Douglas, who in *Fatal Attraction* and *Basic Instinct* was not exactly reticent in bedroom games.

However, this was new ground, boardroom games. Best-selling author Michael Crichton's book, and the movie taken from it, asked who really is the boss in the high-tech workplace. Surveys say that by the next century women will rule in the corporate world. Crichton and others were arguing that nudge-nudge and leering will no longer be a mainly male prerogative. And, in keeping with her track record, Demi Moore was the first to take things by the balls. Literally and figuratively in the film.

She went to Las Vegas to accept her award as Female Star of the Year – 1995 from the owners of America's major cinema chains. These businessmen were happy that her past three films had each earned more than $100 million in America alone. For them she was an uplifting woman. 'Don't you think I was perfect casting?' she asked, with a light laugh. In real life she got her man, but rather more romantically. Bruce Willis was so overcome by her that he flew her to Las Vegas for a 'surprise' wedding. Half a dozen years and three children later they are one of Hollywood's few stable power couples. They share the chores and the kids but have separate film production companies. In Hollywood love is having his and her hit movies. At present she's ahead of her *Die Hard* action man, although he recently won rave reviews for *Pulp Fiction*.

Ms Moore can cope with fame and family but still wants more: 'I just want the end result of things to be the highest quality they can be. I want good work. I want things to be the best they can be. I want greatness.'

Well, you can't knock ambition. She's proved it's possible to juggle motherhood, a high-profile celebrity marriage and superstardom. Her daughter Rumer (after British novelist Rumer Godden, author of *Black Narcissus*) was born not in some trendy Hollywood hospital but in the tiny town of Paducah, Kentucky. Bruce Willis was on location there. He had arranged with the movie's producers to have his pregnant wife with him on location and the best facilities available for the birth – which he videotaped.

But even his superstar clout and negotiating talents pale against his wife's. She has a reputation for being relentless in the pursuit of getting what she wants. When she produced the thriller movie *Mortal Thoughts* in 1991 she cast Willis as the abusive husband of a friend of her character. 'I don't think we'll work together often but if something like that comes up it's silly not to do it. Bruce really responded to the character – and it made it easier for the family to be together,' she said. The family that stars together stays together? 'I'm very embracing, very maternal, and I think I'm a grounding force, a centre that I provide for Bruce. But together we have created a tremendous foundation of a family.' In California-speak she went on: 'Bruce made me feel important. That filled me with a strength to step forward with a courage that if I stepped a bit further I knew I wasn't going to fall. And if I fell it wasn't going to be quite as hard. It's very easy for me to see what I've got and where I've come from – but you don't know. You don't know. I can be OK and know what I've got today but what's going to happen next year? What's going to happen in the year after? I don't like to think too far in advance. Maybe I'm super-stitious, afraid that what I've got may go away. But I'm not cautious about what I'm doing. I plough ahead like there's no tomorrow.'

Moore is building an amazing celluloid portfolio. In 1994 she completed *Scarlet Letter* based on Nathaniel Hawthorne's classic American novel – with Britain's Gary Oldman as her co-star – and moved on to *A Gaslight Addition*. She got $5 million for *Disclosure* – Michael Douglas was paid $12 million – but made an even more lucrative deal with *Striptease*: she was paid $8 million to star as Erin Grant in the film version of Miami-based journalist Carl Hiaasen's genius of a book of the same name.

Is she worth it? 'The reality is that I feel that I am good but I'm not great. I have the potential maybe to do some really great things but I don't feel like I'm extremely gifted. There's a part of me that just thinks: "Well, I have something, I don't know what it is or why it works but I'm happy that it does. Because I really like doing what I do." And I know there is a part of me that can convey real, honest emotion and affect people.'

Asked about her role models, she offers Katharine Hepburn and Susan Sarandon. Hepburn, well, for being Hepburn. Sarandon? 'I think she's laid the groundwork (and some others) for those of us who are coming up to trying to find important characters in later life.'

You see it first from Monte Cielo – 'the mountain to heaven' – and it sits so high up in the hills that the Mexican tiled-roof appears to be touching the clear Californian sky. This is horse country and you get here by driving forty-five minutes on sweeping, curving roads to the north of Santa Barbara. Then, it's bouncing on dirt tracks until you spot the arrow with a red heart tacked to a telephone pole pointing the way to the electronic security gates.

That's the only Tinseltown touch in the lifestyle of Bo and John Derek. They're Hollywood's back-to-basics couple. And it was a life that kept Bo in good enough shape to adorn the pages of *Playboy* magazine again. Fifteen years after her début she was the main cover in December 1994. Inside she was the stapled attraction in photographs taken by her husband.

The Dereks live lavishly but not at all in the way we might think glamour queens do. Or maybe should. Their Spanish hacienda is stunning and so is Bo, who bounces around bra-less in a white sweatshirt and faded working ranch jeans. She knows the other sort of genes were generous to her and says she still feels guilty about it. She will be forty in 1996, but for Hollywood and, clearly, *Playboy* remains a *10*. After that huge hit she more or less bowed out of mainstream Hollywood. Until the mid-1990s, her life had been her home and her husband. Times change. Necessity brought her back to the spotlight.

It was the money earned from that box-office success – she was paid a comparatively modest $35,000 in 1975 to be Dudley Moore's dream girl – which helped make the down-payment on their lovingly nourished twenty-six acres in the Santa Ynez Valley. The movie that made Moore a Hollywood star and self-confessed 'sex-thimble' – a reputation he has proved again and again – also established Bo Derek. She has fond memories of Dudley and says: 'Nothing would surprise me about him. He's cheeky and likes to have fun. Which is fine if no one gets hurt. I just hope Dudley and his ladies are OK.'

John and Bo Derek were living in an apartment in Marina Del Rey out on the west side of Los Angeles when Bo became a worldwide fantasy girl and not just of cinema audiences but of every producer with minimal eyesight. 'John saw the necessity to get out right away and have a place. We didn't have the money but with the few dollars we had we made a down-payment and thought we'd worry about it later. It's been my sanity this life. And it's not just the ranch and the animals [twenty-seven horses, cats, dogs and parrots] but being with real people who have nothing to do with the film business. We're involved with the community – if someone is in trouble or has problems everybody tries to help. We're more social than I ever believed we'd be. Now there's a big invasion of film people up here. I don't like it because they don't leave their business down in Hollywood. We'll be sitting around having lunch with friends and someone who's in the business will come in and they can't talk about anything except how much money they just turned down, how much they're worth, how much the picture made and, oh, it's so boring . . .'

What is not, she says happily, is her life with John Derek, the former matinée idol turned film producer, photographer, husband and Svengali to blonde Ursula Andress, blonde Linda *Dynasty* Evans and to a beach-loving blonde Californian teenager called Mary Cathleen Collins. He called her 'Bo' and helped create a phenomenon.

Derek was still married to Linda Evans when he met her lookalike on a Greek island. Although he was thirty years older they were smitten by each other. And still are. 'I'm just about the luckiest person in the world. I've only known love. I went right from my family who love me to John. I found my love when I was seventeen years old and my love is one hundred per cent honest. We've never had any ugly, rocky things to overcome. This love and this lifestyle are everything I hold as the ultimate thing to have in life. This is something to envy and I'm so happy to have it. Others would rather have jewellery and cars and furs or whatever is opulent. But this is opulence to me and I'm ashamed to have it sometimes. I work hard for I feel I have to earn it somehow, to do more than just have a straight nose.'

The Dereks designed their gardens and stables and, over the years, have added outbuildings and horse-working areas. Every plant, every brick on the property has been personally approved. John Derek would put in trees before lunch and then take them out afterwards and vice versa. He is a fickle perfectionist. He has always wanted everything around him to be beautiful. By the front door is a navy-blue lap pool put in to help Mrs Derek keep her exceptional shape. She has displayed it in films like *Tarzan, The Ape Man* and *Bolero*, but she denies that she's made 'sexy' films: 'I feel like such a prude now. I never thought I would feel prudish in this business and about film projects. You haven't even begun to see the films that are coming. I've been reading screenplays . . . these vulgar women, these wild sex scenes and I mean they just . . . if they don't get more inventive there's nothing else you can do.

'It's been done to death and it's vulgar just to be vulgar. I find them so unappealing and so unattractive. The next group of films is just unbelievable. Sharon Stone? It all boils down to who she's making love to and why she's making love in the story. The gymnastics pretty much haven't changed. I think Madonna is the only one who goes over the edge on that.

'I played a definite part in it. I guess the things that I played in films and the way the nudity and the love scenes were handled were really different. What now stands out to be unusual is that in the love scenes I did the people were in love. It wasn't kinky, deviant – any of these things that seem to be most popular right now in the 1990s. There's an incredible fascination for that and that goes with violence in pictures.'

She is not concerned for actresses getting involved in torrid scenes: 'I don't feel sorry for them at all. What's there to feel sorry about? They're simulating sex in a film. I find it much worse to simulate sick violence and glamorize it – that's something to worry about and that I would have trouble with my conscience doing. Glorifying violence is terrible. Simulating sex is nothing – it's something so impersonal really.'

She keeps reading scripts and, in 1995, was gently putting herself back in the Hollywood workplace. She drove down to town in the week for meetings and stayed with friends. And she can still laugh at the days when the world's producers were constantly knocking at her door. We had people walking into the office with suitcases full of money and talking millions and millions and big percentages of billions of dollars and it was so overwhelming. When I look back on it, it was so much fun to turn down, more fun than accepting it. I get a kick out of it and I smile when I think about it. In the long run I've had much more fun having turned them down.

'A lot of people think I've missed out but I don't think I have. It's always been my decision. I've got experience now in how to defend myself against a monster director – I couldn't before, I didn't know the game.

'We moved here because we couldn't stand the bullshit that goes with being a so-called celebrity and living in a glass house. We love making movies but we don't like all the hangers-on, all the pretence that goes into this business. I have a reputation for being difficult as well as being under John's influence. They think I'm just a body for him to channel through.'

She and John Derek have for the most part been a working-couple package. Now she travels and does deals on her own. 'I never felt dependent on him but at the same time I think I knew deep inside that this was all too much for me to handle alone. It's a certain type of dependency but it's also a partnership and sharing. Looking back on myself, I could never have handled all the attention *10* brought.

'I met John in 1974. It's amazing, isn't it? I've changed so much. I thought at the time I was very adult and mature and grown, but now when I look back at myself, at sixteen, seventeen, eighteen, nineteen, twenty – up to about thirty-two I was very young. But you never realize that at the time. I wasn't a woman.'

She is now. And part of the *Playboy* deal and the publicity was aimed at keeping the family's future intact. She also appeared in the chilly thriller *Billy The Third*.

John Derek, now sixty-nine, had a heart attack eight years ago and suffered a slight stroke in 1991. It made him even more aware of his own mortality and the thirty-year age difference in his marriage. He thinks often of fifteen years down the line and says: 'It will be awful for her because I will be slowly falling apart and no matter what she says the person she fell in love with won't be there any more.'

He knows his wife. She dismisses his concerns with: 'I'm not going to worry about anything until it happens. It's not my nature. I live for the moment and if it's a good day it's a good day. As I mature, the age gap and the personality gap and all these things just start to get smaller and smaller and you become more similar. Rarely does he ever get me confused with his other blonde wives now ... He used to say: "Remember when we went here or there and did this?" I'd say: "No, that wasn't me." We'd argue and he'd say: "Oh, that was the other blonde."'

In the past she has said that she was waiting until the right time to have children but now admits: 'I don't want children now. John has always been open to having children if I wanted but they're not his favourite things.'

Michael Jackson's Neverland ranch is a short drive away. 'Elizabeth's wedding was there. We have Steven Segal and Kelly Le Brock now. We have Jimmy Connors and his Patti, who's a very good friend of mine. They've been here a long time though. We have John Forsythe – he just moved up and bought a really cute goat farm here. We have Cheryl Ladd and her husband Brian. There's Fess Parker and Ray Stark the producer and Doug Cramer the producer. The Reagans don't come very often now. It's a very remote place they have and it's a nice old house but it's not luxurious.'

They are also surrounded by rumours. There was one that she and Ursula Andress and Linda Evans – John Derek's trio of wives remain close friends – were going to open a restaurant together. 'I used to take the rumours seriously and now I just exaggerate. When they call and ask about the restaurant I say: "Yes, we're opening on Rodeo Drive in Beverly Hills and then having twenty-six more across the country. Sort of Italian Hard Rock Cafés." The last rumour was that we were so broke we were selling our ranch for $20 million. I loved that. I'd love to have assets of $20 million.'

✼　✼　✼

Tim Robbins is a player but he is also Hollywood's egghead, an actor of conscience who suddenly found himself a leading man of the 1990s. He remains involved with a string of projects and able to concentrate on them despite the distraction of his long-time lover, Susan Sarandon. Robbins finds it sexist that *his* leading lady is renowned not just for her remarkable acting talent but for being voted as having 'the best breasts in the world'. But, an understandably happy man, he said he must simply shrug such things off. He said it with a smile.

Since the baseball movie *Bull Durham* in 1989 – in which he co-starred with Kevin Costner and where he met Sarandon by whom he now has two sons – Robbins has been pitching winners. He's worked for Robert Altman in *The Player* and *Short Cuts* and for himself (he was producer and director) in the political satire *Bob Roberts*, which was followed by *The Hudsucker Proxy* with Paul Newman, and the 1995 Oscar contender *The Shawshank Redemption*. He's incredibly tall and his lean body makes his six-foot-four frame seem even higher. When you do a double-take he's got his stock answer: 'When you're so tall you have no one to look up to.'

Robbins admits he is becoming much more adept at 'selling' his work and says: 'I have a family to think about. I can't just be indulging myself in pet projects any more. I have always wanted to do mainstream movies – films that entertain and also have a message.'

Tim Robbins is a serious fellow but then: 'Anyone who has danced around the truth to create a widely palatable perception of themselves is playing politics. A minor example is an actor doing an interview. What do I mean? It's a joke. Life and movies – anything at all – is all about selling ourselves or the image we believe has the most currency value. We're all dancing around the truth.'

But life has not always been an amusing game for Robbins. He and Sarandon have a tight, content, happy family unit. They live in a rambling country house in Westchester County, New York, with their two sons, Jack Henry, six, and Miles Guthrie, three, and Sarandon's daughter Eva Maria, ten, from an earlier relationship.

Sarandon, famed for performances in *The Rocky Horror Picture Show*, *Thelma and Louise* and director Louis Malle's *Atlantic City*, won an Oscar nomination in 1995 for her role opposite Tommy Lee Jones in the film version of John Grisham's *The Client*. She brought the kids to visit Robbins on location for *The Shawshank Redemption*. 'It was a great break from the pressures of the prison atmosphere,' said Robbins, sporting the usual two days' growth of beard. 'I try not to talk about Susan and the kids. It's a kind of "No Trespass" area for me but I'll make every effort to be polite. It's just that I feel there are certain areas of your life that you must protect. I know all about being a performing artist and the risks that involves but I've never been able to figure out why that should intrude on the private life.

'I know, I know! If you're out on the stage you have to take the attention. I don't mind it as long as it doesn't interfere with what I'm doing. But every little personal thing you let out turns out all wrong. Can you blame me for wanting to keep my privacy? What does the public want to know? My personal feelings? I want to save those words for who they are meant to be heard by. When we were having Jack everybody found out from the papers before we could tell them. That's a shame. I missed the joy of breaking the news. I felt cheated. I have a life just like everybody else and I want to be able to share the joys and the sorrows with my friends on a personal level. Susan? Well, we all know she's special. Very special.'

In the spring of 1995 Paul Newman wanted him for another movie and so did Robert Altman. There was also talk of a gritty tale with Martin Scorsese and Robert DeNiro. His friend Tom Cruise was also interested in directing Robbins in a gangster movie. 'You make your own moves, your own luck. If you simply listened to the talk nothing would get done. I am trying to keep a balance like any other guy between work and family. I don't want to be away from my family for weeks at a time. It makes no sense. But, yes, if the right thing comes along . . .

'You make deals with the devil in yourself. I've seen it all my life. My father was a folk-singer in Greenwich Village in New York and my mother worked in a publishing firm. It was definitely an eclectic place to grow up – the Village was filled with progressive thought. Very few people came out of there with closed minds. I saw heroin addicts shooting up when I was eight years old. I was propositioned when I was ten, saw guys being led around on chains by their nipples. I mean, I saw some sick shit but it was normal to me. From my eleventh birthday I've learned that anything is possible. Belief is a lot stronger than talent sometimes.'

He and Sarandon are a politically correct couple. But

they are not a couple who do it for awards or cocktail parties. Sarandon has been an activist for most of her public life and Robbins now holds her hand in her causes. 'This is not something I'm doing to keep her happy – we both believe in the same values. What's dispiriting is the people that don't believe in anything. I'll listen to your argument – but you have to have one in the first place. There are so few people out there who are thinking. I'm thinking all the time . . .'

Elaine Young loved being a movie star's wife and was shattered after her divorce from Gig Young. 'The first couple of months I needed to go to a psychiatrist. It was wonderful being Mrs Gig Young. I could walk into a restaurant and we didn't have a reservation, they could sit us down and fifty people could be waiting. And then when we'd divorced, I'd go to a builder, a doctor, they'd make me wait two hours. Funniest story about that is that Gig and I used to go to auctions and we used to get the most gorgeous furniture at the best prices. We got a divorce. I went without him. They bid me up to the very maximum. I went, wait a minute, what's going on. And I realized they let him get away with it because he was a movie star and they wanted him there so everyone could see him. So I was paying more when I wasn't Mrs Young than when I was. So I couldn't believe it. No, they love stars here. I couldn't get a seat on a plane, you know, like I could before. Things were difficult.'

TILL DEATH . . .
Chapter 6

'A trophy wife has a short span in this business.'
Palimony lawyer Marvin Mitchelson

Hollywood has a history of heartache headlines. There were marriages that were thought unbreakable and, because of happy-for-ever-after fan magazine coverage, when they disintegrated shocked even more. Janet Leigh and Tony Curtis, Debbie Reynolds and Eddie Fisher (who lost his new wife Liz Taylor to Richard Burton) and Robert Wagner and Natalie Wood, whose first marriage was split by her relationship with *Splendour in the Grass* co-star Warren Beatty.

Oscar-winner Lee Marvin was taken to court by his long-time live-in lover Michelle Triola Marvin and California's 'palimony' law was established. That got Nick Nolte, Rod Stewart – from Britt Ekland – and a string of others into lawsuits. Rocker Rod also left Alana Hamilton and Kelly Emberg before settling with his present wife, supermodel Rachel Hunter.

Julia Roberts jilted Kiefer Sutherland at the altar, got together with Jason Patric but left him to marry country-

and-western singer Lyle Lovett, from whom she then officially separated.

The marital merry-go-round is constant in Hollywood, with the search for trophy wives. And husbands.

Sylvester Stallone got engaged again in the spring of 1995 after long-time affairs following his legendary marriage break-up with the statuesque Brigitte Nielsen. Roseanne married again soon after losing husband Tom Arnold.

It goes on and on. Roger Moore's 'perfect marriage' to long-time wife Luisa is over. So is John McEnroe and Tatum O'Neal's.

Like everything else involving Hollywood People there is no sure thing and the romance is never really what it seems.

Marriage, separation and divorce have been Marvin Mitchelson's business for decades. His answerphone plays 'You've Lost That Lovin' Feeling', and when they contacted him many of his clients, from the late James Mason to Bianca Jagger, Joan Collins and many others had. Of mythical stature for establishing 'palimony' in the California courts he is an expert on Hollywood couples: 'Hollywood women have always had power, sexual power, the power of allure, and anyone who might be interested in them will give them power. But they didn't have power in the sense of equal protection of the law, or I should say equal application of the law – and I've tried to do that, and my colleagues have as well, over the years. We've had a lot of changes in the law and we now try to divide property equally that's been acquired during the marriage.

'Many women have high positions of power today and their earnings are taken into consideration. They don't need to have a man support them. So it works both ways. I represented men in the past, who asked women for some money and who didn't feel they were entitled to at least half of the earnings that they had combined as a couple.

'A lot of people think a woman gets a large settlement, that's wonderful, she's happy, but most people are very unhappy when they go through a divorce. Someone's always wounded, no matter how much they may dislike being married or, you know, have got tired of the process. They're losing something. They're losing a partner. They're losing a way of life. So you can have all the money in the world, you've heard that before, but you still may have bad health and you may have something else wrong. A broken heart is something that money doesn't assuage too easily.

'Money helps. I give them a choice: most people would say I'd rather have the money and you'll see a sign here or there that says to be rich is the best form of revenge. It's probably true.

'You can at least get a new start when you have some money. That's one of the worries you have. You have your health, you have your love life, you have your work, you have financial considerations. So there are the several problems in life and if you eliminate one problem you have others you can concentrate on better, but if you're fighting poverty *and* a broken heart that's even tougher.

'A poverty problem in Hollywood for a woman who's had everything is tough. *Sunset Boulevard* – the show tells us what happens to an ageing star who has lost her money, her fame and her age. That's not a good position to be in for a Hollywood woman. Many find themselves in that position.

'We all know that the roles are more limited for women as they get older. A man can go on ten or twenty years longer, be a screen hero in his sixties, perhaps even as far as seventy. Palimony? I always tell everybody that palimony, even though it's attributed to me, that I invented it or I established it, began two hundred years ago in England. It was all palimony in the sense that of 90 per cent of the people who lived with one another, ten per cent had ecclesiastical marriages but most people just lived together and they were considered to be man and wife. Hence common-law marriage. But what happened was that young inebriated couples would walk out at night. Lo and behold, someone would jump out from behind a lamp-post selling a secret marriage licence for a ha'penny or a penny.

'They'd wake up the next morning, they were married. So Lord Harwicke decided to put an end to this nefarious practice, went before Parliament, had the first Marriage Licence Act passed. Hence no common-law marriage.

'I think there is a fear of women in Hollywood. Men fear losing their assets. You see, men look at it like this: this is mine, I made this money, I did this, I painted this painting, I wrote this song, I was the star, and they resent someone particularly when a marriage breaks up, someone taking half of it or part of it, but the idea of marriage is to share what you have. That's hard for people to do. So they fear the power women, and they fear that they may take everything. With women's rights today and all of these lawsuits over sexual harassment there's a fear of women. Now you don't have to be married to be sued so I've added something by coming up with the palimony concept. It's divorce without marriage and I always used to be opposed to pre-nuptial agreements. The only one I ever tried to defend was Joan Collins. I did that successfully because Peter Holm was such an overreaching person.

'Competition in Hollywood is there, like in any other field, except more so. Every good-looking woman probably thinks that she wants to be, secretly or otherwise, a movie star or a model and there are lots of beautiful women. It is very difficult for women who have a short life-span in the film and entertainment business compared to men and they're fighting tremendous competition in a very overcrowded field. That's gotta be a real concern to women and spawn a lot of jealousy, competition and fear.

'The woman who doesn't really have an option of being a movie star, just a good-looking woman on someone else's arm or the wife or girlfriend of a famous person, they're in for a rough time because they can't compete film-wise or entertainment wise. They're just an appendage of someone else and there's so many good looking people. Now we hear about all the Hollywood divorces. Today you've got a 50 per cent divorce rate in America – almost all over the world for that matter – so divorce is easy to come by and not hard to find. The man who's famous or a well-known actor, he's travelling all over, he's having new women to look at all the time. The competition is brutal and it's pretty hard. You might wanna stand by your man but it's pretty hard to hold him.

'The shelf life of a trophy wife is probably about as long as the success of Academy Award winners. I wouldn't imagine more than three/four/five years. There are notable exceptions. Jimmy Stewart has had a long marriage and it's nice to have a good marriage. It may be even worse to be married to someone in the business because the partners are always going off in different directions. A marriage is like a plant. If you don't water it or nourish it it won't last long. You have to go down a road together sometimes. I don't know what is worse: being a trophy wife where you have nothing to do but be on the arm of your husband and try to make him happy and bore him to death, or to be a competitive wife, having your own high-profile image and going off to Asia to make a movie while your husband's making one in Europe and never the twain shall meet.

'A trophy wife is one who makes sure that she's in the pictures her husband takes when they're out together, when they're doing the eating circuit, wants to make sure that they're not too many beautiful woman close to her husband or they keep their distance, will usually get involved in extra-curricular activities. I don't mean extra-curricular in the sense of affairs with other people but be involved – overly involved – in charitable events or whatever they're trying to do and is not one who's liable to be in the limelight but tries to stay in it by virtue of being married to the star or being on the arm of the star.

'There are people very happy at not being in the

business and not being in the limelight and very productive people, but the ones that don't have much to do except for just try to make their husbands happy have a hard time. It's indigenous in people's make-up, I think, to wanna do well and have security and I think that some really get involved in marriages just to come out financially ahead. There's no question that people need to make a living, need to get ahead, need to have security. It's important to a woman. Particularly in a day and age where marriages don't last very long. So this is not necessarily a bad thing to want to marry well. For generations people all over the world would marry off their children the best way they could and try to have what we call a "good" marriage.

'I've always been pretty much against pre-nuptial agreements because I consider them to be a recipe for divorce. People who have pre-nuptials usually worry about the terms and whether the relationship is going to break up. When it happens, they make very little provision for the other partner. Usually it's a one-sided deal, but there are those people, of course, that have had bad marriages. Joan Collins had three of them. She had three that didn't take and she had enough, as she put it, paying all these husbands off, to get rid of them. So Joan, at this point of her life, was doing the *Dynasty* series and was very successful but realized that that might not last for ever and wanted to be somewhat careful and frugal and not just go head over heels in love and give everything to her husband.

'Peter Holm was sort of a novice at the business. He fancied himself as some rock star, which he really wasn't, and he was out to take Joan, it was later proved during the trial, with this affair with – what we called Passion Flower – the lady he used to meet at Mulholland Drive every morning and have an affair with after Joan went off to work.

'Joan asked for a pre-nuptial agreement and Peter Holm drew it up himself with her help. It was crudely drawn but I fought to uphold it because it was what she meant to do. She gave him 20 per cent of her gross. That's a lot of money. When you pay your agent and your hairdresser and everybody else that's pretty close to 50 per cent.

'Peter Holm, not satisfied with this largess, wanted to set aside the pre-nuptial and get 50 per cent of everything, which would have given him several more million dollars. Fortunately the judge saw through it and we showed what Peter's true motives were. The judge upheld the pre-nuptial agreement so there's a case where I had one upheld when normally I try to set them aside. Peter Holm made us look good because he was so overreaching that it was obvious to the court. I think anyone could have won the case. So I don't give myself too much credit there but I was happy for the win.

'Peter Holm was overwhelming in his bad behaviour. He would picket her home, he would have signs there, he would march up and down protesting, saying, "it's my money too," and he made himself thoroughly obnoxious and it didn't help him at all. It didn't look too good in court.'

HOLLYWOOD KIDS
Chapter 7

'Doesn't he know Porsches are passé?'
Beverly Hills teenager on graduation gift from Dad

Life as a child of Hollywood people can be strange. It is a bizarre world for many children who are indulged and pushed into work. They literally live on Planet Hollywood, in their private twilight zone where even great-grandmothers don't want to be old.

A camping trip? Cute idea, thought the parents of the trendy tykes who attend the upmarket private school on Melrose Avenue in West Hollywood. They went out to buy specialized camping gear for the school's first overnight trip. There were Louis Vuitton bags for the kids' Guess pyjamas, jeans and sweatshirts. They went off to Abercrombie and Fitch for tents and sleeping bags. They already had the customized lunch boxes with their children's names spelled out in stars. They went to Georgette Klinger and Elizabeth Arden on Rodeo Drive in Beverly Hills or the Skin Spa in Encino for the specialized lines of children's skin creams, Mustela de Paris, and some got cashmere sweaters from Sarah Patterson's on La Cienega, and so it was that many thousands of dollars later our intrepid group were outfitted for the call of the wild.

It was early evening and most of the tents were occupied. There was a crunch of gears at the entrance to the National Park on the outskirts of Los Angeles, and the Hollywood producer arrived with his mobile home. He was concerned about his daughter's first camping trip and wanted to be in the vicinity. He had an aide with him to mix his martini before the dinner his chef was preparing in the kitchen of his home-on-wheels. But his daughter slept in one of the tents. Her nanny slept beside her.

Hollywood children *are* different. All the way from push-carts to Porsches to psychiatrists. Even before they are born they are being prepared for a life that for many is way over the top. Mothers-to-be don't talk to that swelled bump in their lives but play cassettes of nursery stories or soothing music – the current favourite is the work of Esa-Pekka Salonen, the romantic leading-man-looking conductor of the Los Angeles Philharmonic. Then there is the grand entrance from the womb in the fourth floor maternity ward of Cedars-Sinai Medical Centre. It's on average a $10,000 production between arrival and mother and child being taken by wheelchair from the ward to the waiting limousine or valet-parked car. That's if you don't count Father's meals across the street at the Hard Rock Café or Chasen's, and shopping sprees around the corner at the tempting and incredibly user-friendly Beverly Centre.

But, with luck, it will be a couple of years before Junior discovers the delights of the mall. For now it's the nursery. And nursing. Mother can contact Breast Feeding

Lauren Bacall, a survivor of Hollywood's 'golden' age and a class act who can still turn heads.

Photo by John Rogers

Actress/comedienne
Roseanne's, fifth child
was born following
in-vitro fertilization
in August 1995.
Buck Thomas weighed
8lb. Her former body
guard became her third
husand after her divorce
from Tom Arnold.
Photo by Eddie Sanderson

Victoria Principal,
married to one
of Hollywood's leading
cosmetic surgeons,
has interesting views
on the quest for the
body beautiful.
Photo by Alex Berliner

Zsa Zsa Gabor – the image of Hollywood glamour.
Photo by Alan Berliner

The legend of Marilyn lives on. **Anna Nicole Smith's** claim to fame is her remarkable resemblance to this Hollywood icon.

Photo by Alex Berliner

Pamela Anderson – a new icon in the making? Shapely star of hit show *Baywatch*.

© A. Crollalexza, Rex

Judy Lewis – discovered that she was the love child of Loretta Young and Clark Cable. Her resemblance to her famous parents could have given her away.

Photo by Eddie Sanderson

Theresa Russell
Has strong views on just how far she'll go for success.

© *Carlton UK Television Ltd*

The Wagners
– Robert and his two daughters. A Hollywood family who've survived the hard times.
Photo by Eddie Sanderson

Catya Sasoon
Hollywood kids have a tumultuous ride. Only some make it.
Photo by Bernard Fallon

Elaine Young A true Hollywood life. She lived the high life as Gig Young's wife but paid a price for trying to cling to youth.
Photo by Alex Berliner

Therapy comes in all forms in Hollywood. **Wanita Holmes** will cure what ails you through crystals.
Photo by Eddie Sanderson

Angelyne, a Hollywood woman famous for being famous.
Photo by Bernard Fallon

Jennifer Flavin
Sylvester Stallone's friend.
Photo by Alex Berliner

The Hollywood quest for perfection, like everything in Tinseltown, is pushed to extremes and the gym is one of the more normal ways of achieving it.
Photo by Bernard Fallon

Fortress Hollywood. Fame creates fear. Bodyguards, guns and shooting practice are common currency. Former *Dallas* star **Deborah Shelton**, *left*, seen here at target practice with her instructor.
Photo by Alex Berliner

Fashions in Sunland for the *de rigueur* nursing wear of the moment, or possibly Mothers With Style in Glendale. On Wilshire Boulevard there are breast pumps for rent at the Pump Station and Velcro nappy covers. Bundle of Convenience delivers French and German lotions, disposable nappies and a variety of baby-care products. Bare Bottom Diaper Service in Malibu offers pick-up and delivery service of all-cotton nappies as well as instruction classes for mums and dads. Love 'n' Kisses Kids in Encino specialize in infant clothes but also do a booming business in Comfort Silkie security blankets with satin binding, handwoven cotton throws and cashmere baby booties that will not fall off. Harry Harris Shoes for Children is ready for early walkers with baby cowboy boots, sparkle fashion shoes and dress shoes with rhinestones, pearls and appliqué. A must is a visit to Flap Happy for products to protect baby's face and neck from the California sun. The hats are in brushed cotton, Arctic fleece and flannel and in ten different styles to match junior sunglasses. The shop also offers rompers and Baby Bumper knee pads.

Other productions are needed for the child of Hollywood. First Steps Baby Proofing is one of a couple of dozen companies who move into the new baby's home and advise on everything from stair gates to motion detectors and Plexiglass barriers. The advice can cost up to and beyond $10,000. But think of the peace of mind.

What do you put on the walls? Grandma Whoopi Goldberg and Chevy Chase head for Every Picture Tells A Story. The art gallery that sells original art from children's books is the in-place for today's children-orientated Hollywood when even bad boys like Warren

Beatty and Jack Nicholson are now super-indulgent fathers. Lee Cohen, a co-owner of the gallery, said: 'Some of the buyers are collecting art for themselves but most hang the paintings – they cost from around $15,000 – on nursery walls.'

Baby will have a full-time nanny, probably arranged by Renee's of Beverly Hills. They charge a $2,000 fee and the live-in gets $500 a week, plus room and board, television, stereo, Nintendo and her own telephone line. When Oscar-winner Richard Dreyfuss's nanny decided to get married and have a family of her own, Dreyfuss couldn't find a 'suitable' replacement and moved nanny and her new husband and child in with them. Ryan O'Neal and Farrah Fawcett paid $1.7 million for a house next door to their Bel Air estate to accommodate domestic help and the beloved nanny of their eight-year-old son Redmond.

'Our nannies get anywhere from $300 to $700 a week according to whether they live in or out or work around the clock with very young babies,' said Claudia Kahn, the co-owner of Baby Buddies, adding: 'The perks are usually terrific. They get a limousine to drive them everywhere or maybe their own car. And the nannies get to go on movie locations and vacations in Europe.'

Bodyguards for babies are another essential. With kidnapping a big fear in Hollywood, celebrity parents hire guards for public events. Bruce Willis and Demi Moore even took a guard when they went to a cartoon movie screening with their daughter Rumer. But just plain Hollywood parents will already have the Universal Child

Fingerprinting Kit. All those aged more than three years old can be 'printed' with this non-toxic, inkless kit which puts the fingerprints on an official, colour-coded FBI card preformatted for a nationwide computer data base.

The children, not surprisingly, are more interested in their surroundings – and possessions – than security. At Baby Motives, a Los Angeles baby store, owner Wendy Pennes sells glider rocking chairs with custom-made ruffled covering for $329. Whitewashed or natural wood cribs are popular at $599 and the traditional canopy bed is a big seller at $809. 'People spend $10,000 to $20,000 on floor to ceiling decorating,' said Ms Pennes.

Others spend much, much more. At HaRry's (correct spelling) owner Paul Kunsberg does big business in 1950s-style chrome dinette sets for children with a table for $950 and chairs at $550 each. And there is the cheerful and delightful Bunny Novick. She's a children's interior designer and runs Kidspace out by the beach in Santa Monica. When we met she was 'working with' a local ten-year-old: 'Her parents gave her the cheque book and told her to get on with it. There doesn't seem to be a budget. She keeps writing the cheques.' Bunny ('everybody calls me Bunny') reported on one family that gave their children the front room: 'Really, they gave the three kids the living room. We designed it so each had space for their individual televisions, VCRs and Nintendos. And the bedroom was something else. They all have duvets covered with fabric from Germany and hand-painted. It's about $100 a yard. And they each have different duvets to use depending on their mood. I will only work with children. It's their space that we're creating. Obviously, the parents are involved but most of them just let us get on with it.'

Fun Furniture in Beverly Hills will customize any child's dreams. One three-year-old wanted Goldilocks and the Three Bears to sleep with her. The parents simply wanted her to sleep. Marcia from Fun Furniture spent $10,000 creating a Goldilocks House within the toddler's enormous bedroom. It has four rooms and from one window a slide goes out to an imitation pool with frogs and forest animals. On three armoires with vines and roses sit Mama, Papa and Baby Bear still allowing room for the TV, video and CD collection.

At eight months the Hollywood child will most likely get its first swimming instructor. Popular is Happy Swimmers, which offers a mobile service, which means they come to your pool, and Happy Sun Private Swimming Lessons, which do much the same except the instructors smile all the time. The children will be ready. They will have been working out at My Gym in Santa Monica where Tiny Tykes (aged three to ten months) get flexibility classes or Waddlers (eleven to eighteen months) are into gymnastics. Or at Jed Heller's Junior Gym in Van Nuys, where those aged more than six months are 'introduced to the rings, bars and balance beam'. Some children will already have their own personal fitness trainers.

By the first party, parents will have employed Chuck's Parking, who specializes in valet parking for such important child events. Cristal champagne, at around $140 a bottle, is the etiquette drink for wetting the baby's head at age one. At two, the Hollywood child will get his or her personal stationery usually from For Lahaav, which boasts its merchandise leaves 'lasting impressions'. Most certainly girls will have a gold or silver tennis bracelet from Otero's Jewelry.

Before the age of five, he/she will have a doctor, a dentist, an orthodontist, a dietitian and cosmetic dermatologist, like Beverly Hills's Letantia Bussell. And a hairdresser. Kiddie Kuts are popular: they charge outrageous prices but they offer Disney movies and baskets of toys. Hairdresser Jose Eber – best man at Elizabeth Taylor's last wedding and a Nicky Clarke hype type – cut a ten-month-old baby's hair the other week. It was the first cut so he charged the going rate of $275. The trimming of the curls took four minutes.

Dr Oliver the vet will be called in to teach children how to take care of pets. Ava the belly dancer may also have paid a visit to instruct on her art. One mother complained that the recession had ruined her Saturdays. She used to have a clown around the house every Saturday to keep the children happy while she had a facial. From an early age most Hollywood kids' rooms look like toyshops – $300-model, two-foot-long $2,000 Rolls-Royces to get a feel for the future – which starts early.

'Education begins at two,' were the words of Dr Isabelle Buckley, the founder of Buckley School, one of *the* places of status scholarship. To give a child a chance to get into schools like Buckley, Curtis, John Thomas Dye or Campbell Hall, parents send their two-year-olds to the Centre of Early Education. Barbra Streisand's Jason, Cher's Chastity and Diana Ross's Tracee all went there. The fees for these youngsters are upwards of $3,000 a term. It gets more pricey as children move on to Buckley (Frank Sinatra's grandchildren) and the others with fees ranging upwards of $5,000 a term. But that doesn't include the birthday parties.

First, the invitation, please. Around the world a note might be sent to classmates inviting them for cake and ice cream. Not here. A film producer wanted 230 invitations printed in gold leaf on a scroll, packed in a satin-covered box with Mother Goose books and freshly baked teddy-bear biscuits, tied with a ribbon embroidered with the initials of the birthday child. He also wanted the invitations delivered by hand by messengers dressed as Mother Goose characters. The cost was $100 for each invitation – but it's image not the price that counts. Which is why Marc Friedland's company called Artafax is booming. He arranged the Mother Goose invites from his office in Hollywood where he has sixteen employees and $2 million a year in revenues. When Melanie Griffith and Don Johnson wanted to announce the birth of their daughter the cards were decorated with tiny pearls, pink bows, little bunnies and alphabet beads.

Theme parties are favourites. For younger kids it's usually the present Disney release: now it's *The Lion King* but swimming-pool parties still centre around *The Little Mermaid*. For the sixteenth birthday, when teenagers can get a driving licence in California, Hansen's bakers do a special cake that looks like a licence and has the birthday person's photograph on it. It's usually presented at Jimmy's in Beverly Hills but former husband and wife

Lesley-Ann Warren and super-producer Jon Peters did their son's thing at Spago.

Children sometimes demand carnivals in their gardens, and companies will provide balloon arches, craft booths, face painters, disc jockeys, magicians and games like electric basketball shooting. The Party Factory can go even further and provide backyard circuses with elephant rides, lions, tigers, jugglers, stilt-walkers, organ grinders (and monkeys), high-wire acts, acrobats, square dancers, ethnic dancers, street dancers, rap acts, magic acts with live doves and rabbits, marionette shows and Ferris wheels (small, medium or large). Rod Stewart is one of the many Party Factory clients – others include Sylvester Stallone, Cheryl Ladd, Mick Fleetwood, Lesley Ann Down and James Caan. At one of Rocker Rod's parties guests put on goggles and plunged their faces into rows of lemon meringue pies searching for $20 bills. The first to discover a total of $100 won a $5,000 mini-Mercedes.

Oscar-winner Sally Field spent $200,000 on a baby suite for her Beverly Hills home. Bruce Willis spent $85,000 for a playhouse for his daughter: it's stucco with a Spanish tile roof with two rooms, a bathroom and full air-conditioning. Farrah Fawcett marked an early birthday for son Redmond by buying an $8,000 miniature pony equipped with special child saddle and bridle. The boy was decked out in designer cowboy gear for his first ride.

At Bloomers for Kids on Sunset Boulevard Arnold Schwarzenegger outfitted his kids for the ski trips to Aspen and Tellruride. *Après ski* they might wear one of the leather bomber jackets designed by actress Morgan *Dallas* Brittany. Her kids' line called Stunt Gear is very popular and jackets sell for $250.

Beverly Hills teeth are important. They don't just have 'braces' to straighten teeth. Orthodontists, like Dr Richard Grosman of Beverly Hills, correct wayward teeth with a 'hidden device' which costs about $5,000. Meanwhile, a plastic surgeon like Dr Frank Ashley will straighten your nose and pin back ears for about $2,000. They're working on spots.

If the new look gives a child an identity crisis there are plenty of child psychologists. Dr Irwin Lehroff is a favourite, and not just because his office is conveniently across the street from Neiman-Marcus, which has now become America's premier department store. But it does give the mothers somewhere to hang out while the offspring get their brain fixed.

Pre-teens – known as 'weenagers' – are the most indulged group. To truly witness the coddled Hollywood kid it takes a Saturday-morning visit to Balboa Park where the youngsters play official soccer games. If the team is winning, all is well. If things go wrong ... actor Beau Bridges' wife Wendy lost it when her son's team looked like losing. So much so that a mum with a son on the opposing team looked like getting her Armani T-shirt twisted around her neck in an argument. Actor William Katt – a true Hollywood child, he is the son of Barbara Hale, who played secretary Della Street for forty years in the *Perry Mason* TV series – is the coach of one team. Or, rather, was. When his team was losing 3–0 he lay on the ground and stopped coaching. 'It's not over until it's over,' he was told. He looked at the ground and muttered, 'It is for me.'

'Everything has a pay-off price and a price tag to it,' says Marilyn Ruman, a clinical psychologist based in Encino. 'Children have enough trouble coping with their parents and vice versa without the burden of coping with their parents' exalted status. Celebrity children often have problems with identity. And that celebrity doesn't have to be in the movie industry. This is a town of wealth – and a wealth of opportunities. Not winning and being told "no" are not something that Hollywood kids hear a lot. It can mess around with values during growing up and later.'

By the teenage years Hollywood children have discovered Westwood, the video arcades, music at Dillon's, watching the weirdoes and eating burgers at Fat Albert's, trending on Melrose Avenue, taking Harleys over Mulholland, surfing at Zuma Beach, playing the Malibu dating game and hoping Dad's booked the Hotel Jerome and not the pretentious Little Nell in Aspen for Christmas.

If the school grades don't look good the Hollywood child probably has a tutor. Parents just hope this is a better investment than the judo classes, deep-sea-diving course, five years of piano lessons, dance and acting classes. And the elocution lessons which can make a child say, 'Leave me alone!' perfectly. Or possibly a vowel-perfect, 'Give me a break!'

One teenager on his graduation had strong hopes of being given at least a VW Rabbit convertible and at best a Ferrari. On the big day Dad took him out to the garage. This was going to be awesome, dude!

Dad pushed the remote control and the garage door swung open. Inside was a spanking new Porsche, $65,000 of driving machine. The lad hid his disappointment but would later tell friends: 'Gee, Dad's so out of it. Doesn't he know Porsches are passé?'

The streets of Hollywood may be palm-lined and driven by Porsches, Rolls-Royces, Mercedes and avarice but life is not all easy for Hollywood Kids. It can be a chance or a curse to be a 'celebrity' child. Often parents are more wrapped up in their own lives than their children's. And vice versa. It happens worldwide – but Hollywood, as always, magnifies the happiness and the horrors.

Elaine Young epitomizes the Hollywood Wife (several times) and Hollywood Mother. With her actor husband Gig Young she had a daughter Jennifer: 'Jennifer's my only child. I love her madly but she was like having ten. Growing up in Beverly Hills is not easy. Too much of everything. When my daughter was going to school, if you drove by Beverly High there were Rolls-Royces, there were limos, there were people picking up their children with chauffeurs. When my daughter was sixteen, graduating, it wasn't good enough that I got her just a *car*. It had to be a Rabbit, it had to be a Ferrari, it had to be something really exquisite, and at that point I was a single mother selling real estate, trying to build the business.

'I wasn't like all the other really, really wealthy parents. I was a mother that raised my daughter alone, which was very difficult. Kids here give lots of parties when the mother's away – you're lucky if you come home to anything left in your house.

'But she had a lot of wonderful friends, a variety of friends. Nicholas Cage, who grew up to be a big star, and Heidi Fleiss was a friend of hers.

'When Jennifer was a teenager I wasn't really privy to what she did in private or with her friends. I would see her friends when they'd come over and they'd hide the liquor if they had liquor. Everything was hidden from Mommy. They'd come over to my house 'cos I was working and they could have a ball there. I would see beer bottles and things. So I knew there were a lot of parties going on.

'A lot of them didn't take life too seriously because there was too much of everything. I was born here and my lifestyle was quite different because then California was like a small town – I used to ride my horse down Rodeo Drive. My dad was one of the heads at Universal Studios and when I was little I lived in the Valley because it was near Universal and we had horses and we had chickens and we had vegetable gardens. People don't even think about that today. My last house I had fifteen fruit trees. That was the best I could do to bring back the way I grew up and what I really like.

'I remember one thing that was sort of funny, 'cos I've never lived anywhere but California so I don't have a great comparison but I do think I have values. I was doing an interview with *People* magazine and I'm trying to tell the lady I think I'm a very normal person, I'm a good mother and I'm reliable. She said, "Well, how many times have you been married?" I said six. She said, "How many cars do you have?" I said three. She said, "And you think you're normal," and I said, "Oh, maybe I'm not and I just think I am."

'I have a very interesting story. I went from riches to rags and then riches to myself. My father was one of the richest men in the poorest neighbourhood and I felt horrible about it. You know how kids feel about being poor? I felt just as bad having money 'cos all my friends did not. At Hallowe'en, my father would take me to Universal Studios to the wardrobe. He'd dress me up as a fairy princess with diamonds and jewels and this long dress, and I'd go to school and the kids had sheets on with eyes cut out and they laughed at me. So I would start to take money from my dad and give it to my poor friends. It always bothered me. Money was always sort of a problem for me and then my dad lost everything when I was twenty-four. I was going to UCLA to become a lawyer and I started working part-time in a real-estate office answering telephones and that's how I got into real estate.

'When I was a teenager I guess I would be considered a bad girl. I was pretty wild. I hated school. I ended up going to UCLA for four years and getting great grades but during that time I didn't want anything to do with studying. I wanted to go out. I was boy-crazy, which most people were. I was popular because we had a studio in the back of our house, a theatre and everyone came over and watched television and, of course, they could have food and drinks 'cos I came from a wealthy family. I grew up very popular.

'I thought it was wild time. But I didn't drink, and a lot of the kids now drink beer, and I didn't do drugs. I don't even know if they did then. I'm fifty-nine. I guess a wild time was just having a lot of boyfriends and being in love all the time. Today it's clubs, going out, rock 'n' rolling, dancing all night.

'It's very common in this town to come from a dysfunctional family. The word dysfunctional has certainly become a classic word around here, but I don't think it should be a cop-out and that's what I tell Jennifer. I have absolutely hammered into her that you're better having a mother that loves you, that's there for you, than both parents that don't care about you. You can never take away the fact she didn't have a father but you can't dwell on sympathy and blame your past life and never ever get it together. My parents were together and it was horrible for me and I have overcome it.

'I think it's much harder to have a famous father and not see him. Think of the people married to actors, who are madly in love with them – when they die, it's very difficult. They see their husbands on television like they're still alive. We even forget who dies 'cos we see them in old movies. So for Jennifer it almost keeps him alive in her mind and he isn't and she has to get that into reality.

'A lot of actors are too busy with their careers and they forget they have children. They forget they have wives! When men or women make movies they have to travel and sometimes they can't take their family. When Jennifer was two Gig did *The Music Man* all over the country and I took Jennifer and she would cry. He'd say, "I've never sung before, I can't concentrate on my role, that child has to stop crying." What could I do? I wanna be with my husband but I wanna be with my child too. It's a great problem, the industry and being married to someone in it. You make it up to your kids by throwing money at them. Clothes, cars, freedom. Freedom's worse than giving them money. No discipline is worse than giving them money. Freedom, then they have no values. They don't know what to do. They're running wild.

'Jennifer had too much freedom. She went through being wild but she's starting to calm down now. She still has fun, but she's getting more into her career and more stable. It's getting embarrassing. I'm not that old and now she's sort of treating me like the daughter. She's saying, "Mom, you shouldn't do that, you shouldn't give your money away," and "If you listen to me you wouldn't sign that contract."

'Clothes, clothes, clothes. One time when my daughter was like twelve, I think, I said, "You've gotta get a job, Jennifer, even if you only make two dollars a week." So she got a paper round. One day I come home and see this taxicab and I say, "Jennifer, what are you doing?" My paper round, my bike broke down. So her paper round cost me money. I had to pay for the cab. She didn't wanna let anyone down but that's typically Beverly Hills. A paper round from a cab.

'I think the biggest bill Jennifer brought home charge-card wise was $4,000. It's a lot of money. I worked hard for that. This is a fierce town for competition, even with the kids. They feel it at a very young age. They've gotta compete. Well, Susie has a brand new Rabbit, maybe I should get one too, or she's got a Gucci purse, I'd better get one too. They keep saying to you, but Mom, everyone else has it. What about me? And it's difficult.

'Some people don't have enough food to eat and your daughter's saying, "I wanna Gucci purse 'cos everyone has one,' and that's like three, four hundred dollars. That feeds a family for a week, and you go, wow, something's wrong with this picture.

'Did I buy the Gucci purse? Yes. Shame on me but I did. I always gave her love but you think giving things will help, too. I was a very young parent raising my daughter alone. I was married five times after she was born. She got along great with the men, it wasn't like a deep-seated problem for her that Mommy had five husbands. She enjoyed it. It was fun. They always took her places and it was always something new for her. So I mean she did enjoy it and she liked them and they liked her.'

Jennifer Young is an aspiring singer. 'I'm a singer, I like to act and eventually I'd like to have my own entertainment show. I've been singing since I was a little girl. My mom always jokes that when I was a baby she used to put a radio by my crib and ever since then I've had a love for music. I've performed at the China club, which is a very hot nightclub around here, a nightclub called Spice, Club Lingerie, the Palomino. I performed in Japan for about five weeks, not too long ago I sang live on *Joan Rivers*.

'They just did a big write-up on me in *Buzz* magazine and they compared my voice to Dolly Parton. I come from an entertainment family, my father being an Academy-Award-winning actor, and my grandfather. My great-uncle was a famous conductor, Jan Garber. Being in the entertainment industry, it's just in the genes.

'I have vague memories of my father because I didn't live with him long. It was hard for me 'cos my mother and father got a divorce when I was about four and my memories of him are just seeing him on television shows. They had a kinda bitter divorce and I was kinda the scapegoat. I got used in the situation, you know, so my father didn't see me much and that was hard on me.

'The day he died was very difficult for me because I was so into music I could not sleep without the radio on and it was on every news channel. I opened the door, cameras were flashing in my face. I didn't know what was going on. It didn't really hit me till that night I saw it on every news channel and then it was on every radio station. And finally I couldn't take it any more. I just turned it off and that's when I broke down hysterically.

'I was fourteen, and I stayed home for two weeks just so no-one would come up to me and say, "Oh, I'm so sorry." I thought it would die down. And the minute I went out I saw Katie Wagner, Robert Wagner's daughter. She came up to me on that first day, "Oh, I'm so sorry about your father." And I thought gosh, I stayed home for two weeks. I really didn't wanna talk about it. I wanted to bury the feelings.

'As I get older now I'm starting to learn a lot more about what happened. I think to myself sometimes if I could just have ten minutes to talk to my father, and then that ten minutes turns into one hour and then that one hour turns into one day and the one day turns into one week . . .

'So it's never enough and I just really have to bury it. But, if he hadn't been such a big name and if he didn't

Hollywood thrives on sex but sometimes the boundaries are pushed and young children are caught on a seedy and possibly violent treadmill.

Photo by Eddie Sanderson

Dr. Lois Lee – runs the Children of the Night, a shelter for child prostitutes.

Photo by Eddie Sanderson

TV family – the Waltons today. *Above from left to right* – **Eric Scott** (Ben), **Mary McDonough** (Erin) and **Jon Walmsley** (Jason Walton).
Photo by Eddie Sanderson

Brogan Lane – ex-wife of Dudley Moore.
Photo by Bernard Fallon

Plastic surgeon
Dr Rosenstein – with
a tool of his trade
Photo by Eddie Sanderson

John Wayne Bobbit
– has become a porn
star since his brush
with fame.
Photo by Eddie Sanderson

Kevin Costner
– star of Hollywood's most expensive film, *Waterworld*, whose divorce from wife Cindy could cost him almost as much as the $200,000,000 movie.
© *Rex*

Val Kilmer – the new Batman has separated from British actress Joanne Whalley.
© *Rex*

Melanie Griffiths and
Don Johnson – they've
split, too, again.
© Dave Hogan – Rex

Richard Gere
and Cindy Crawford
have also gone their
separate ways.
© Rex

Susan Sarandon
and **Tim Robbins** –
still together and still
going strong.
© *Peter Brookner – Rex*

Bruce Willis
and Demi Moore
© *Rex*

Clint Eastwood
© *Rex*

Meryl Streep
© *Alexandra Boulat – Rex*

John Travolta
© Facelly – Rex

Sean Penn
© Rex

Jessica Lange
© Alison Waggner – Rex

have a star on the Hollywood Walk of Fame and if I wasn't reminded of it probably on almost a daily basis it'd probably be a lot easier for me. But the fact that he was a famous name makes it more difficult. I think I've turned out okay with it but it's hard.'

Jennifer can see the funny side of her mother's many marriages. 'I had a lot of stepfathers ... My mom has been married – oh, God, six times, so there were a couple of good stepfathers. I had one favourite step-dad. I actually had a bodyguard from the age of eleven to fourteen and he was Mr Universe at the time. I later discovered my friends could not understand why I had a bodyguard, and it was funny because he was kinda Italian Mafia-type and he was my favourite stepfather. He was very good to me. He took me on my mom's honeymoon with them. He took me everywhere and I guess maybe he'd be in a little trouble here and there. I couldn't figure out why I had a bodyguard all the time but he was always watching over me, protecting me and it was definitely different!

'The big-star-name kids also had bodyguards. I carpooled with Glen Campbell's kids. I grew up with people like Tatum O'Neal and Griffin, her brother. And I also grew up with Leif Garrett when he was real popular. Beverly Hills High is not like your average high school. I don't know if I would want my kids to go there! I've learned a lot from it but the competition is so fierce that it can really destroy you. I mean it's unbelievable. If I didn't have that four-hundred-dollar brand-new sweater or if I didn't have those brand-new Montby's shoes and keep up with all the kids in my school I did not feel whole. That's how they made you feel. The competition was so incredibly fierce. Kids got anorexia, starved themselves so they'd look great. It's very fierce competition. I never had anorexia although I was told I looked very skinny. I would look at myself and I would think, Gosh, I look skinny but I think it looks good, you know. Everyone wanted to have the best body. Everybody wanted to have the best clothes in Beverly Hills High. Everyone had to have the newest thing that was coming in, whatever would hit the stores, the newest fad – you had to keep up with the trend or you were talked about.

'A lot of rich kids at Beverly Hills High were driving up in Ferraris and Porsches at sixteen years old. Even men and women in their forties don't drive around in cars like that. There's a thing called the Tracts here in Beverly Hills and if you had a house above the Tracts where all the multi-million-dollar houses are, you were considered up to par. If you had a house below the tracts, you'd be talked about.

'I have some very good memories of Beverly Hills High. I went with the king of the high school. I was popular so it was fun. I was kinda a little bit more into the boys than my homework but it was a fun time. Everybody'd all get together and go out and I mean there was constantly parties. There was always something to do and it was just a happy, fun time. I used to throw some pretty wild parties! In one of our houses there was a liquor cabinet; my mom would put all the liquor at the very top so it was hard to reach it but the guys would figure out a way. She would go out, I'd call all my friends, invite every one of them over and they would tell their friends and they would tell their friends. They'd get the liquor out and they'd start pouring it.

'But all of the competition comes back to money. All of it. It was always, Mom, please, I have to have this. I love you so much. You have to help me. Everybody's got this now why can't I have it? I was a bit spoiled growing up. But I think I turned out okay. I think that with her being a single parent, she felt the need to give me everything I wanted and so I didn't really have a problem keeping up. I was lucky. I'd get the new thing just in the nick of time!

'I had a lot of charge credit cards, although they were my mother's. The most I ever spent in one day was about one thousand dollars. Maybe a little more. I didn't go crazy – I always looked at the price tags. Not only would I buy clothes for myself but whatever friend was with me. My mother was so giving.

'Every time she'd make a multi-million-dollar deal she would buy a house. I always call it like Monopoly. Basically she would buy a house, we'd live in it for one year and then we would move out and this would go on and on. We ended up owning eight houses, which I thought was real brilliant of her. Some of them above the tracts, some of them below. In high school I lived below the tracts so I was made fun of. To this day we still own these houses and, hey, they're worth good money!

'I tried to make my own money. I had every conceivable job you can possibly think of but back then what the hell is four dollars an hour gonna do for you? Absolutely nothing! I worked at David's Cookies. I worked at Benihana's restaurant as a hostess. I worked in a nightclub during the day answering the phones, then night-time would come and I'd do the cash register. My paper route was the funniest thing. My bicycle broke down and I thought oh I've gotta take care of this paper route so I called a taxicab. My mom had to pay for the taxicab and the day's work ended up costing probably double what I would have made.

'My mom had a hard time punishing me. She was very easy-going, she kinda couldn't use the word no with me. A lot of the time she couldn't be home for me. I was left a lot with the housekeeper, even though my mother and I were very close, I loved her more than anything. She had to work to support me. There was no father so what was she to do? She just kinda gave me anything I wanted.

'My mom thought therapy would be a good idea and I had a male psychiatrist. Just being around a male once or twice a week probably helped me a lot. I tried to find my father one day and I missed a therapy appointment. I took two buses to get to his apartment. I got up to the door and I said, "Is this Gig Young's apartment?" and they said, Yes, it is, and I said, "Well, his daughter is here." He was there at the time and I got through the doors, I got up to the door ready to knock and all this fear started going through me. What if he slaps me? What if he turns me down? What if he says I don't have a daughter? All these what-ifs and I was just about to knock and I didn't. I got home and my mother said, "Where were you, you missed your appointment?" It was very expensive back then, and my father was only giving me about two hundred dollars a month, child support, and I started crying. She was shaking me and I said, "I tried to go find my father," and she just lost it. She broke down and she started crying so hard. It must have affected me pretty much.

'I'm not the only kid in this world without a father but I think it's harder when you have a famous father figure or famous mother figure. I just wanted him to acknowledge me. Look what I've grown up into. I'm your daughter. I just wanted him to say hi. Just for you to notice me and that's it. If he would have given me a hug I sure would have loved one!

'I regret not knocking to this day because maybe he would have accepted me. The only reason I regret it is if he would have accepted me. But I have a feeling he may have slammed the door in my face. That would have killed me. So I just decided not to knock.

'My father did not acknowledge me after the divorce. One thing that made me very happy is that my best friend's mother ran into him in a tennis shop and she said, "My daughter is best friends with your daughter, Jennifer Young, and they play at your daughter's," and he started asking her a bunch of questions. So I thought, at least he cared enough to ask.

'He won an Oscar for *They Shoot Horses, Don't They*, with Jane Fonda, and right now I'm trying to get my father's Oscar. As I've gotten older it's become such an obsession with me to have that Oscar. I saw a little bit of the movie on TV and I will tell you what I did. I ran up to the TV and I put my arms around it and I started crying and I said, "That's my dad, that's my dad," and I was just crying and crying and crying. Why can't I see my dad? I went nuts.

'My mum wanted my father to see me too but he was

such an ego-maniac that he figured, "I know Jennifer is the most important thing to you, Elaine, and I'm gonna destroy that. I'm gonna not see her, I'm gonna make you miserable." My mother got my father sober for one year, you know, and then people would say, "Oh, Gig, you're no fun, liven up, have a drink." So he started drinking again and my mother couldn't handle it any more, so she wanted a divorce and he flipped out!

'There's so much divorce here. If you lived in Hollywood you would be able to see why. This whole town is full of competition. You have to be better than the next person. You have to look the best. You have to act, you have to be the smartest, you have to be above everybody. I was born and raised in this town, Hollywood, California, and I'll be the first to say that this town can chew you up and spit you out if you're not careful!'

Jennifer is also candid about drugs in Hollywood. 'I was pulled in a bathroom stall by three guys one time in the men's bathroom – hey, you're kinda cute. The next thing I knew they were pulling out drugs and I was like, Oh, boy. This is a little bizarre! I thought one of them was cute so I just kinda hung out and watched. The drug scene, it goes with the territory. This is Hollywood. It's all ages. As young as thirteen years old or as old as sixty-five. There's so much pressure in this town that I think people use drugs as an escape, or alcohol or marijuana or what have you. I'm not an angel, you know, but I don't have a problem. I've tried certain things in my life but there's certain things I would stay away from. Ecstasy was a real big fad here, everybody was doing it. I try to stay away from things like that. It's like a trend here. A new drug'll come in and everybody's gotta try it and then it fades out and then the next one comes in and everybody's gotta try it and then it fades out. I've had a very close friend die, OD – Charles Bronson's son. That affected me a lot. I really cared about him.'

Jennifer's friends include supersexy blonde star Nicolette Sheridan, one-time step-daughter of Telly 'Kojak' Savalas. 'Nicolette and I were very close. We were inseparable for about two, three years. We did everything together. We'd buy the same outfits but different colours and we'd wear them together! I'll never forget when I had a Thanksgiving dinner with Tatum and John McEnroe before they were married. Victoria Sellers and I were inseparable for quite some time. I had a lot of fun with her. Victoria had the first convertible BMW in this town and everybody went nuts. Everyone tried to pull her over and say, "God, your car is so hot!" So her licence plate said, "I know." When Britt [Ekland] would go out of town, I'd spend the night over at Victoria's house. She could be a little bossy at times but I thought she was so cool. The craziest thing we ever did was have our boyfriends at the time spend the night at her house when her mom was out of town. Nothing severe went on. We always got into the cool parties. I also grew up with Jennifer Nicholson, Jack Nicholson's daughter. I met Heidi Fleiss through another friend. Heidi and I just clicked. I've known Heidi for like ten years and when we lived together it was great. We roomed for about a year and a half in Beverly Hills. Heidi and I have just now made up and I don't wanna say anything wrong 'cos journalists turned us against each other for almost a year.

She was the best friend I ever had. When we lived together she was just there for me. I went through some really rocky relationships and Heidi just was there for me.'

Jennifer has been at her mother's side during her horrific plastic surgery problems. 'I don't know why my mother had to do it. She was beautiful and she got all this plastic surgery done to her and it affected my life because she started getting it when I was very young and I didn't know how to deal with it. She would walk in with two nurses, all bandaged up, and I used to shake in my pants. I would freak out. It was so scary to me and she kept going back for more and more and as a result it backfired on her. She almost died from it. She's had thirty-six eye surgeries and had her entire face removed, you know. Her face was taken off.

'She had one hundred and eighty-seven stitches in her head with a blood bottle coming out. I used to have to take care of her after the plastic surgeries went bad, and it's been a long haul for her. I believe that silicone is something that you would probably stick in cars or something like that and these women just don't understand. I don't understand it, 'cos they're so pretty to begin with so why do they need to have plastic surgery? But everyone's gotta be prettier than the next person, you know.

'The most popular plastic surgery in high school was nose jobs. I will tell you that when I was in elementary I was made fun of all the time because of my lips. I started to cover them and I started to run and cry. Then this guy said, "No, they're great." and people started having lip collagen injections. So something I was made fun of for, is now an in thing!'

Victoria Sellers, daughter of Britt Ekland and the late Peter Sellers, has been one of the most mixed-up of celebrity Hollywood children. She's frank: 'I like to know about all aspects of all life! And a lot of people find that unacceptable. There is a lot of prejudice among the Beverly Hills set when they know that I have black friends and my boyfriend is black. When I go somewhere Beverly Hillsish – and I love to do that, dressed how I wanna dress, with my friends, and they're good people – I can feel the whispers, I can feel the vibe of the people that are thinking, He don't belong here. They don't give you a fair chance at all, I don't think.

'I used to dwell on buying a collection of some clothing or something, I used to be like, I've gotta get that, I've just gotta, I won't eat and I won't pay this bill but I'll get that. Now I think, How could I have been interested in that? For example, my room-mate Darren bought me some new Adidas, some grey corduroy Levi's and two huge white T-shirts and tube socks. Like that is like the best new outfit to him and I like that a lot too. He hangs his T-shirts up, he irons his T-shirts. He wants to do his own laundry just so that nothing gets damaged. He looks after what he owns and values his few possessions. But there's other people who'll rip you off, become your friend to know who your friends are that have money.

'There's a lot of people out there with guns. Young people. It's like a power thing. My friend was pulled over in my car and he throws his gun on my lap. I didn't even know he had it! We got pulled over and there's a gun on my lap. It was all over the papers. I think a lot of children between thirteen and eighteen have guns. That is more a problem now than drugs. Now if I'm driving someone I don't know that well I just ask if they've got a gun, and if they do, I say, "Don't come in my car if you have a gun!"

'How I know that someone really wants to know me as a person is really hard to tell. It sounds so awful but I have to put someone through a little test or something. That only comes after being screwed over a lot of times.

'So much has made me angry. My God, there's so many different circumstances! This guy that I thought was my friend, he took my bank card, put cheques into my bank account and they were bad, withdrew money, tried to steal my car, threatened my life. Just small things like that, I don't know! He seemed so nice, and a friend, I thought.

'I've had a lot of people rip me off and use me for money and take my clothes and my belongings and all that. That's why possessions aren't as important to me as before.

'I don't think LA is that dangerous. I just think it's what you get caught up in. I mean people ripping you off and I mean drugs. Drugs and the wrong people. Also you can get really depressed if you don't have any money and you don't have anything coming in or any new opportunities. I think now people are more smart about drugs – but the wrong people, that's a really tough one, because I'm so open myself at first. I trust people, I give them the benefit of the doubt. I just cannot believe the things that happen to me because of that.

'I have experienced drugs. When I was younger I used to do cocaine and I did not know how I was ever gonna not do that. I went to a rehabilitation place. I went to two places. One for thirty days and then I went to a six and a half months one and that one they were like "get your arse to bed!" That's how they talk to you there and I was like, okay. That was one where I became a drug and alcohol rehabilitation counsellor. Can you believe me? I was a counsellor in the drug rehab, helping other people that came in because everybody that worked there had been through their programme and was a former drug addict. I hate the way that sounds but I guess that's what it's called. I've smoked marijuana, had alcohol, and cocaine. I took it because of the people I was around a lot, Beverly Hills people. A lot of Beverly Hills people do cocaine but back then drugs were more in and more talked about. Now it's unacceptable. It really is. I took it at my friends' houses in Beverly Hills. People throwing up in their marble bathrooms ... The weekend before I went into my six and a half month rehab this girlfriend of mine, who's on a soap opera, I saw her high and I was, like, my God, have I ever looked like that, and I wanted to go to that place. My mother and my stepfather sent me to the rehab. Back then drugs were being used a lot more and there was a lot of commercials on television for drug rehabs and if you don't get help here get it somewhere else. I was in AA for three or four years, where I was greeting people at the door, bringing the coffee, and that was really good for me too.

'When I came out of my rehab, for about two or three years after that I hung out with people in AA. I felt comfortable and I was safe and I was better, and I just did not feel right around the other people that I was friends with before.

'I think all teenagers and young adults and children know about drugs and it's like, don't do that! And people wanna do that, and it's readily available at all street corners and it's everywhere. But I think now it's, like, crack time, and I would never even think of that.

'My parents would ask me about drugs and check my things. It wasn't something I could have at home. That's why I went to my friends' houses. A lot of their parents weren't as strict. My mother, I think, is on the stricter side but that's good, not that I was happy with it then but later I think I was. And a lot of my friends, their parents would let them have anyone sleep over, be it girl or guy, and their parents would be gone. I always had a nanny there and she would not be exactly the nicest person that's ready and willing to let me do whatever I wanted. So I'd go to my friends' houses where they'd have the whole place to themselves and people'd come over and that's how it would happen.

'I guess I was a wild child. I felt like I was a rebel because I went into the punk rock thing and then into a Beverly Hills thing. Now I like to go and meet interesting people. I'm more open to that than a lot of other people are. My dad [Peter Sellers] wasn't as strict as my mother. That's why I went to his house on the weekend because he'd let me drink champagne and, you know, I was like thirteen or fourteen. And he'd let me go to Westwood and if you were really cool you were in Westwood on a Friday or a Saturday night and my dad would pick me up and drive me there and my mom was like, you're not going there! After a while I knew that I couldn't ask my mom 'cos I know the answer's gonna be no. I'll go to Dad. Things like that.

'Divorced parents are so common here I don't think I know anybody's two real parents. I have one girlfriend and I thought her parents were like the perfect couple. They lived next to Lucille Ball. My friend had a powder room and a dressing room, a bedroom as big as a house. We were about seventeen. Her parents were still married and I used to think that that was just neat. Her mother was from England and they always did the same thing every Christmas, went to a certain ski place, and Easter they went to Hawaii. I used to think that was really nice. And then it turned out her father was seeing another lady and then he moved out of the house and then the mother was living there alone but it's such a gigantic mansion to be in by yourself so she moved.

'My friend had to go to a school that wasn't as good and she sort of blew school off. Her parents just gave her money to make up for the divorce. I mean she was driving different cars and had a Rolls-Royce when we were eighteen. Crazy things like that. I saw her going through a lot when her parents were getting a divorce and I was thinking, My God, it just seems normal to me because my parents were divorced when I was five.

'I was a spoilt kid. I had a lot of nice things when I was little and when I was seventeen I got a convertible BMW. I was in my punk rock stage and my parents were trying to get me out of it and encourage me to like nicer things. And so I did and then they were, like, Ooh, we don't like you like that either. Well you made me like this!

'When I was in the drug rehab I had therapy with my mother for six sessions and they worked really well. I was terrified, I was like my God, you want me to tell my mother the things she does that bother me? Are you crazy? No way. No, with her sitting next to me, no, no! And you had to. There was no being at that place and not trying to share your feelings. They didn't let you hide and be quiet. There was none of that. It was strict. I can still picture me being pulled into that office. I wasn't but that's how it felt. Since that time we can talk about anything. When I was younger I used to sometimes hate my mother and now I think of her as one of my best friends. I can just openly talk to her about anything.'

Victoria claims she wants to put her 'wild child' life behind her. She wants, she says, a 'normal' life. 'Married with children, and I wanna have a career too. I'd like to be acting, and just to be happy and healthy and that's about it. But I don't wanna bring my children up here. I'll probably bring them up in London. It was really a strict life there but it was the way it was and I was used to that. It's not like here at all and it will never be, so you won't be open to all the sort of things that can happen to your child in a town like this, that will happen regardless of whatever you try to do. I'm not saying that it's that terrible here but I'm not gonna bring my children up here. After they're done with their school, when they're eighteen they can do what they want, just like my mother said to me. "When can I do this?" I'd say. She'd go,

"When you're eighteen," and I'd be like, God, that's two years!

'If I wasn't me I would most wanna be Madonna. She's a woman that went out there and did it and got everything she wanted to and she's talented on top of it. But it's usually only men ever come out in the position that she's in. In her life right now she's like a mogul and I look up to that. She did it all herself, coming off the streets, so I like her a lot!

'I also admire my mum and dad. I'm always asking my mum advice like what skin cream should I use for this and what I should do for that. And my dad, if I'm really working hard at acting, when I'm being really good I can like look at something, a piece of work of his and try to bring something of him into myself. Like for *Saturday Night Live* I need a character, since I'm not a stand-up comic, and I look back at my father's movies and we look at his characters and his voices and when he was an Indian or a Frenchman and that helps me.

'I do have regrets but it's too bad! All things happen for a reason, but I don't wanna say what they are. It's mostly about people, just being wary of people in this town or probably anywhere but mostly in Hollywood, California!'

Judy Lewis has lived a remarkable Hollywood story. And she tells it here in detail. She was born following a secret love affair between Hollywood's 'King' Clark Gable and Oscar-winning actress Loretta Young. Her mother's pregnancy was concealed to avoid what, in 1935, would have been a headline-making scandal. It would have ruined the careers of Gable and Young – they both had morality clauses in their studio contracts. The 'mistake' baby was hidden for eight months and then placed in an orphanage. Nearly a year later Loretta Young reclaimed her and broadcast to Hollywood that this was her 'adopted' daughter.

Loretta Young, who won an Oscar for her role in *Farmer's Daughter* in 1947, was paranoid about the Hollywood power players making the connection between Gable, who died in 1960, and Judy. One characteristic that Judy inherited from her father was his big, protruding ears – Gable had them glued back for *Gone With The Wind* – and her mother made her wear a bonnet year-round. But it was school playground taunts that made Judy plead for something to be done. She had painful plastic surgery and the obvious link with her father was literally severed.

She was twenty-three when she was told of her father's identity. But she could not believe it until she heard it from her mother when she was thirty-one.

She might have had her father's ears, but she also had – and has – her mother's face and that warm smile which brightened movies like *The Bishop's Wife*, *Along Came Jones* and, interestingly, *He Stayed For Breakfast*.

She talks slowly and happily about it: 'I was raised by my biological mother as an adopted child. I first learned Clark Gable was my father when I was twenty-three. I was about to be married and I said to my fiancé that I couldn't marry him because I didn't know my background. He told me it was common knowledge my father was Clark Gable. That's when I first heard that. But I couldn't believe it until I asked my mother and heard it from her lips, and that wasn't until I was thirty-one.

'When I finally got the courage to confront my mother I was married and a mother. I'd been in therapy for a number of years and I was doing a soap opera in New York. I flew 3000 miles to California where my mother was and I said: "I must know, is my father Clark Gable?" And she said, "Would you like him to be?" I said, "Yes, I've heard he's a wonderful man." She said, "He *is* your father."

'And then she told me the story about how they met on a film called *Call of the Wild* and they fell in love. He was married and she was single. That was in 1935. And in Hollywood, in the thirties, it would have been a terrible scandal had my mother let it be known publicly that she was an unmarried woman and pregnant. So she had to hide her pregnancy. They finished the picture, my father left his marriage, separated from his wife, and my mother went to Europe on a trip. She told everyone she was going on a vacation and then snuck back into Hollywood and she went to a small house in Venice, California, and that's where I was born. Then, I was kept hidden in that house and for a time I was sent to an orphanage, and then when I was nineteen months old my mother introduced me to Hollywood as her adopted daughter. She did that through Louella Parsons, who was a famous Hollywood columnist. Only she didn't say that she adopted one little girl, she said she adopted two little girls as a smoke-screen. Then a week later she said that the mother of one of the little girls wanted the child back so that left my mother with one little girl, me. But the strange thing is that in the thirties single women were not allowed to adopt. So really nobody was fooled but everybody kept her secret.

'Why didn't they marry? My father was still married and my mother was a Catholic, and he kept trying to see her and trying to be close to her. He visited me a couple of times when I was an infant in that house in Venice. She told me she kept pushing him away. She was so afraid people in Hollywood would see them together and they could lose their careers. It would have been a terrible scandal. Hollywood in the thirties was very different from Hollywood in the nineties. In the thirties there had been three main scandals.

'And there was the "Hayes Code" which was Hollywood producers censoring their own films. There was also a morals code attached to the stars' contracts at the studios. Had my mother's pregnancy been discovered both my parents would have lost their contracts and also their careers. So it took several years for my father to become divorced and by that time he was going with another lady. Has my mother ever publicly acknowledged me? No. To this day she hasn't. At this time my mother's public statement is that this was a romantic rumour of a bygone era which some people want to believe for their own reasons, and she gives it no further credence. It saddens me that to this day she still does not publicly acknowledge me.

'I only had one meeting with my father and at the time I didn't know he was my father. So it was bitter-sweet now that I talk about it. I was fifteen and I was in

Merrymount High School, and I came home from school one day and I walked into the living room and there's Clark Gable. And he's alone and he says: "You're Judy, aren't you?" He knew who I was. And I said: "Yes, and you're Clark Gable." And he burst out laughing, said, "That's right." And then my mother came around the corner and I thought he was there to see her, of course, because they'd just finished doing a film together, *Key to the City* (1950). So I excused myself and I started to go upstairs and my mother said: "No, wait ... spend some time with Mr Gable." So I thought, What am I gonna say to Clark Gable? I'd just seen him in *Gone With The Wind* and so I was very enamoured of him.

'We sat on the living-room couch and he began to ask me questions about my life and I began to talk to him. And as I was talking I looked up and my mother had left us alone. And he quickly put me at ease and he wanted to know all about my life, about my school and what I was doing and my friends and my boyfriend and we spent a lovely two hours together. I was very much aware that he really wanted to know about me and he left and as he left he gave me a kiss on the forehead. But I didn't know he was my father. Had I known that Clark Gable was my father I think my whole life would have been different. It's too late now. He was dead many years when my mother told me Clark Gable was my father. It's sad.

'It's so hard to talk about him because I didn't know him and when I talk about him I talk about him only as a loss. So naturally the child in me wants to know why he didn't rescue me, why he didn't come up on his shining white horse and say, here climb on the back of my horse and I'll take care of you. So the question is like the end of *Gone With The Wind* when he turns to Scarlet and says, "Frankly, my dear, I don't give a damn." I wonder sometimes if that's the way he felt about me. And it's hard to know because he's not here to ask.

'The first time he saw me was at the house in Venice. My bed was a dresser drawer. According to my mother, he reached into his pocket and pulled out a wad of bills. He'd been very poor as a young boy and he liked being able to reach in his pocket and feel money, that he had a lot of money. And he kept a wad of money rolled up. Apparently he peeled off four one-hundred-dollar bills of this wad of money, handed it to my mother and said: "The least you can do is buy her a decent bed." My mother said: "That's the only money he ever gave me for you."

'It's very difficult for me to watch my father's films knowing that the man on the screen is my father and I can't reach him, know him, touch him. I cry most of the time, all the way through them, it's a loss for me. From what I know of him and see of him on the screen, he was a real guy, he was a man. And everybody that knew him and people that have talked about him said that I would have loved to have had that relationship with that man. I missed that. So it's a big loss to see that man on the screen and he's my dad.

'It's hard for me to watch my father as Rhett Butler in his scenes with Cammie King, who is a friend of mine, playing Bonnie Blue as his daughter. He's so darling with her. He's so warm and tender with her. I wish it were me. I wish I had been there and I like to imagine that he was thinking of me when he was playing those scenes.

'Somewhere he is quoted as saying, "The only time I liked myself as an actor, felt I was anyway, half-way decent as an actor, is in the scene when I learned that Bonnie Blue had died." And so it helps me to imagine that he was thinking of me when he played those scenes.'

She remains resentful that she was never told who her father was for all those years: 'I remember the moment my fiancé told me. I was so angry. I was angry at him for keeping this most important secret to me away from me. And everybody I talked to after that, and even today when I ask people and I say, "Why didn't you tell me? Don't you know how important it was for me to know that?" Everybody said, "It wasn't our place to tell you. It was your mother's place to tell you." And total strangers knew. It was common knowledge, and my closest and dearest friends kept thinking that my mother would tell me. They'd wait for my sixteenth birthday and my eighteenth birthday and my twenty-first birthday, and finally they thought, Well, she knows. And indeed I didn't until I finally confronted my mother at thirty-one and it was too late.

'My mother and I last spoke in 1986, on Mother's Day, ironically enough. She thought I was writing a book. It was stated in a New York paper that I was writing a 'tell-all' book and I was not. And I assured her I was not but she didn't believe me. And she asked me to leave her house. And I said, "All right, if that's what you want but before I do leave I need to know one thing. Will you ever publicly acknowledge that I am your child and that Clark Gable is my father? And she said no. And we have not spoken since.

Loretta Young was determined to keep her secret. Judy said: 'I was born with my father's very large ears. And they were not only very large but they stuck straight out and so there was no way really to hide my ears except for my mother to put bonnets on me, which is what she consistently did. Everywhere I went I wore a bonnet because I was supposed to be adopted and here I have my father's large ears. Even as a child I remember thinking there's something very wrong with these ears of mine, people keep covering them up. So if there wasn't a bonnet I would brush my hair over my ears to make sure that they were covered. And it got to a point when I was seven and one birthday party that I went to at Barbara Warner's house, Jack Warner's daughter, the movie was Walt Disney's *Dumbo*. And, of course, here is this wonderful little elephant with these enormous ears, and the film finished and I heard a couple of little girls pointing to me and saying, "Dumbo, Dumbo," and I was devastated and I went home to my mother and I said I hate my ears. And she said we can fix that, and sure enough I had plastic surgery on my ears when I was seven and they were fixed. At seven years of age what do you know about plastic surgery? I had no idea of the pain I would undergo. And, of course, my mother was thrilled because, by having surgery, it severed the one connection I had with my father which was his big ears. I am told I look a great deal like him, and I also look like my mother, which is rather ludicrous since I was supposed to be an adopted child.

'I remember going to my mother, as any adopted child does, it's very natural, asking who are my real parents and why did they give me up? And she would divert me beautifully by saying, "I couldn't love you any more than if you were my own child." That didn't answer anything. It left me totally confused and also left me knowing this is a question I shouldn't ask.

'And then I remember a friend of mine who was Irene Dunne's truly adopted daughter, Mary Frances Griffith, who said to me, "How come you look like your mother?"

'It was more and more of a mystery as I grew up.

'In 1935 in California single women could not adopt so I was never legally adopted. And the very fact that my mother announced in the papers that she'd adopted two children amazes me that she got away with it because everybody knew single women couldn't adopt. Also a biological mother can't adopt her own child. However, this was Hollywood in the thirties. And it was a small town and everybody protected everybody else. Everybody knew the story but everybody kept my mother's secret.

'I didn't see my birth certificate until I was married and a mother so I was in my mid-twenties. My husband had to go down to Los Angeles City Hall and get it for me and he told me he was so terrified that somebody would be following him that he felt like putting on a moustache and dark glasses. That's how much this secret carried down through the generations. The only certificate I had of any legality was a baptismal certificate and that was a phony because the name on the baptismal certificate was Mary Judith Clark. My father's name was William Clark and my mother's name was Margaret Clark. And what my mother had done is she had chosen my father's first name for my last name. The name on my birth certificate was Judith Young, father unknown, mother Margaret Clark.

'My mother dealt with my life as if it was a movie. I was born and it was convenient to write me out and then I was written back into her life. And then I was written out again and when it was convenient to show me off I was written back in again and I came out in my bonnet and curtsied and went back again. It was very strange.

'In Hollywood in the thirties, forties and fifties it was very different than in the nineties. Today stars have children out of wedlock and it's no big deal. They're human beings. They even announce it in the press and they don't get married.'

Holly Palance, daughter of tough-guy and Oscar winner Jack, is an actress and writer. 'For people who haven't grown up in Beverly Hills one of the ways they could feel what it's like is to watch the show *Beverly Hills 90210*, which is very much like my experience of Beverly Hills High. Everybody driving up in these fast, expensive cars. Everybody dressed to kill. I even had a friend whose parents lived in a hotel suite. Every time I see that show it just gives me the willies. I just think that's exactly what it was like. Too much, too soon, too fast.

'At Beverly Hills High there are a real range of students. I mean not everybody is wealthy, not everybody has famous parents. I don't know if there is a typical day. There was a typical day for me and the crowd that I ran with. We were the bad guys, though. There were a lot of people there who were in the Honours Clubs and who, you know, went on to Harvard and Radcliffe. We were busy hanging out on the beach, smoking dope, going to the car wash, getting fast foods, doing anything that we could do to avoid going to school. At one stage we went to the stationery store in the middle of Beverly Hills and bought a machine that would duplicate the machine that they had in the office at Beverly Hills High so that we could run our own passes and get ourselves in and out. We were using our intelligence. We just weren't using it in the ways that they were hoping we would. At one time I was actually charging people to do their passes for them. I was just terrible. I just can't believe I wasted so much time but at the time it felt like fun.

'I remember that every morning I would have to get up very early like about six o'clock in the morning to put on false eyelashes. I wouldn't wanna go to school without them. I wouldn't wanna be seen without them so I would go without breakfast to put these on. That is pathetic now, but at the time this was very important.

'We didn't need to have credit cards when we were in high school because our parents had charges at the local department stores. So we would just go and our names were on there and we would just pick up a few things. I did have some taste. I wasn't a completely crass person. I did put some limits on myself. There's only so many pairs of black trousers you can wear. What I would do is I would buy enough so that it wouldn't draw attention to the account, because that would get it taken away from me. The business manager would check the account. At no time did he take me aside and say, "You're really spending too much." My business manager does that now but nobody did that then.

'I used to go to a lot of concerts but the mother of all concerts was the first time the Beatles came to the Hollywood Bowl and I was desperate to get tickets, so desperate that I actually asked my parents to get them for me, which they did. They included themselves at this concert and I had to sit there with the two of them and my brother and sister. I was so humiliated. I was so desperate to get away from my parents – I did not want to be seen, it was just the ultimate bummer to be seen with your parents – I charged the stage. I ran down with everybody else on to the stage and I was brought home by the police! Very nice. They drove up with the police car, because I got separated from my parents, which was my plan but I just didn't expect to have the police bring me home.

'I only got taken home by the police once. I was a good girl. I was just a directionless kid with too much money on my hands. I wasn't shooting up in the hallways. I wasn't harming people. I wasn't stealing property. I was hurting myself. I was sad and it took me a long time to get past all of that and I wasted a lot of time. I regret a lot of that but I don't think I was so different from a lot of kids who grow up in wealthy environments around the world.

'I used to cross my father all the time. I guess I felt I had licence because he wasn't there and to get him back I would just kind of tell it like it was, and I also felt that he had sufficient guilt about not being there that he wasn't gonna cross me. So we kinda worked it out that way. He never had any opinion on what I should do with my life. He was one of those parents who loved unconditionally and whatever I wanted to do was okay.

'The other day at breakfast my daughter asked my father for his autograph and I have to tell you I was taken aback. He gave it to her and I thought, Geez, maybe it's time to get out of town, it's happening again. I asked her if she knew what it meant to be famous and she said, "Yeah, means people know who you are," and I said, "That's right, but it's not necessarily a good thing," and she said, "Why not? What's bad about it?" I thought, Oh, God, we're gonna have to get out of town more often!

'In the case of my early life and my children's life at the moment, the fame is vicarious, it isn't your own. It doesn't mean to you what it does to the famous person who has worked for it, who has earned it and I want my kids to be people in their own right. I don't want them to be shadows.

'To get into the best schools in Los Angeles people will stop at nothing and it's highly competitive and it's a very star-studded crowd. My son is about to go into kindergarten so we had to take him up for his testing the other day and I was sitting there and all of a sudden the door opened and Steven Stills walked in of Crosby, Stills, Nash and Young and James Spader walked in with his child and the head of one of the studios walked in and various producers. My daughter attends that school and she's a little bit older. I got a call when I got home from one of the top executive producers in this town asking me for help to get into this school and one of the ways you do this is by donating items, auction items. All schools have silent auctions which are fund-raising events for the school and there's a very well-known school that had their auction the other night and one of the auction items was to sing back-up with Bruce Springsteen on one of his tour dates. That item went for $23,000 which is a lot of money by anybody's estimation. That's the kinda things people will do to get their kids in.

'Everybody'll tell you I don't want my kids going to school with other industry kids. I want them to go to school with a diverse crowd but it doesn't work out that way. There's ten schools and they are on the west side where most people in the industry live and so kids of industry parents end up there and on the playground you hear people talking deals. That happens all the time. I was shocked when my children first started being invited to birthday parties and people were working the room. There's a clown in the corner and the adults are wandering around seeing what deals they can make.

'I guess the most outrageous kids' party I've seen was also the saddest kids' party. They had hired a hot-dog vendor, a balloon vendor, various clowns and different entertainers to wander around and entertain the kids and only four kids turned up. It was sad and we didn't even know this little girl. Her mother had invited us from meeting in the park. They were not in the industry but they were very wealthy.

'These children have schedules as if they were running the government. I try to pare this down because any parent will tell you that you don't wanna go to a birthday party on both Saturday and Sunday with industry people where you've gotta be dressed and you've gotta be on. You wanna relax, you wanna put your feet up but you've gotta be on at these events. You have to judge it for yourself but these kids are overbooked. The thing about Hollywood is that people are never off unless they're in their house. Business is done everywhere and anywhere and if you bump into the head of a studio at a party you may not have another opportunity to pitch an idea to him. So you take the opportunity and run with it. You're doing deals while six-year-olds are running around your feet.

'I'm not a member of AA but I know it's a star-studded group. The group in Santa Monica and the group in Malibu is very star-studded. They go to do the business of being in the twelve-step programme and then on the way out, Oh, God, look who's here. Well, you know, don't look a gift horse in the mouth, and they use the opportunity.

'In the fifties and sixties there was not the crime that there is now. I have an alarm system on my home. I would not allow my children to be photographed with my father. I don't want them to be seen or known and I'm very careful where I take them and where I let them go. They never go anywhere unaccompanied and that's very sad.

'They don't have a bodyguard. My dad is well known and he's also been incredibly lucky to have such a long career, but he's not a superstar and he never was. Now Arnold Schwarzenegger's or Steven Spielberg's children would need a lot of security. Mine, no. I remember being in New York with my god-daughter and bumping into Sean Lennon in Bloomingdale's with his two huge bodyguards and it was so sad. There he was, this sweet little boy, who was never alone, who was always aware of who he was and the danger that that brought on to him, but my children are not in that league.

'There are dangers. People like Michael J. Fox have had crazies writing them letters or David Letterman has had people coming into his home. I think the dangers to my children are no more because their grandfather is a celebrity than most other children in Los Angeles. There're kidnappings, there're shootings. It's a dangerous town.

'I think acting's a wonderful profession. It's a lot of work and there's a lot of personal rejection and you've gotta be ready to take all of that. I wouldn't allow my children to do a part as a child actor. I'm just not interested in them doing that. My son does brilliant imitations of Macaulay Culkin. I'm practising being the kinda parent who is non-judgemental so hopefully by the time they're eighteen and tell me they both wanna be actors, I'll get there.

'Gosh, I mean Macaulay Culkin, what a pressure is on him! I think you may have seen that he withdrew from the Oscar presentation at the last moment because his father objected to some of the script that Whoopi Goldberg was going to say. His father has put tremendous pressure on him. His father is not a well-liked man in a lot of Hollywood circles. Some kids survive it [pressure], some kids don't. Remember Jodie Foster was a child actor. She has triumphed brilliantly and some kids don't. I don't want my kids to have to go through that at that age. Hopefully they have other aspects to their personality besides their cute quotient that they can deal on. People like Winona Ryder are making the transition right now and doing it beautifully. If we put them in a box and say, like Shirley Temple, that they're only worth money if they've got those ringlets, then that's very sad for them. You should be allowed to grow and explore all the areas. Hollywood tries to put everybody in a box. For example, Clint Eastwood is an action star, but doesn't do serious pictures. Well, now he does do serious pictures so he broke out of the box. Julia Roberts was everybody's sort of favourite *ingénue* until she ran off and got married and said she wanted to play grown-ups. She broke out of the box. People have to break out on their own because Hollywood does like to typecast them. What does the industry do to child stars who are no longer bankable? I guess they're just out of work. They're gonna have to find a new life for themselves. There's a tremendous pressure in Hollywood to stay young. Oh, God, we all feel that. I wrote in one of my columns that the great thing about Europe was that in Europe ageing was a process and not a crime and here it's such an unfortunate thing that people go through and then they're washed up. There were women on the Academy Awards the other night of whom I thought, Oh, God, she's too old for that hairdo, what is she doing? But it's business. If they don't wanna sleep with you they're not gonna hire you. Actresses who are past a certain age are not getting work.

'And neither is the kid who is no longer cute. How can a kid fill the void when they're no longer a desirable commodity in the movie business? It's something I don't want my kids ever to have to find out.

'Parents think they're gonna find a meal ticket for their family. I'm afraid that that's what most parents who bring their children to Hollywood are wanting and that's tragic. I would guess that was probably the number-one reason – that their daughter is so adorable, their son is so adorable that their life will be made.' Obviously Brooke Shields went through that process and has had a relatively difficult time establishing herself as an adult presence in the industry.

Actress Tippi Hedren, mother of Melanie Griffith, who watched her daughter run wild when she was barely a teenager, talked of Hollywood Parenting, of the temptations children have when one or other parent is a star. And of a mother's dilemma: 'I really didn't have any kinda dreams about being an actress. I was doing well with the commercials and with my modelling career and yet you can't model for ever. It just doesn't work that way and my career was ebbing when I got a call from Universal Studios asking if I was the girl on the Sito commercial, which was a diet drink, and I was asked to come in and meet with one of the executives there because a producer was interested. I was not told who the producer was and that was on Friday 13 October 1960. Alfred Hitchcock wanted to sign me to a contract. Melanie was born in 1957, so she was just a little girl.

'Melanie was happy about the move to the coast because living in New York your child has absolutely no freedom whatsoever. I think she was happy. She seemed to be. I don't think Melanie realized that I was famous. I certainly didn't feel like I was famous. I was working very hard. Being an actress is not a glamorous job. The hours are horrific. The work is difficult. It's demanding and there's really very little glamour in it.

'When Melanie decided to go into the acting profession I was surprised because she had not only seen how difficult it is, how hard you work, but it's also you have to have a skin of alligator hide because you are thought of as a commodity. Your feelings can be hurt very deeply. You can think you are perfect for a particular role and you don't get it. There're many difficult aspects in being an actor. You're always looking for a job. It's not easy. I didn't encourage or discourage Melanie into being an actress. I thought this is something that if she wants to do it that's the best part. To encourage someone is important after they've made a decision but I think it's important for anyone to do what they wanna do and then encourage them. Melanie fell into acting similarly as I did.

'A friend of hers had gone on an audition for *Night Moves* and was told that she was too old for the part. I think she was sixteen, and she said, "Well, I have a friend who would be perfect for the part," so she brought Melanie, and Melanie got the part. She was fourteen, fifteen, something like that. It is a very crazy world for a fifteen-year-old to enter. However, she took it very seriously and she was very good in her first role. She went on to studying in New York and look at what's happened to her.

'I was divorced from Melanie's father Peter Griffith in 1959. I think divorce always has a profound effect on children. It's very sad that something can't be devised to make life perfect. I think it's a difficult decision for adults to go into a divorce. Very often the child thinks it's his or her fault and it's important that the child doesn't feel that way. I don't believe that Melanie ever felt that it was her fault. I certainly never would have allowed that kind of feeling. She spent time and still does with her father, but there's no way that you can say it isn't difficult. It's difficult on everyone.

'I know there are many people in Hollywood who have children who are actors, and very good actors, so maybe there is a genetic situation there. I know Melanie's very good. I think she's one of the finest actresses in Hollywood today. Talent is one of those magical words that it's hard to explain. There are some people who, once they are up on a screen, something happens, something magically is triggered.

'I think as far as the acting ability goes, you have to have a great sensitivity, you have to have a lot of make-believe in your make-up. Acting is a very important profession. A great deal can be told through stories on the screen, on television, because it can be very meaningful, very forceful. I also think it can be a lot of rubbish, unless you choose scripts that have a meaning that will lend quality to our lives.'

Danny Bonaduce, voted one of Britain's top ten ginger-haired TV favourites in 1995, is the former *Partridge Family* child star. He hosts his own radio talk show in Chicago, and also *Danny!* a weekly television talk show made by Buena Vista, a division of Disney.

Before that, Bonaduce hit the skids: he had problems with drink and drugs and trying to feed himself. However, he never lost his sense of humour, no matter the predicament in which he found himself. He's since been reunited with his *Partridge Family* co-star, David Cassidy, and they have talked of future projects together. But it was tough. He never complained – and doesn't have time for child stars who do.

'I'm relatively successful, financially speaking. I have one of the top-rated radio shows in America but five years ago when I was completely broke I got the joke. I realized it was funny to be a famous waiter. That made being a waiter more difficult than it already was but it amused me. Wouldn't it be funny to be getting served lunch by Danny Partridge? This cracks me up. I got almost no tips, 'cos they assumed I was doing it as some kind of lark. Nobody assumes you're trying to feed yourself. There are kids today making $75,000 a week and if they piss their money away I'm gonna have a hard time feeling bad for them in ten years. Shut up, stop whining, get a job. That's exactly what I'm gonna say to my kids.

'Being a kid is a hassle period. That's all. It's being told what to do and having to do it. I was told what to do and had to do it on the set where if I didn't do it people asked me please. Where every other kid is forced, I got to stay a kid longer.

'I was fourteen when I stopped being Danny Partridge. Well, actually, I was fourteen when I stopped being paid to be Danny Partridge. I did car shows and opened supermarkets and things like that for years to come.

'I had such real traumas at my house that normal

childhood traumas didn't seem important. The first pimples, first dates, that kinda thing, I had different dilemmas and they didn't occur to me. Nothing about being Danny Partridge was difficult. I'd love to have a problem and I'd love to say "Oh, really, I'm this hideous wreck you're talking to right now because I was Danny Partridge." The easiest thing in my life was being Danny Partridge.

'Home was a hassle. Mum and Dad divorced and we were very dramatic in the Bonaduce household. It was not impossible for someone to get hurt.

'I really think that just mostly people in California make AA their home. We have some seriously screwed-up people. It's just a bullshit town and there's more bullshit piled up. Really, these guys are crazy out here. This isn't the real world. I live in Chicago where it's seventy below this winter! I have a real problem with people in their Ferraris with the roof down in December telling me they have any dilemma at all.

'People are prettier in California – men and women. I went to the gym and lost thirty pounds and was looking real good and I came out to LA to do some television show and I had one of the best bodies in Chicago and I was the fattest guy in Los Angeles, all at the same time!

'There's more to do out here. There's more temptations out here. Relationships are hard in California but not just because of those things. People are predisposed to make things harder. It shouldn't matter that people are better-looking here. You're married, that's that. Divorce is more acceptable than it should be. It's okay to leave your wife 'cos you met someone prettier. That doesn't seem right.

But I don't believe there's anyone prettier than my wife, so that won't happen to me.

'I lived on my boat and I'd wake up in the morning and I'd do lots of drugs and drink lots of alcohol and that was pretty acceptable for me. I thought, Wow this is cool! I just wake up and do drugs all day! What a life! I was in a Japanese restaurant drinking Mai-tais and the two waitresses were talking in Japanese. I didn't completely waste all the drug years: I learned things on drugs. I happen to speak Japanese fluently. So this waitress, I guess, feels pretty comfortable speaking Japanese in front of a drunk redhead, thinking I don't get it, but what she's saying is that she has two full-time jobs and goes to school full-time and her visa has expired and she feels like a criminal. I just leaned up from my Mai-tai and told her to get her paperwork and I'd marry her if she wanted. She said OK and we got married some time later and she got a Green Card and then she went about her merry way.

'My second marriage is even goofier than that one. I really think that God has a very good sense of humour 'cos this should not have worked at all. I married my wife – she's ten weeks pregnant – the first night I met her. We got married on our first date, seven hours after we said hi, nice to meet you. She wouldn't sleep with me. I really am a great first date. I'm good up until the end of the first week. So we went out and I was killing. Oh, she was having a wonderful time and I thought sex was pretty much guaranteed so we get to my house and I went for the sex and she looked right in my face and said, "Oh, I'm sorry. I'm a good Christian girl and I won't do that till

I'm married. And I said, "I'm ninety bucks into this evening already, doll," and I called a minister. We got married in my house and I got sex and I woke up in the morning just appalled. I've done some stupid stuff, drunk. I have tattoos with girls' names: I have no clue who they are. That's dumb, but being married in the morning and hung over ... This is a pretty shitty morning and I woke up and I thought, Oh, my God, I've got to get out of this. I know, I'll be a huge jerk and she'll just run away. She'll see that she married a jerk and get out quick. So I woke up and I was gonna give her some long explanation and I started of by saying, "Listen, I don't even know your name," and she looked at me and she said, "It's Mrs Bonaduce. Try not to forget it." And from that moment on I said, "This is the girl for me." I love this girl and I swear to God I love her more every day. I could never conceive getting along without her.

'Totally lucked out. I can't believe that I'm married to this saint of a woman. The only reason that I have an exceptional career now compared to when I was a child, that's all Gretchen. She's the only thing that changed my life. She changed all my habits by force. She gave up her whole life for two years.'

He also got outside help. 'Everybody in this town has had therapy. It's how you tell how cool you are, who's your therapist. It used to be what kinda car you drive. It's now how much you pay for your psychiatrist. By the way my psychiatrist drives a cool car, so I'm well up there! I've had therapy. It helps you work out any issues. I've spent maybe five hours on a psychiatrist's couch. I told a bunch of really cool stories and he went, "And how do you feel about that?" and I gave him $150 an hour and then I went home.

'When you sign a long-term contract for showbusiness you have to be seen by a medical doctor and you have to be seen by a psychiatrist because movies are so expensive. If you flip out half-way through and they have to start over it can cost somebody as much as $20 million. It's not like I sat on couches and told my deepest problem. At times you have to go, it's part of your job. I think everyone has to do it but maybe they were just kidding me. Maybe they thought I was nuts and just made me go and told me that story. Macaulay Culkin probably does what he wants. I'm gonna have a real hard time ever feeling bad for him. What's he making? Eight million a picture now? He shows up with problems later and I'm just gonna smack him. I have no problems that eight million dollars a picture won't cure.'

It's not always easy being the sons and daughters of Hollywood People. Katie Wagner, thirty in 1995, is the daughter of Robert 'R.J.' Wagner, one of the most admired actors in town, from his marriage to Marion Donen. He has two other daughters, Courteney and Natasha, from his marriage to Natalie Wood. R.J. is one of the most admired men in town for his ongoing goodwill and generosity. Kimber Eastwood is Clint's daughter from the affair on the set of *Rawhide*. They grew up differently but are both Hollywood kids.

Katie Wagner is a television interviewer and happily says: 'There are hundreds of girls here that just want to act. It's not something I wanna do. I'm glad they're out there for it means more people for me to interview.

'Hollywood is the backdrop of my life. It's been really helpful. Often I've been in line at a film opening trying to get interviews and I see people I've grown up with. Between my grandmother, who is in her nineties, and my younger sister who is a teenager we know just about everybody in town. It's helped and it's made me comfortable. Being a woman with a microphone helps – it's so phallic. I find myself flirting a lot with people but not in a sexual way. It's my weapon.

'My father being famous has helped me in so many ways. It hasn't been a downside for me at all. Everybody that knows my father loves him. I have never heard anybody saying something that is not nice about him – except maybe my mother once or twice. I'm so fortunate to be following into a business environment where both he and my stepmother Natalie Wood were so well respected. But because I am not doing what they do I have a better chance, I think. He really helped me get my foot in the door. I don't dance like my dad, or sing like him or talk like him. I just sort of smile like him. We're great friends so it's only helped me to have the name Wagner when it's got such great respect. It's nothing but a joy.

'I am a Hollywood brat. I love it. I pretty much have always gotten what I wanted but that doesn't mean that I am difficult. It's just that my mom and dad gave me what I wanted within reason. I'm a Hollywood brat but that's better than being a Brixton brat. Life is good here for the most part. My sisters may find it tougher because their mother was the Hollywood woman in their family. But like me they'll always have Dad.'

Kimber Eastwood has only recently *really* had Dad – publicly. She grew up away from Eastwood, his then wife Maggie and children Alison and Kyle. The kids are now all friends but Kimber acknowledges that for a long time she was something of an outcast. Clint Eastwood's illegitimate daughter by actress Roxanna Tunis, who worked on her father's TV series *Rawhide*:

'Growing up in Hollywood it's fast. It's a fast town. You grow up seeing movie stars around and I grew up going on the sets and on the studios and going to public school and private schools. People try to keep up with everybody else. It's like trying to keep up with the Joneses, even when you're ten, eleven, twelve. You go to private school and you have a lot of money.

'Fashion's a big thing! What cars you drive – and what car did *you* get at sixteen years old? Fashion-wise I was always trying to keep up. That's about it. I just wanna be me. I don't wanna keep up with anybody.

'I think people wanna get to know me for my dad, but not everybody's like that. There are people out there. How do you root out who your real friends are? You just have to get to know them and it takes a while to weed them out but eventually you catch on to it. They'll go around telling everybody who they're with, and who my father is, and eventually you catch on and you just drift away. I had a lot of pressure because a lot of people didn't believe me when I told them who my dad was. No-one ever saw me in magazines so I wasn't talked about. They thought I was just spreading rumours, had this great fantasy. I think I'm used to reading about him in the paper, just like people ask me what's it like seeing him in the movies. I grew up reading about him and watching him and I don't know any other way. That's just the way it's been. If he was a nine-to-five guy and came home every day I don't know what I would do! Because I don't know what that's like.

'As a kid I saw him as often as I could, about three, four, five times a year. Had he been around all the time I think I would have been exposed to the public more and I would have been in the spotlight all the time. I don't think I would have grown up as private as I did.

'I want to be an actress. My dad encourages me and he wants me to stick with it but he wants me to prove myself, to do it on my own. Then he'll know I'm serious about doing it.

'I auditioned for one of my dad's movies but I didn't get the part! I think he doesn't want people to think, She's a crummy actress and she got the part because of who she is! And I don't wanna be like that either. I wanna be a good actress and I wanna prove myself. I don't want it to be just handed to me and rumours around Hollywood. My dad is a big influence because he struggled to make it in the business and he became so successful by himself, on his own, that I think that's just a great Hollywood story. It's a lot of work – an overnight success of twenty years! It's a challenge and I like a challenge.'

Catya Sassoon was twenty-six in 1995 and had faced more than enough challenges. The daughter of superstar hairdresser Vidal Sassoon she left him to marry when she was fifteen. She has had drink and drug problems and gave birth to a boy in 1995. Often estranged from her family and father, she named the baby London Vidal Sassoon.

'Getting pregnant was not planned. I lost one of the biggest movies I might have ever had. It was either an abortion or the movie. And for the first time in my life I wasn't selfish. It wasn't right to have the abortion. I've had an abortion before but I just knew in my heart it was not to happen this time. And so I chose to have the baby and give up on this huge movie project. And I never even got a pat on the back from anybody. I gave myself one because, for once, vanity and ego didn't get in the way. I was not selfish. I put a child I didn't even know first.'

Catya, daughter of Vidal and his second wife, Hollywood actress Beverly Adams, says her attitude has changed. 'It used to be: "I can do whatever the fuck I want. If I wanna take drugs, if I wanna sleep with whoever I wanna sleep with it's none of their business." But when it comes out in the papers and my father reads it after the reputation he has built up, I can understand how much it hurt him.'

She says she's always been a rebel: 'I would say my rebellion started when Mommy left Daddy, when my parents started fighting. Our life was so public that everything was always smiles and everybody was always happy. And then when we got behind closed doors . . .'

Catya, despite her tough take-on-the-world attitude, cried several times during her interview usually when the conversation turned to her relationship with her family, especially her father. 'I didn't know what was going on and then I found out they were having a divorce and it was Mommy left Daddy, and Mommy left Daddy for booze. That's what my dad says. That my mother left him for the bottle.

'My mom hasn't had a drink in nine years and he still won't let her go, which really bothers me. I remind my father of my mother so much that I think it sickens him. He'll look at me and I'll feel the anger. He'll say: "You're just like your mother." He's always saying that I've been doing things for the past ten years. He doesn't realize I'm getting older. I just wish we could start again. I want my dad to have a relationship with my son that has nothing to do with anything but love. I don't want my son being around people who are going to hurt his feelings, call him names. When my father gets angry with me his temper gets loose. My father's very polite to anybody else but he talks to me like I'm a drunken sailor. That's the hurt that comes out.

'Cat was the black sheep. Cat was the drug addict. Cat was the bad girl who got married when she was fifteen. Or was it fourteen? I was the bad one. I didn't graduate from college. And I was the rebel.'

It began in the early years: 'We had the strangest backyard. There were three tennis courts and nobody played tennis. It was very strange. There was an Olympic-sized pool and another pool. My dad insisted on the Olympic pool and the other one was for me and my two brothers. We'd fill the jacuzzi with Vidal Sassoon shampoo and the whole backyard would be bubbles – it went for miles. You'd see suds everywhere and we'd piss off all the security guards. That was our fun.

'We had a laundry chute and if we wanted to ditch the butler or the housekeeper or the cops we'd just use that to get out of the house. My nanna, Janet Salisbury, brought me up. There's nannies, there's cooks and butlers and other people, and they all do different things. I usually didn't know half their names because there were so many. The house was so big I identified everything by colours, the red room, the blue room . . .

'My upbringing must be to blame for the way I am, or was back then. It's like I grew up with things that most people don't even dream about. There was just so much of everything. It was so intense and so amazing the way I grew up — and then all of a sudden, Dad decides to get remarried and I got cut off. It was like, what the hell am I supposed to do?

'When I was doing movies and they were running on cable TV he would stop and maybe watch one. He'd call me up and go, "Why would you do a karate movie?" I would think, Do I ever do anything right? I love you so much, can't you just accept that? This is the way that I am.

'We were all brought up differently and not by our parents. I hate when my father talks to me about dignity and pride and self-respect when he's cursing at me or swearing at me. Wait a minute, who's talking here about dignity and pride?

'Did I get to see much of my dad growing up? Not much. When I was a little kid my dad used to put me on his shoulders and run through Central Park. I remember one time that he dropped me on the ice and I broke my nose and he ran all the way to the hospital screaming through traffic. And it was like *my* daddy. I could never say balloon, I always got "boon, boon", so every time my dad writes a card, he always writes, "Don't forget the boon." That's the only thing that he remembers about my childhood.

'I did *Playboy* and if they offered me the cover again I would do it again. I wouldn't do anything sleazy and I wouldn't do anything tacky or trashy and I don't spread my legs. I would never ever do something like that.

'What hurt my feelings is that my dad gave my brother his offices to work out of. I'm really proud of my brother – he has his production company and everything, but I was kind of hoping that my father would've said, "Well, why don't you put your sister in the film?" But I was pregnant at the time, so I couldn't do it then. My brother does wanna work with me, so we are gonna work together. And it's exciting and we're both really looking forward to it. I wanna open up a modelling agency called Sassoon. It's my sister, my brothers Eden and Elan and myself, we all wanna do it, and we'd all be partners. And are we gonna get sued by my father? I have to ask permission now, I guess.

'There's no better name in fashion than Sassoon. It's known all over the world. People can't afford toothpaste but they buy shampoo. And that's not what my life's about, you know. I don't think I should be reprimanded. It's been a lot harder for me because I'm a Sassoon now. People don't think that I need to work and that's why they'll give the job – even if I work ten times harder – to somebody else. It makes me so furious because the one thing that I am good at, and the one thing that I put everything in my power into, is my work. My love and my passion in my work. And my love and my passion goes through my family, through my husband Kevin, through my baby, through my life, that's what I live off.

She says she is determined that she is going to bring up her son London. 'We didn't go with our parents anywhere. We were left at home with other people. When a parent isn't with their kid, they lavish gifts and they send money. That was how I was brought up. My parents were building an empire, so I can't blame them. God, I missed my mother so much, because she was my mommy, you know. But I was the kid . . . we were all the kids that were driven to school in limousines. My brother Elan used to jump out of the limo two blocks away from school and run to school so nobody would see him get out of the limo, and I would make sure that I got out of the car at school, which was just the way we grew up, totally different. But now, my brother would be sitting right next to me and we'd both get out of that limo together. He's changed. He's grown up. He's now Mister Producer, and it's a different lifestyle.

'When I was a little kid, I was Hollywood. I was proud of it. But I was a little snot. If we were gonna be cruising in a limo I wanted to get out right where I wanted to get out and be picked up where I wanted. I wasn't embarrassed at all about who we were and what we were. My brother was. He didn't want anybody to see.

'I went to Beverly Hills High School and then I went to professional children's school for a while. I didn't really go there. I enrolled there. Daddy paid for it and I kept getting modelling jobs and I would sit in the classroom and all I could think about was – what am I doing here? And I'd leave. Cos if you had a job, they'd let you leave and go to work. I got away with never going back, but passed anyway.

'Beverly Hills High is not like the series *Beverly Hills 90210*. No way. Please! It is sex, drugs and rock 'n' roll. Spoiled, druggy, rich kids that wrote their parents' names in cocaine and snorted it up for fun, stupid things like that. But that's how we were. And I guess that everybody else went through their phases. Because I was in the public eye mine wasn't considered a phase. Mine was considered a disaster and a huge problem and how dare she!

'School was like a blur – I showed up, signed up and left. I didn't give a shit about school. I wanted to make money and I wanted to work. And that's what my dad did at fourteen. He didn't have a choice. I did. But I believe that I made the right choice. I don't wanna change any of my history. Unfortunately I hurt a lot of people in my family and I finally realize that now. That's what the baby has done for me. I can understand why my parents went to hell and back in a bucket because of me.

'But it wasn't just me. Whenever there's a problem, it's Catya. Just because I love to do wild things does not mean that I'm sitting in a corner shooting heroin. I like doing things and, believe it or not, I haven't even done that in nine months. But I was doing it when I was younger. That almost killed my parents. They were totally freaked. And I got into car accidents. Once I hit twelve parked cars from the Porsche/Audi dealership. They were all lined up on the street and I just drove by and hit every single one of them and kept on going and the passenger door ripped off. They didn't appreciate that. Things like that kept happening and after a while I guess they just got numb and sick of it and just fed up with me and didn't wanna deal with me. All I wanted was Mommy and Daddy and all I got was Beverly and Vidal.

'When we were fourteen, thirteen we were trying out stuff. But it got heavy. I was a heroin addict. I went to go stop someone from shooting heroin and she ended up shooting me up, which was a terrible nightmare. I was sixteen and it was only for like a couple of months, because I couldn't stand it – it wasn't my drug. Now I'm a totally different person so I can talk about my past and the drugs and all that stuff. Yea, I used to shoot dope, okay. Big deal. That's over with. On to the next.

'My God! I went to school with everybody. I went to school with Christian Slater in New York. I went to school with Chynna Phillips – she was my room-mate for a while. Victoria Sellers, okay. She was a good friend of mine. The money that was left for her in her father's will her stepmother took all of it. So Victoria went nuts. You know, she really had a serious problem. And some of the things said about her, that she's hanging out with gang members and all that stuff, I don't see that side of her.

'A lot of kids that come from famous families get cut off and get into stuff. I've never done anything like prostitution, never, ever. And I never will. Ah! I remember one experience when I was in New York and I had this fling with this really rich man and he left me to go to work one morning and by the side of the bed he left me ten grand in cash. I was so offended. I tore it up and left it there all over his bed and never spoke ... I was so angry. He was so mad that I tore it up. It was, like, "You could've just left it there." And I said, "No." To me it was dirty money, he didn't deserve it and I didn't either. I didn't do this for money. I mean that's just not me at all. I love sex, I'm not gonna deny it, but I'm certainly not gonna screw anybody for cash.

'A lot of celebrity kids resort to selling drugs in mass quantity or like pornographic stuff or strange things. I didn't just turn into like the Virgin Mary, you know, but those things I wouldn't do. There have been times in my life, God knows, where I've been completely flip but I'm not willing to pay the penalty of going to jail for selling my ass.

'My dad thinks that there's nobody on earth worse than me. But he doesn't know about all of these kids that are doing what they're doing. I am definitely, without doubt, a Hollywood kid.'

But she believes her new attitude to life will please her father who now lives with his fourth wife Rhonda: 'I'm getting older and it's time to stop screwing around, it really is. It's not a game any more, it's not fun any more. It's great every once in a while to go out and have fun, but I don't need to be the centre of attention in the nightclub when I'd rather be the centre of attention in a major motion picture.

'Jackie Collins and I have been kind of doing the circuit 'cos she considers me to be the ultimate Hollywood kid. And, you know, if I do end up playing Jordanna, which is the heroine in her novel *Hollywood Kids*, I wouldn't even have to act. Not at all.'

IN ANALYSIS
Chapter 8

'The image of every Hollywood producer who sleeps
with every star is not about sex, it's about ego'
Dr Barbara De Angelis

Chance and temptation are, of course, seductive bridges
to dreams and desires and vice versa. But they are always
ready to collapse. When they do and the crush on the
brain and soul becomes too much, there are always the
'experts'. Psychiatrists are only equalled in number by
cosmetic surgeons in Beverly Hills and it remains a
growth industry.

In Hollywood advice is expensive, but interesting.
There are 'experts' on everything. They use crystal ball
and hypnosis or whatever works for their clients. Dr
Barbara De Angelis wrote a book advising men to eat
pineapples because it made their semen taste better. She
then won her own Hollywood talk show. She has had
countless unhappy couples, lovelorn women and showbiz
swingers crying on her designer shoulders. 'People in
Hollywood are more conscious of the personal growth
process. If you stop anybody on the street in Southern
California and you say, "What are you doing for your
personal growth?" they will probably say, "I take yoga

classes," or "I don't eat meat," or "I go to this group." If you stop somebody in New York or Chicago and ask them that, half of them will say, "What'd'ya mean personal growth? What are you talking about – do I go to the gym?" So there is a consciousness here which I love that has to do with growing, introspection, and with spiritual philosophy which I think balances out a lot of the superficiality in this town.'

She's noticed a change in the way women, in particular, work the Hollywood system: 'Some women in Hollywood want prestige, they want to feel that somehow they have an entry because of who they're with, they want to be taken care of and have the bills paid and not have to think about anything, and I think that's very sad. I think those are women who are really cut off from their own sense of power and womanhood. They really give all women a bad name and they take our whole cause back centuries.

'The younger women in Hollywood are putting their foot down and saying, "I want a real family, I want a quality of life with my partner, I don't care how many more movies you make, I want you to spend time with the kids, and I want an equal relationship." You do see these relationships more and more. I think when you look at the relationships of some of the stars maybe twenty or thirty years ago, they're different from the ones now when the women have been brought up in a different generation and are more demanding. It's not enough to have the house and the maid and the car, they want a husband and they want a husband who can communicate with them so I think younger women are more demanding on the

Hollywood man perhaps than women growing up in the forties or fifties would have been.

'But I don't see many happy marriages anywhere in Hollywood. Whenever I give speeches, I'll ask my audiences to fill in the blank – I'd like to have a relationship just like ... and think of a couple, and most people sit there for a few minutes, and I say think of five, and they can't do it, they can't even think of five couples they'd like to emulate. In this town there are some happy marriages, there are some marriages which are arrangements, where they kind of stay together but not "in love" any more, and then there's very unhappy marriages where there's a lot of infidelity going on.

'What people need to understand about sex is that sex is an addiction like a drug, like alcohol, like gambling, like anything else. The image of the Hollywood producer who's sleeping with everybody or picks up a hooker, who sleeps with every star, it's not about sex, it's about ego, it's about power, it's about control and it's an addiction exactly like an addiction to cocaine. There are a lot of sick addicts in this town because the substance is readily available, it's free, it's everywhere. You're producing a movie and you go in and sit in that casting hall and a hundred beautiful women show up and they're dying to get that part. That's like a cocaine addict with bags of it sitting in front of him. There's a temptation there. That's not an excuse for doing it, but I think there's more of a temptation than there would be for a man in a normal job. And that is a dangerous thing.

'There are some Hollywood marriages that have lasted for forty, fifty years but I'll bet you anything there's been infidelity along the way and that the wife had just accepted it and forgiven it. And that's why the marriage stayed together because she gave him the room to dally round and do what he wanted.'

For all the Tinseltown temptations Dr De Angelis is optimistic about the future of marriage in Hollywood. 'I have a lot of compassion for Hollywood marriages. Marriage is hard enough anywhere. In Hollywood the pressure is tremendous and if you can make a marriage work in Hollywood you have really created a miracle.

'I think most young Hollywood wives who have children are really into monogamy. They've seen what's happened to the women before them. They don't want to end up with a broken home, they don't want to go out and be having affairs while their husband's having affairs on the set, and they're working very hard on their relationships to stay married and to avoid the trap that a lot of other women have fallen into. It's difficult because of all the temptations especially when both stars are working and they're in different parts of the world for three or four months at a time, but you do see a lot of young Hollywood couples saying we will not do two films at a time, I'll go with her and she'll go with me, almost as insurance to make sure they stay faithful to each other.'

This will obviously have a beneficial effect on Hollywood kids, says Dr De Angelis. 'In previous years children of Hollywood marriages have been notorious for being dysfunctional because of the tremendous insanity – three, four husbands, travelling all over the place, living in the spotlight – that's gone on in their lives. A lot of them have become famous and written books about their terrible childhoods. I think that parents who are stars or are behind the scenes as producers are very aware of the dangers and are trying to bring up their children in a normal environment, often sheltering their children from the public. People don't even know what some stars' kids look like. They're trying to give them a sense of normalcy so they don't grow up to become Hollywood brats.

'This doesn't mean that the fascinating chain of Hollywood relationships is going to end. There was a really funny cartoon in the *Los Angeles Times* where they tried to draw the genealogy of all these different stars in Hollywood – who each one had slept with and then who that one had slept with and they had just about every star sleeping with every other star and they ended up tracing it all back and the last person was Warren Beatty!'

It's also a most politically incorrect town, says Dr De Angelis. 'Unfortunately I believe women are seen and treated as sex objects and there is a real battle going on about that, with women trying to break out of that mould. But in this town, unfortunately, women are still judged by their sexuality. You don't see women who aren't beautiful in romantic film roles. You don't see overweight women in a romantic role, you see them in a comedy role, and that, unfortunately, is the way is it and I think it's the way it's always going to be.

'The criticism is that Hollywood puts too much emphasis on sex and glamour. The problem is that sex and glamour sell so the same people sitting at home saying, "Oh, these Hollywood producers, they all make these sexy films, it's ridiculous," they're the same ones who, when they see the cover of a tabloid and it says so and so caught in bed with so and so, they grab the magazine right away!'

Sex may sell on screen but Dr De Angelis claims that, behind the scenes, Hollywood is not a sexy, glamorous town, it's a sham. 'I can tell you that it is an illusion that this is a party town. Hollywood is a working town. When tourists come to Los Angeles and they're looking for Hollywood, they're amazed to find that Hollywood is an ugly section of Los Angeles where nobody goes. No stars live there. It's basically full of drug addicts and prostitutes. I'm sorry but that's the truth. The stars are embedded in the sidewalk and there are some old buildings but no one lives in Hollywood, they live in Malibu, they live in the San Fernando valley, they live in other parts of Los Angeles. There are not wild Hollywood parties every night. Everyone is too busy working. If you're doing a television show you're working twelve to fourteen hours a day. I know because I've had one. If you're doing a movie you don't have any energy to go to a party. Hollywood stars could count on one hand the number of parties they go to every year. Their idea of having a good time is coming home, taking off their make-up, taking a bath and putting in a video and watching it with their family.

'There has been a mini exodus out of Hollywood to other parts of America by certain stars, to Northern California, Montana, New Mexico, Santa Fe, because of some of the problems in L.A. More Hollywood women carry guns, more of them have been taking classes where they're learning to protect themselves. Even more they're concerned about their children and bringing them up here, and you do see them trying to move out of the town. Nobody really lives in Beverly Hills any more who is, I'd say, under forty years old. The people living in Beverly Hills are the old stars.'

Dr De Angelis, who lives in movie-star style in a beautiful home overlooking her Pacific Palisades neighbours, Steven Spielberg, Sylvester Stallone and Goldie Hawn, has been teaching a seminar called 'Making Love Work' in Los Angeles for fifteen years. 'People fly in from all over North America and some parts of the world just to spend the weekend with me and go through what is a very deep process of emotional transformation. I teach them everything we should have been taught about relationships, what works, what doesn't, I help them deal with a lot of the old emotional baggage that we all carry in from childhood and from our other relationships so we're not dumping that on our partner or passing that down to our children, teaching people how to break the chain and heal a lot of the wounds that we carry in our hearts. It's a very powerful experience because it is an experience, it's not information. They literally come out with a completely different outlook on themselves and on their partner and many a time fall back in love with each other again instead of having to get divorced. I love doing it.

'I usually have a few people involved somehow in Hollywood each weekend but the rest of the people are just normal people like anyone else. About half are couples and half singles, and they're all there for the same reason. They want love to work more in their lives, they wanna understand how they can prevent themselves from getting hurt again and they realize they haven't learnt how.

'A lot of people who are single have met through my seminars and married or begun relationships, which is really nice but it's not the purpose of it. It's not some kind of singles grab bag when you're there, because people are pretty much looking at themselves, but it is a place to meet people who you know are going to be fairly conscious about love. The in places in Los Angeles to meet people these days are not the bar, or the party scene, it's the twelve-step programmes, it's the self-help groups, it's the therapy groups, it's the seminars because so many people have turned to those things and they know if they go there they're going to meet somebody with a similar interest. Of course, this is how Elizabeth Taylor met her husband, and that's the kind of thing that's happening a lot.

'What Aids did was just accentuate a process that was already happening in Hollywood. People were not sleeping around any more anyway because they figured that it didn't work. People were not going out and partying all the time, maybe young rock stars were but that's about it. However, I think with Aids it gave a lot of people an excuse and what I've heard from a lot of women is whereas before they could say to a man, "I'm just not into sleeping with people any more in the first few months of a relationship", now they can say, "Oh, well, because of Aids I don't want to have sex." It's given some people an excuse to do what I think they really wanted to do anyway, which was to say no.'

❉ ❉ ❉

Hollywood is a haven for self-help groups. They cover everything from cross-dressers to one-legged men with parrots on their left shoulders. Hollywood people are willing to pay millions upon millions of dollars a year to learn how to cope. Elsewhere, people just get on with their lives, roll with the punches and get pleasure out of the good days. In Hollywood you see somebody for help with your problems.

Wanita Holmes specializes in the treatment of many of life's problems. 'I'm a clinical hypnotherapist and I work in every area you could imagine, from breast development, biting fingernails, relationships, impotence, Aids, cancer, pain, migraine, headaches, weight, stopping smoking. On and on ... Often young ladies will come to me with undeveloped breasts but they don't want to have surgery. They would like to use hypnosis to develop their breasts. It's quite successful unless there's a hereditary factor involved. If the breast development has been stopped in the puberty stage hypnosis can increase the breast size. I can't do a 32A to a 36D but you could take that 32A to 32B or maybe C. The best results I've had have had the saddest beginnings. The girls may have had an incestuous relationship or be afraid of their own sexuality or their father may have wanted a boy so she may be fearful that if she developed breasts her father wouldn't love her any more.

'There is absolutely no harm in undergoing hypnosis. The minimum amount of sessions would be about twelve. It is permanent. You are working on the client, changing her feelings and thoughts about herself, convincing her that she enjoys being female, that she is entitled to a beautiful body, that being voluptuous is wonderful.

You're really teaching her to love herself. It's a very simple technique. It's getting them to focus the energy. So if you focus on the breast area and the breast tissues you bring the blood and the hormones into the breast tissue and you enlarge the breast.

'Our minds control our bodies. We are what we think. You can't escape it. If you can make yourself have a hysterical pregnancy or blindness or deafness or paralysis ... Our thoughts have a physiological effect on our bodies.'

Wanita Holmes's sessions cost $175 for the first introductory visit and $75 a time thereafter. 'It does not cost as much as surgery. Breast surgery or augmentation is usually around $3000. So it is much cheaper and certainly less invasive.

'I think for women to have plastic surgery to get breasts is horrible. The dangers ... Most of the time women want breast reconstruction not for themselves but for the men in their lives. For us to cut up our bodies to please somebody else is an abomination. But growing up here is very difficult. You're in a kind of beauty contest from the day you drop from your mother's womb in Los Angeles. It's not just difficult for young women, it's difficult for every age. It's on-going. My clients are usually aged from eighteen to thirty and I work with eight, on average, each day.

'There are 600,000 therapy sessions going on in this country every day and I think 300,000 of them are going on in Los Angeles. If you don't have a therapist you're nobody. I'm not sure people here are neurotic. They are more self-centred.

'I see children as young as five, six and seven. I think half the families in Beverly Hills have a psychiatrist or a psychologist or a hypnotherapist or a therapist of some kind for their children. One of the number-one problems for children in Beverly Hills is weight. Not just because of the availability of food or the indulgences of the child but through love hunger. Often the parents are not there for them and they have maids or housekeepers or au pairs looking after them. They eat. When Mom and Dad come home they indulge them again with even more food. Bulimia and anorexia are very prevalent in both males and females.

'This is a tremendous pressure cooker for children. There's such expectations put on them. There used to be a modelling agency for children here and the children would be dragged in screaming. They would have bows in their hair, ears pierced – three years old! God forbid you should have acne or a flat chest.

'Drugs come into it because of the tremendous pressure to be beautiful at any age. And if you can't live up to it you tune out. There are tremendous addicts in this town. There are AA meetings and all sorts of other addictions meetings going on all day long, any hour of the day or night. And they're packed. It's the thing to do. Everyone goes to AA meetings.

'And there are tragedies like River Phoenix's death. His death was an example of the exploitation that people in power inflict on these young people. They haven't any interest in the well-being of the young people. It's what the end dollar is going to be. The sad part about River Phoenix is that people did not know that he was using drugs. He kept it very well hidden – certainly that's what the public has been made to believe.

'It's a mess. Teenagers in this town are having nose jobs at twelve. I remember a surgeon telling me that a twenty-three-year-old came to see him and said, "I want my nose back. I was born with another nose but my mother made me change it when I was thirteen. She had a picture of herself back then. They redid her nose. It's tragic but I'm an exception. I also don't believe you should pierce babies' ears. All of it is a pretty sad commentary about how and where we live.'

Stan Ziegler is an 'adolescent psychologist' working in Beverly Hills. He works with child actors and with adults who were once young stars. He also advises children whose parents are celebrities. His office is right next to Beverly Hills High School (his zip code is 90210) so he works with a lot of the kids there.

'Sixty per cent of the people I see are teenagers. They usually come because they think their parents want to kill them or their teachers are threatening to throw them out of school. Somebody else is paying for it so they're ambivalent.'

But for $175 per fifty-minute session three to four times a week Stan Ziegler will do all he can to help. 'Hollywood's pretty neurotic. It's about ambition and competition. I treat a lot of adults who are studio executives and entertainers and they come and they are miserable. They hate it. They are not going to stay in showbusiness any more. Then a deal goes through and they're happy. Therapy is often necessary to get them through the bad patches.'

Dr Melvyn Rosenstein of Beverly Hills provides a more physical therapy for men: he enlarges penises. A qualified neurologist since 1971, Dr Rosenstein found a new speciality in the 1990s. Describing it as 'minor surgery', he will lengthen a patient's penis for $3900. For the same amount he will thicken it. The charge for a longer *and* thicker member is $5900. The way Dr Rosenstein tells it, the forty-minute procedure is relatively simple, involving snips in the right places in front of the pubic bone to allow the penis to hang forward. Fat from the patient's abdomen is used to increase its diameter. 'I've carried out about 4500 operations without any problems. The recovery time varies – some people are back in the gym after a few days while others take time to heal. Of course, all surgery is minor if it's happening to someone else.'

He happily admits that only in 1 or 2 per cent of cases is the surgery required for medical reasons. So, do men undergo it to impress women? 'If someone wanted the operation to become a better lover I would not go ahead. Being a good lover requires more than my help. The main reason men want the operation is for the locker room – they want to look good in the showers. They don't want to feel inferior in the size department. For years women have had their breasts reshaped and now men are regard-ing this operation in the same way. Most of my patients are "normal" but they want to change. It was something that was taboo for many years but more and more men want to have this procedure.

'I've worked with some famous actors, Hollywood studio executives and eight chairmen of major companies – they just want to feel more confident and this helps. I've dealt with dentists and lawyers. And it's not an age thing, for my patient list includes both young and older men. I see nothing wrong with the procedure. It is a physical therapy which helps many people.'

The procedure is, as Dr Rosenstein says, not about sex but about ego. He echoes Dr Barbara De Angelis. Power and how they are perceived are two of the most important factors in the lives of Hollywood People.

But surgery and augmentation and hairpieces and therapy to boost confidence can only do so much to slow the clock.

GROWING OLD . . .
Chapter 9

'Cheese ripens with age. Wine ripens with age.
Why can't people? Does everybody have to be plastic?'
Lauren Bacall

Michelle Pfeiffer who co-starred with Sean Connery in
Russia House is acutely aware of Hollywood's attitude to
women ageing. When they made the film she was thirty-
two. Connery was sixty and had just been named the
Sexiest Man Alive by an American magazine. Pfeiffer
said: 'I'm not complaining about age but I am very aware
there is a window of time. When I'm sixty years old, are
they going to let me do a film with a thirty-two-year-old
leading man? I don't think so. You see the statistics and
you see the longevity of a female career as opposed to a
male career in this business. It is just so much shorter.'
All her colleagues agree – they just deal with it differently,
from acceptance to drastic cosmetic surgery and all the
beauty regimens in between. If the beauty business is
worth billions of dollars annually, Hollywood People
spend more than most. English doctor's daughter Jackie
Bisset, who was born in 1944 and has gone from glamour
girl to serious actress, talked about growing old in Tinseltown: 'I always used to say that when I'm older I will go

and live in Paris. Recently, I've been thinking about going to live in Paris and I thought, Well, does this mean that I think I'm older? Is it time for me to move? I thought, Bloody hell, do I have to make a decision about this? This is not a decision I want to make. I feel fine. I feel like a kid. Is there an age when you're supposed to get scared and go off somewhere and behave disgracefully? Well, there are days when I'm frightened of this. I used to be frightened of changing in Hollywood and losing my grip on things and becoming spoilt. That was the thing I was most fearful of. I'm not spoilt. What's amazing is, I've found I'm not frightened of that any more. I say, "Oh, well, to hell with it." I'm not worried about that any more. That's one more thing I can get rid of.

'Nobody likes to see things falling and lines and all that stuff, but there's a degree of beauty that comes with age and when I look at my idols they're all much older than me and they're all frightfully lined and have bags and God knows what, and I think, Well, I s'pose I'm not the only person who has these idols and we admire people who are wise souls. Maybe there'll be other people around who will have the same feelings towards me as I had to other people, like Jeanne Moreau.

Victoria Principal, who is forty-five, left *Dallas* to produce and star in her own movies. She is married to Beverly Hills plastic surgeon Dr Harry Glassman and knows about fear of ageing in Hollywood first hand. But she insists: 'It's more important who someone is than how they look, but if how a person looks reflects how they feel about themselves then that's the best of all worlds. The rest of the world thinks beauty is only skin deep. I live in a town that thinks beauty is only skintight. Every year I have a talk with myself about my self-worth and the important thing to me is that when I look in a mirror who I see is who I feel I am. I cannot imagine looking in a mirror and not recognizing myself. Africans believe if you take their picture you steal their soul. I can't imagine allowing this town to steal my soul.

'My face is a reflection of who I am and it's not perfect but I like it. It's healthy and I like that, and I think it shows care and I like that too. I'm going to grow old with this face and I'm sure there'll be times when that's painful and when I'll have to make deep personal decisions, but I don't ever want those decisions to be based upon what this town dictates. I want them to be based on what I dictate to myself in terms of how I feel about me because in the end all I have is myself.

'I'm in the oddest situation. I am married to one of the leading plastic and reconstructive surgeons not only in America but in the world and so I am constantly the "victim" of scrutiny! So it's a push–pull because sometimes someone will say you look so good, what did you do? Well, there's a compliment in there some place but it's not a compliment I really want. I would rather someone say, "You look so good, obviously you take good care of yourself." I love my husband. I'm very proud of him and his work, but it doesn't necessarily mean that I partake of his work.

'My husband thinks I'm perfect and I'm going to leave it that way. I think that there are some women where cosmetic surgery is absolutely a viable choice. Whether it is heredity or age or lifestyle that catches up with them and they look fatigued because their eyes are baggy and it's getting in the way of their getting work, then there's a choice to be made but it's theirs. They may choose not to have cosmetic surgery because they're going to take that look and use it to move on to a different kind of movie role. It's so personal. It varies with every woman. I know women who've said that cosmetic surgery changed their lives, that they like who they see when they look in the mirror, that they feel so much better about themselves, that perhaps their nose had been the bane of their existence, their lines or their breasts or their eyes. Or there were fat deposits on their body and since having those surgically removed for the first time they could make love with the lights on. If that's what they wanted and it makes them happy that's their decision. I know other women who said that if they could turn back time and not have had cosmetic surgery, they would undo it because they were left not looking like themselves and unhappy.

'What do we all mostly fear about ageing? Losing the ability to jump out of our chair and run over to someone we love and throw our arms around their neck, losing the ability to remember our last thought, losing the ability to make plans or have hope for the future. Those would be my greatest fears about ageing. Not if I looked more tired or if I couldn't wear the same size.

'I take good care of myself. I eat well. I wrote books about it. (My books really are mine and they really are my lifestyle and have been for a long time.) I think the twenties are meant for us to find out what's right and what's wrong. The twenties are when you abuse yourself and then at the end of the twenties you're okay and you think, Now how am I going to live for the rest of my life? I made a choice in my late twenties/early thirties about how I wanted to live and I think and I hope that my looks reflect that, that I eat well, I get my sleep, I pursue a career I love, I'm married to a man I love with all my heart and I have found a wonderful place here.

'I do know that people who think that your marriage takes care of itself are the people who are gonna be married many times because marriage is work. Any relationship is work, I have some simple philosophies. My husband has never walked into the house at night that I didn't get up and go to greet him. I never want him to think that his arriving home doesn't mean something special to me. I think If we could all remember to treat the people who are closest to us with the courtesy we would treat a stranger, that it would go a lot further.'

Ageing and how to cope is something Margot Kidder finds bizarre. The actress who played the big screen Lois Lane in *Superman* with Christopher Reeve said: 'It's very much a man's town. When you reach my age you're supposed to disappear or get six face lifts or eye jobs or tit jobs or whatever, which I'm not gonna do, and come back when you're a respectable grandmother at sixty. It's extraordinarily sexist, run by men. I don't feel that we're really gonna make inroads until there are more *Thelma and Louises*, and more female directors and screenwriters writing stories about us, and we prove in a business sense that we are as profitable as men's buddy-buddy movies. And until we stop bitching and complaining, laying blame on the men, and take the reins in our own hands, create our own product and our own audience, I don't think anything will change until then.'

Comic actress Phyllis Diller has played it for laughs throughout her long career but not when it came to trying to stay young. She wanted to stay in business in Hollywood and felt that she had to take certain steps: she has undergone extensive plastic surgery. 'The reason I had surgery at first – I guess I was fifty-five and it was 1971 – I saw myself objectively on a television show, the old *Sonny and Cher Show*. I was playing a witchy role, wearing a black dress with a high collar and I threw my head back and it must have been real bad lighting and something came poking out of my neck and I thought, What is that? It was just looking so bad. When you see yourself in the mirror every morning or whenever you look, you get used to yourself, little by little, and are not aware that it's all gone. The very next day, I couldn't wait to call a doctor. I called my skin doctor and asked him to recommend a plastic surgeon. Fortunately, he recommended the top surgeon in the whole world, Doctor Franklin Ashley.

'He did a complete facelift: nose, chin, eyes, neck, everything. Now he didn't wanna do it all at once but I explained that I don't have that much time off. I had to have it all at once so he accommodated it and that first operation took four and a half hours. You go through the rainbow of colours and swelling and you look like a monster, especially for the first week. It's scary. People rush to latrines and vomit! You look like you've been in a head-on accident. They warn you about that, specially with the nose surgery because it involves bones, because you see all this surgery is surface surgery. It's not deep or invasive and that's why it really isn't that dangerous.

'There is really no pain. You are dreadfully uncomfortable and if you have a nose job and it's packed and you can only breathe through your mouth, you're certain that you'll die! You know you're gonna choke to death or the breath is gonna just get cut off. It's not true. You'd be amazed what the body accommodates to keep you alive! But there's never pain, truly. It's uncomfortable.

'The surgery I've had on my face — I will never know whether it affected my career one way or another or whether I still get witch roles because that is who you are rather than what you look like. I played the Wicked Witch of the West two summers outdoors and they put back my old nose! I got kind of a kick out of that. My personal life took an about-face. I have a great romance going with a fabulous man and I don't think he would have been as interested in that other woman! I've always had a romance going but this is the best one!

'Let me tell you about men. In this town they have plastic surgery to look young and macho, of course, but they make the terrible mistake of having too much and it's their doctors' fault. Doctors should know better. Men should only have their eyes done and the neck wobble. They shouldn't mess with anything else because mileage on a man is acceptable and men start looking like someone else. You wonder, "Who is this guy?" because they've done too much lifting. So many men look like wax figures.

'Women can get away with it. I wanted to do as much as I could to make my face as perfect as possible. My teeth were crooked and they needed straightening and then I whitened them. Your eyes, of course, are terribly important. I've had them done three times because they come undone! You grow more fat particles around them and your upper lid gets heavy and closes your eye. Then I had some body surgery. I had a breast reduction and tummy tuck. I have never had liposuction, where they simply suck out the fat. That's a very popular operation now. There are some dangers with that. People have died. If you get a liposuction instrument in the hands of an inexpert practitioner you can run into real trouble inside your body. You see, that's invasive surgery.

'The breast reduction was because I always had large breasts and I'm small, plus you can't be chic with breasts. Those women who show their breasts and the cleavage, there's nothing chic about it. Flatness is chic! I was 38C. I'm too short for that. Besides they get in the way. Nothing fits right.

'When you go to have your first consultation with a plastic surgeon, your first question will be does it hurt and he says no, the second will be how long will it last and he says five to ten years. Mine went the whole ten years. Don't go for the mini lifts – save your money. It makes no difference at all. Wait until you really need it and get the whole thing.

'I had an acid peel, too. It takes away fine wrinkles – plus all the freckles come off. It takes your outer layer of skin off and then you grow new baby skin and it is smooth and soft and beautiful. I also had cheek implants.

They have three sizes: small, medium and large. I have medium and he got them in just the right spot and they don't even make an incision. It's inside your mouth, they stick them in there and a little string holds them steady till they get stuck where they're supposed to stick. The chemical peel hurts for three seconds, when the doctor takes it off – or I should say rips it off. If you knew how that was gonna feel you'd say let's just leave it on. I'll live with it. I like it. I've become accustomed to it and we'll just paint the face on this mask and leave it! I don't believe I'll need another peel. I'd have to live to be about 140. I had an upper brow lift. That's where they just lift the top half and it takes care of the upper eye.

'I've never relied just on looks. You can go on for ever if you're in comedy because the funnier you look the better. The uglier you are the better. I may have harmed my career a little by making my looks better but I don't care. I have a lovely career going and I'm happy and I like looking better. I feel very sorry for the beauties – people like Mary Pickford, Marion Davies, who one day simply went up into their rooms, closed the door and never came out again and drank.

'I think it's almost fortunate that Marilyn Monroe went while she was still young and beautiful because she would have had a terrible time dealing with age and ageing. If you aren't really solid inside and have a centre, specially if you've relied all your life on beauty, you don't develop anything else – you don't have to. And then it's tough and when you get the tragedies.'

❋ ❋ ❋

Barbara Carrera is a survivor. The former Bond girl and *Dallas* star was the woman in the Duke of Northumberland's life until Naomi Campbell's mother Valerie took over. She has lived the life of a Hollywood sex symbol for more than twenty years.

'After *Never Say Never Again* I hoped I would get an opportunity to do better work. It didn't work out that way. I'm still bombarded with scripts to play *femmes fatales*. I think the Bond part may have scared some of the leading men in Hollywood because she was a very strong character and there's still apprehension and fear about women showing any kind of strength. So it's typecast me and I'm still fighting it.

'The nature of this industry is today you're the top and tomorrow you're the bottom and then the day after you're on the top and the day after it's bottom. One has to take it the way one takes the clouds going by. I reached a period after the Bond film in which I got burned out. I toured the world for two years, always working and living out of hotel rooms. Then I met someone and decided I would like to try a different kind of life, and I married the person and dedicated most of my energies to making the marriage work. However, it didn't work and I have now thrown myself back into the lions' den!

'It all hype here, you know. Before I came to Hollywood, I believed all the nonsense that I read in the magazines about the stars, but then I soon found out that it's all hype. I think Hollywood is over-obsessed with itself. They take themselves too seriously and they have forgotten that what they do is a service to mankind: we offer the world entertainment. It's a service and that's all it is, and I feel sorry for those people who get so caught up into it that they lose the essence of what they're doing.

'In *Dallas* I was playing a character that was more or less a female JR. They were trying to make a tough woman out of her but I was still seen as a sex symbol. That's the only thing a female can become in this industry. I'm hurt that I'm not given an opportunity to express myself more and I speak now for a lot of actors, actresses in the industry. We are tired of being shown as one-dimensional. One of the most exciting things about humans is their nature to change. All we need is to be given the opportunity to express this. However, women have become Barbie dolls. They have to be these perfect-looking creatures and they must smile a lot and act as dumb as they possibly can, or be neurotic or a killer or any kind of a sex symbol. There're too many intelligent women in the world who are capable of much more than this. It's good to be a sex symbol but there are all those other things one would like to express. I'm just offended the way Hollywood treats women in general. There's not enough respect.'

Producer Robert Evans, ex-husband of Ali MacGraw, said Barbara is 'One hundred per cent woman. She knows how to make a man feel like a man.' How does she make a man feel like a man? 'The same way you make a woman feel like a woman. I've noticed something in England that I find very disconcerting: they've been conditioned and brought up not to accept the greatness in themselves. They find it easier to put themselves and others down than to accept their greatness. I've never seen that have a positive effect on anyone.'

Barbara says she has 'learned how to survive' here: 'The danger I find in Hollywood is that there's a lot of envy and people tend to use age as one of the tools to poison another. So they get great pleasure in discussing the ages of beautiful women when they're getting older and they have no qualms about making them older than they are, just to be mean. Sometimes a decade older than they really are.

'We're so obsessed with age that the minute we pass our teenage years we all feel old. When we pass our twenties we think we're old. We're constantly feeling we're old – it's only when you get older and look back you see how young we were. I feel sorry for the men and the women here: they lose all their happy moments because they're afraid they're going to lose youth. How stupid to worry about something over which one has no control. I think it's much more interesting to try to develop an inner beauty that will last for ever. And this obsession with plastic surgery – I don't laugh at it because I understand from where it comes, why people feel it's necessary. They feel that to survive in society they must learn the dance that is being danced. If I'd found that it was necessary for my survival, why of course I'd have plastic surgery. But this town is obsessed with it for the wrong reason. Young women are led to believe that if they want to succeed they have to look like Barbie dolls. They're being told that they have to be absolutely perfect otherwise they will not get anywhere. If you have an inner beauty that is radiant and brilliant it doesn't matter if your nose is not the right shape but no one's saying that. They're just agreeing with all the hype.

'You're seeing me now and I'm looking good but when I'm here alone do you think I'm worried about my hair and all of that?! Not at all! I don't care. When I go out in Hollywood to make an appearance I know what the public wants and I give them that. When I'm not around people who expect to see a movie star I'm just myself. I get dirty in the garden, I get mud in my nails. We're just like everyone else.'

Elaine Young was one of Hollywood's first cosmetic surgery casualties. Silicone injections in her face in 1979 paralysed one side of it and have left her permanently disfigured. 'Women all over the world are turning to cosmetic surgery. If you can look better I think it's great but I think people are going to extremes. I did it because I grew up with tremendous insecurity. Starting with my mother and father. Adding growing up in Hollywood. My parents said I couldn't do anything: I was fat, I had adolescent acne. I had more dates and was more popular than the beautiful women but I still thought I was ugly. No one could convince me different. And in 1979 a lady walked into my real estate office and I said, "You look great, what did you do?" She said, "Nothing more than silicone in my cheeks. You should do it." The next day, I was at the doctor. Didn't check him out. He started injecting me. And for me, it didn't work. And so the reason I've done such a campaign against silicone was because no one should go what I went through. I've had thirty-six surgeries on my face. My face – left side – was paralysed for a year and a half. I couldn't close my eye. My mouth hung down. Finally I got lucky with a very good doctor who operated again. I'm not putting all plastic surgery down. I believe in face lifts if you need it. Check your doctor. Go to the right one.

'I think my surgery had everything to do with Hollywood. Oh, yeah, it was a combination of my parents and Hollywood. Every commercial shows a model that is so beautiful. You're either starving yourself or putting injections in your face. If I were in Iowa, I probably wouldn't have done it. I wouldn't have the same parents either probably. So that would have been different too.'

But some of the screen's most glamorous stars believe in ageing gracefully. 'What's so terrible about growing older and having wrinkles?' asks Lauren Bacall. 'I think the preoccupation with youth is terribly depressing. It's as if the only alternative is suicide. A friend of mine recently said, "Oh, you've had your face lifted." I said: "Are you out of your mind?" Can you imagine a "friend" saying something so cruel? Listen, I've stuck with this face. God knows there's room for improvement. I've earned every one of my wrinkles. Cheese ripens with age. Wine ripens with age. Why can't people? Does everybody have to be plastic?'

Does Sophia Loren feel vulnerable about her age? 'No, absolutely not. I try to keep myself in shape but getting older is wonderful. You mature. You experience so many things. Joy. Sorrow sometimes. But I've had a wonderful life. I *have* a wonderful life. And I *will* have a wonderful life. My life has been almost completely fulfilled. I said,

"Almost", but I have no regrets. I'm proud of what I've done with myself. And I'm very proud of my children. There's no question that I took from my mother a kind of strength and dignity in looking at life.

'I was born old. I've been in films since I was fifteen – always a woman, never a girl. When I was thirty the world press descended on me to ask how it felt to be middle-aged. I felt like a national institution beginning to crumble at the edges. When I was thirty they said it was a critical age for women and then at forty and at fifty and now at sixty. What counts for me in life are the relationships I have with my family which you build at twenty or thirty or forty or fifty or sixty.'

Loren, bronzed with those hazel-flecked eyes flashing, laughs: 'Everything you see I owe to spaghetti.' Or: 'Sex appeal is 50 per cent of what you've got and 50 per cent of what people think you've got.' Some would be happy with 25 per cent. But she says: 'I look okay – just okay. My nose is too long, my chin too short, my hips too broad. But together all these irregularities seem to work. I don't mind ageing. Everybody gets older – if they are lucky. I have nothing against plastic surgery if a woman is obsessed with the way she looks. But I like to stick with my dear old face. I'm young inside so getting old doesn't make a difference to me. The best thing I've ever done for my looks was to quit smoking.

'Age is a condition. You have to cope with it as best you can. You have to know how to get older or you become a caricature. As I get older I get quieter because now I know myself better. When I was young I was more aggressive, wilder even. Now, I find myself more knowing which is good. I think the secret in keeping young is never to look back, only ahead. Once one starts to look back one feels the age.'

Clearly, she doesn't feel the age one bit. Sex? 'From my young days I have always known that sex should come with companionship but it is not fundamental. So now I put companionship before passion, before love and before sex. At first sex may appear to be the most fundamental element but then a new kind of relationship develops with a man which is better, deeper and far more enduring.'

ON THE CASTING COUCH
Chapter 10

'Women get taken advantage of'
Theresa Russell

La Loren can reflect on sex, but for aspiring players in the Hollywood game it can often be a threat rather than a pleasure. Making it is a struggle for the majority but some take an easier if not always successful route and *make* it with men or women who can advance their careers. The key to the top is a mix of brawn, brains and beauty. There's another B – bed. Or, in Hollywood parlance, the casting couch.

Lauren Bacall, for one, admits that women have never been in control. Men did and do run Hollywood. On sexual harassment in Hollywood, she says: 'That's always existed at any business at any office. The casting-couch theory was always true, in the theatre and in the movies. Lots of executives have their girlfriends in movies. If they're lousy they don't last very long.'

Theresa Russell, the American actress married to British director Nic Roeg, and star of *Black Widow*, *Whore* and *The Last Tycoon*, has no doubt about the business of sex for movie roles: 'Definitely, the casting couch does exist.

There's a lot of women who will unfortunately do pretty much anything to get their foot in the door. If you haven't got talent you get found out pretty quick. It's just there is so much competition. Say they have Mel Gibson to do a film and they go through a list to find a female lead. If it's not Kim Basinger then maybe it's Michelle Pfeiffer. If it's not Michelle Pfeiffer maybe it's somebody else – the women are interchangeable and it's cast on who thinks she's fanciable. It's true, it really happens.

'Women get taken advantage of. Even ones who are semi-established. I did some work with Molly Ringwald (*Pretty In Pink*) and I had a lot of conversations with her. You go into a slump and people want you to come in for readings and wear a bathing suit so they can see what your body looks like. I'd say no and tell them to shove it where the light never goes. I'm not that desperate. The world does not revolve for me around this town.'

Hollywood has been marketing sex since the silent days. Russ Meyer, the producer of super-mammary films like *Beyond the Valley of the Dolls* and *Faster, Pussy Cat*, is a master purveyor. It's his endowment policy. The moviemaker to whom the British National Film Theatre devoted a special season in 1995 said: 'If they wanted to work in the major studios the girls in my films were always told that the casting couch must be a consideration. I won't mention names but big-time guys, some of the most unpleasant men I've ever met, are major film producers.

'I've often said that X-rated film-makers don't have to have a couch, it comes to them real easy, but the casting agents, producers, directors often try to extract the flesh as well. I don't audition people for the sake of acquiring some kind of sexual relief. I'm there to make a film.'

Phyllis Diller, who has been in Hollywood for more than fifty years, says: 'The casting couch is the name of the game in Hollywood. It goes on all the time. I like to think that the people who become really big stars are bright and talented and work hard. However, I know there are stars, especially women, who have made a career from sexual favours.'

Helen Mirren, who endured her own Hollywood upset over the casting of the big-screen *Prime Suspect*, is tough talking about sex on and off screen and the domino effect. 'Sexual harassment has very little to do with sex. It's more to do with power and domination. It's saying I can do what I like to you and you can't do anything about it. Sexual harassment has always gone on in Hollywood. Absolutely. It was a joke, wasn't it, the old casting couch? I always thought it was a joke and now women are saying, well, actually, guys, it wasn't a joke. We never found it very funny. It really pissed us off. And we're going to get our own back.'

She is concerned about the message being transmitted in some 1990s films. One, in particular, angers her: '*Pretty Woman* was so immoral. I couldn't believe it. It was just so unspeakably disgusting and misleading. I live in Hollywood and I know what Hollywood hookers look like. And I know what Hollywood Boulevard is. America's full of people who don't live the glamorous life that's constantly shown on television and in films and I think of the fourteen-year-old girl in Waco, Texas, seeing that film.

'I know what I was like when I was fourteen: those images are terribly seductive, you believe, in your dream world, that that could happen. That's not what happens. That's not what Hollywood hookers are like. Their lives are horrendous. I'm sure that there were many little girls who thought, I know how to get rich and marry a millionaire – by going to suck dicks on Hollywood Boulevard. That was a truly violent film because I'm sure that film was responsible for destroying quite a lot of lives.'

Roseanne, one of the few female powerbrokers in town, never shies from making her views known: 'I was fat so I didn't go through the casting-couch type of degradation, but I was always treated like "the girl", which is basically what the casting couch is about; being reminded constantly that you're the girl and the outsider and not equal as an artist. I just never laid down for anybody. Nobody ever asked me. I'm not above anything that a woman has to do to get what she wants. I'm not against any woman doing that. When they give you limited choices you go with the one that works. So if it would have been easier on me in the long run to go on the casting couch rather than have to go through all the mental and emotional torture I had to go through, I would have chosen that. I would rather suck cock than kiss arse. And I would tell everyone that because kissing arse, well, you have to do that for free, but sucking cock, that's a decent business proposition, you get your money up front. You say: "I'll do this for you, you do that for me." Kissing arse, first of all it never ends and you do it in the hope that someone will appreciate you, which they never do. They just keep piling more shit on top of you. They say, "Okay, now go bring me some coffee and kiss my friend's arse too while you're at it."

'I think Sharon Stone's smart. I think that's cool. I'm not gonna ever put another woman down. More power to 'em – everybody go flash your beaver and get millions of dollars. If that was how it was, I would be out there telling women to go flash every second, get every god-damn cent you can get. You're the one that's raising the kids, you're the one that needs it. Whatever any woman has to do to get where she has to go. Short of murder.'

Jacqueline Bisset might disagree: 'I know that it's not the way to get a job. I've had what is called longevity in Hollywood and I have never done anything for a job of that type. Never. When I first started I had a few people come on to me and try it on. I've seen a producer with a dressing gown come and open the door. But I said this was horrendous. This is something that one has to deal with. I would wear dresses that were maybe quite low and I was much more voluptuous-looking in those days. I was also probably much less centred, but I still had a strong sense that if it doesn't work out in Hollywood I'm going home. When I came here, the first year I had a couple of producers who were a bit sleazy, I could handle it. He's a decent man underneath, I'm sure. He's not rotten. Men like pretty girls, it's normal, and it's normal that if the girl is behaving a certain way the man's gonna take advantage of it.

'I went for the heart and it worked for me. There are probably jobs that I didn't get because I wouldn't do all kinds of things. I didn't want to do sexy pictures and lots of flesh stuff because I'm not comfortable about it. I don't have a moralistic view on that. It's just that I'd rather not do it. But women do it all the time. I think it's part of being a woman. Most women spend an enormous time trying to find the right clothes, the right make-up, the right hair to be attractive and desirable. You put that all together and you set the thing in motion. The male computer says short skirt, nice high heels, good legs because that's the way he's been brought up to react. I think this whole sexual harassment thing is very confusing. I mean, women are now harassing men.'

At least, that was the premise of Michael Crichton's bestselling book *Disclosure* which became a hit movie with Demi Moore playing Michael Douglas's boss. And she wanted more from him than nine to five. Crichton turned out a thriller using sexual harassment in the workplace as a backdrop. Unlike his *Jurassic Park* it wasn't all fiction. The battle of the sexes goes on in boardrooms and bedrooms.

Especially in Hollywood where sex is a constant commodity.

HOLLYWOOD SEX
Chapter 11

'Hollywood is a place where they pay you $50,000 for a kiss and 50 cents for your soul.'
Marilyn Monroe

One of the biggest sex symbols of the 1990s is Pamela Anderson – C.J. on *Baywatch*, which, in 1995, was the world's most watched television show. Blonde Anderson, with her hour-glass figure, is a Monroe-style star. Off-screen her marriage to rocker Tommy Lee, the former husband of actress Heather Locklear – another blonde sexpot in *Dynasty* and later *Melrose Place* – caused as much attention as her fabulous figure. Especially her tattooed wedding band which the *Baywatch* producers felt was a little over-the-top for their show's clean-cut image. But Anderson's fan following is so huge that the problems, rather than the tattoo, faded.

On sex in the film capital she says: 'People think of Hollywood as the sex and glamour capital. I see sex everywhere so I don't just put it in Hollywood. What is called sex here is a kind of externalization of sex. I don't see a lot of real sex here. I see a degree of sensuality, which comes with the weather and people being good looking, but most people are so business oriented. I don't think sex based on business is sex. To me that's not sex. That's manipulation. I don't want to be relating to things that way. I'm aware that if you're not careful you can get used here but my theory is that people are very greedy and that a lot of what happens to them they deserve. Sex to me is about wanting to make contact and about giving. It's also about pleasure, all kinds of things. There are people here who really want to give and a whole lot who really want to take. Now that should balance out somehow but it doesn't frequently come together in a very tender way.

'There's an extraordinary amount of incredible-looking people who flock into this city and try to use their sexuality to get jobs. It's not the way to get a job. It may have been in the old days. It's not a way to be taken seriously.'

Sex sells twenty-four hours a day. Lauren Bacall knows the score. 'If you want anything, just whistle,' she purred to Humphrey Bogart in her début film. She was sultry and sexy but revealed nothing but her dental work in 1944's *To Have and Have Not*. She was nineteen and her act seduced audiences as much as it did Bogart, who married her.

More than fifty years later, actresses are still trying to turn audiences on but are rather more forward. After *Basic Instinct*, and the stunning success it provided for Sharon Stone, scripts in Hollywood now include dozens of pages of material reflecting naked ambition for box-office hits. *Showgirls*, to be released in late 1995, was another effort from the *Basic Instinct* team (director Paul Verhoeven and screenwriter Joe Eszterhas). The X-rated thriller set in the strip clubs and topless revue bars of Las Vegas was blatantly stacked with sex and nudity.

Lauren Bacall believes one pair of knickers too many have been dropped and prefers the style of yesteryear: 'Glamour was great. It was total glamour in the movies and it was so seductive you just wanted to be part of it. It had such an aura and now it's too graphic. Everyone knows everything about how movies are made, what goes on, how special effects are done and who wears what and who's doing it to who. The great thing about what we now call "old movies" is that you were able to use your imagination. You were able to envisage whatever you wanted, whatever you were able to imagine instead of having it all laid out in front of you.

'I think romance is almost a thing of the past, as far as movies are concerned. It's sad because romance is something people always want and look for. It's what you hope for, what takes you out of your reality. The sex thing – I like sex as much as anyone but don't wanna watch it on television or on the screen in a movie theatre. I don't want to watch Michael Douglas at it all the time, thank you. I really don't, cute as he is.'

Bacall talked frankly about the stars of the mid-1990s: 'Julia Roberts – she's only twenty years old or something and she's making a *comeback*. I mean, that's pretty stupid, isn't it?

'Sharon Stone, who came from nowhere, she's made a noise and she's got an old-time movie-star look about her, which is great. There's always a place for that but who knows how long any of these women are gonna last if it's only based on a small thing?

'Madonna certainly was one person who made a wave but I think she was different because she was really so smart about selling herself in such a major way that she's become almost a world unto herself. You can't call her a flash-in-the-pan because she's been around too long. For actresses you can't just shoot your wad the first time out – you have to have some talent that's going to last.

'When I went out to Hollywood I was eighteen and I didn't know anything about anything. Bette Davis was the big star – she owned the Warner Brothers lot. Barbara Stanwyck and Ann Sheridan – they were the top ones. And you had Garbo and Katharine Hepburn and Lana Turner, Ava Gardner, Norma Shearer and Joan Crawford. Endless women stars.'

But sex in the movies is only one aspect of the sex scene in Hollywood. It acts as a magnet for all kinds of activities, most of which you'll find in any big city, but there's just that little bit more in Hollywood. Each year the Hollywood sign attracts hundreds of kids, maybe several thousand. They all want to be stars or make money. Mostly both. Many end up on the streets trying to pay either for a drug habit or acting lessons by prostitution. All along Sunset and Hollywood Boulevards are the male, female and transsexual hookers. Any vice, any kink – if you have the money – is available. Detective Bill Dworin sees the plight of many exploited and exploiting youngsters every day. He is with the Los Angeles Police Department: 'I'm the officer in charge of the sexually exploited child unit. Our unit has the responsibility of investigating crimes of child sexual exploitation, which includes child pornography, child molestation and prostitution.

'A lot of the children in the Hollywood area are runaways. They run away from all parts of the country, from foreign countries too, seeing the glitter of Hollywood, the belief that they, too, can become stars. When they reach the Hollywood area and they don't have a place to live, they can't survive on the streets without going into some illegal activity. They frequently end up into prostitution.

'What we do is build a rapport with the child, hope that child will disclose why she/he ran away, the circumstances behind it, and frequently you'll identify the child as a victim of either physical or sexual abuse.

'You can identify pimps who are using children on the street in prostitution. You can identify people involved in pornography using children, and the use and distribution of narcotics.

'There is no typical kid that ends up in prostitution because every child has their own story, their own horrors, but we find that they frequently come from an abusive home life, or have been victimized outside the home by a family friend or somebody in authority.'

Runaways come into the Los Angeles area by bus and pimps work the bus stations. They see a child come off the bus, there's nobody there to pick them up, the child looks lost, confused. This pimp introduces himself, gives the child a place to stay, food and after a period of time, demands money for the services he renders. When the child is unable to pay it's forced into prostitution.

Often the kids start to use drugs and alcohol, supplied by the pimps. It lowers their inhibitions, they go along with what the pimp wants. If the child is involved in narcotics to begin with, it's just one step to get them more involved, keep them high and force them into prostitution. Other children use these narcotics to block out their activities. They're on the streets probably ten, twelve, fourteen hours a day. They also have a more sophisticated juvenile prostitute, a service where somebody calls up and orders a specific type of child prostitute.

'The clients? We've arrested anybody from the blue-collar worker to corporate executives so it doesn't make any difference, it's what that individual has an interest in that makes the difference.

'Child prostitutes start at a very early age. If you can call them that. I don't consider them prostitutes, I consider all these children victims, in particular pre-pubescent children controlled by an individual. I've seen them as young as five and six.

'Depending upon the individual and what they can afford, that's what the pimp will demand for that child. I've done cases where a person is willing to pay up to a thousand dollars to have sex with a five- or six-year-old child. The child does not usually see the money itself. What they see is something that money buys – a trip to Disneyland, new clothing, new toys or affection and attention again. We have to combat that problem by making it difficult for the trick, the John who wants the child, to find that child. And we actively seek out not only the children who are the victims of this activity but also the people who are taking advantage of them.

'A lot of children involved in prostitution attempt suicide or commit suicide. They just cannot live with themselves for being a prostitute. Others survive by going into alcohol and drugs. Of course there's therapy, something like Children of the Night, a group who's willing to go out and talk to children. A lot of those counsellors were prostitutes so they know what the children are going through, and they relate much better with them than, for example, people who don't know the streets.'

Sex sells. It's also for sale. It is the ultimate guilty pleasure for men who have everything – sex with the women of their dreams. And they desire different dreams or kinks every night, day, lunchtime or teatime.

Author William Stadiem who wrote *Beverly Hills Madam* was interviewed for 'Hollywood Women' and Alex Adams – the 'Madam' in his book – talked on 'Hollywood Vice' about the perils and pleasures of Hollywood sex.

Power players can have whatever style of women or sex they want and pick their lusts from the pages of *Vogue* or *Harper's Bazaar* or the latest television show or cinema blockbuster – women will literally walk off the pages of the glossy fashion magazines or entertainment screens and into bed with those willing to pay a lavish price. And female lawyers and accountants, doctors and dentists can happily be lured into selling sex because of the money available. In Hollywood there is a price for everything. And, seemingly, everyone.

Stadiem says he is a little amused at the shocked faces when people learn that their favourite actor buys sex. He argues that they pay for everything else from Lear jets to dog psychologists, so what's different?

A great deal, of course. But Stadiem is more interested in the what, the why and with whom than the morality, for he says: 'High level prostitution is Hollywood's best kept dirty secret.'

It is the subtleties of the game which are fascinating and intriguing: the customer who runs up an annual million-dollar tab for girls; the cross-dressing and premature ejaculations of famous names; the OPEC minister who has a 'regular', a six-foot-tall former ballet dancer; the sexaholic producer who never sees a girl twice; the accountant who loves sex and wants to work as a hooker to make money and 'meet interesting people' – she's flown first class from Los Angeles to spend time at New York's Carlyle Hotel with a major British chief executive officer. And the hookers who have become wives to major stars, power figures in Hollywood, and famous film and TV stars.

Why *do* men who have everything and can have anything, pay?

Stadiem offers some of the answers in his book *Madam 90210*. It is a tale of stars and sex and, appropriately, vice versa. He was researching a business book about a Hollywood studio takeover but found most people reluctant to talk about dirty money. Dirty secrets were an altogether different matter. He says of his book: 'It's about sex and power in Hollywood told from the point of view of Madam Alex Adams who was the madam to the stars. She's retired now but through her I was able to interview about a hundred of the most beautiful call-girls in the world and many of their clients. In Hollywood it's a status symbol even to have been on Alex's list of customers. It was a very exclusive list, you had to have really, really arrived. It was the equivalent of a good table at Spago. To be at Alex's you knew you were a player, one of the big players. The men were very proud that they could have – and talk about – all the famous women or cover girls they had had. It was great fun. They talked to me about it. They weren't ashamed.

'Alex was just another way for these powerful men to meet the women they wanted. They liked to challenge themselves and put their egos on the line. They didn't mind paying a few thousand dollars to meet the woman for the first time. Then, the challenge was, can I get this girl to sleep with me for free the next time? It was a game.'

And an expensive game for one Beverly Hills billion-aire: 'One of the former call-girls married this incredibly wealthy man but even after they were married she demanded $2 million for fifty acts of sex. It was very much a quota system – she still wanted to get paid for her services. He paid her. It was so good he couldn't resist it.'

Stadiem says he has learned the power of beauty. For it is not just the sex act, it's being able to get the fantasy girl of their choice: 'It's the sheer excitement of being in bed with these women. These are women that you would see in magazines like *Vogue* or on TV. Men would often call Alex and say: "I saw this girl – can you get me her?" And she could do it. She had an amazing network and for X-thousand dollars you could have an affair with this girl. Alex's price started at a thousand dollars for an hour of pleasure and then two thousand for an extended after-noon. For a whole night it could be five thousand. And if they went on trips then the cost was more. The first-class sections of British Airways and Air France were frequently populated with a number of Alex's creatures. If they were starlets or models and someone spotted them they would say they were going on a photo-shoot in Milan but it was something else in London or Milan or wherever.

'A lot of the men pay cash, although some of Alex's clients and those of her successors run up huge tabs – it's not surprising for people to have six-digit tabs. They run up bills just the way they would at Armani or Morton's and pay it off at the end of the month. These people are good for the money. What are they getting for it? It's very conventional sex – very normal, nothing particularly kinky. It's not so much that you want to tie the girl up or degrade her – it's the idea of having her, having someone who you never thought you could have, that's the excitement. It's fucking the unfuckable. This is the same creature this man might meet in a bar and be able to go home for free with. But, in the age of Aids, men – even if they are famous – cannot expect to go to a bar and pick somebody out and go to bed with them that night.

'This is a town where time is money. People don't want to waste a lot of time in pursuing women that all they really want to do is have sex with and will probably never see again. Why should they waste their time? And the watchwords for Hollywood in the 1990s are "family values". These same men have families and they don't want to get caught out having an affair with some teenage model or young starlet. That would just defeat everything. Their box office depends on their image. To paraphrase that old deodorant commercial, the madams take the worry out of being close. It's amazing that people would spend so much money but when they have an annual income of $20 million, a million a year for recreation is a drop in a gilded bucket. There are no bargains in sex. They are not wanted. The more they pay the better they feel. It's like going to an élite French restaurant. They feel that it's safer, it's more glamorous, it's a higher tone experience.

'You know, Tom Cruise and Julia Roberts get $10 million a picture and because of that people think they are seeing a bigger picture and a bigger star. It's the same thing when the same people who are making these big movies want to hire call girls. They want to pay more. The more people pay in Hollywood the better they feel. They feel more secure that they're really getting quality.'

Providing 'entertainment' for stars and executives in Hollywood has long been accepted. Producer Wilbur Stark – father of the Duke of York's one-time love Koo Stark – said that when he was a bachelor he was asked to arrange girls: 'Married friends – top executives – would say: "Willy, you're single, set up a date for us." I was amazed. So I had a list of prostitutes they would call and afterwards the girls gave me the story.'

Stadiem acknowledges the longtime 'perk' of Hollywood success. 'This is the golden triangle of sex in America, the most expensive neighbourhood in the world. Houses on the small lots start at three million dollars.' Up Rodeo Drive and into the Hollywood Hills the $1.6 million ranch-style home of Heidi Fleiss – best friend of Victoria Sellers – is not much compared to others in Benedict Canyon. But it's not drab for a high-school drop-out who moved in on Madam Alex's territory – and was later arrested and convicted on prostitution charges – when the former queen of the game was busted and placed on probation. 'Heidiwood' was the Hollywood scandal of the summer of 1993. It may have scandalized the rest of the world but is shrugged off in Hollywood.

So does Stadiem believe almost any woman in Hollywood is for sale? 'I wouldn't say that. I think a lot of men would like to think that and perhaps everybody has her price at some point. I'd say that a lot of young and ambitious women, women under twenty-five, could use extra money. Unless they have made it in the movies by that age.

'Alex was a florist in town. In the course of that business she met her predecessor, an Englishwoman, who decided to get out of sex and become a dog breeder. She told Alex she wanted to sell her black book. Alex became probably the world's most important madam with movie stars and major politicians and statesmen and some of the biggest moguls in the world from America and Europe. She's had them all – it's one of the great luxury items. If anybody has the money they want to try it out of curiosity. It's very civilized. It's like a dating service, except the dates will cost you a thousand dollars and upwards. But or men who are not price sensitive that doesn't mean anything. These girls are charming. They're from all over the world. I've met lawyers, accountants, development girls from the studios, and they find it an amazing way to make a lot of money in a very short time. Some of the girls have married very well and become Hollywood wives. Others have become Hollywood producers or executives. A large number have become actresses, starlets, models. And a lot of the models when their modelling careers are over and they are too wooden to act marry rich and prominent men.

'In Beverly Hills and Hollywood superficial is fine. If a woman is beautiful that's enough – yet that's why you see so many ugly divorces here. After a while a lot of these women let their mercenary roots show, and the men who marry them are not cured of their sexaholism by marrying perfect call-girl types. They find themselves calling the madams again. It's a hard habit to break. They're often busted by becoming patrons of younger call-girls and their ex-call-girl wives catch them. Nobody can smell a call-girl like a former call-girl.'

Marriage or fame can change outlook, as Stadiem notes with the famous Marilyn Monroe line when she finally became a star: 'I'll never have to suck another cock in this town again.'

Stadiem talks of another starlet, now a famous name, who cost a Hollywood producer tens of thousands of dollars. 'She's a huge star now, one of the biggest. A number of girls have become huge TV and movie stars. You can turn the TV on any time and see them and a lot of them have become prominent social housewives. They've become ladies who lunch. It was a brief window of opportunity in their path. One didn't have to be a call-girl for a long time to make wonderful contacts. They become trophy girl-friends, trophy call-girls, trophy wives.

'When a woman marries a famous man in Hollywood she is immediately accepted in Beverly Hills. Money talks. Power talks. Power derives from money here and if a call-girl marries a rich and powerful man her past is acceptable and forgiven. In Hollywood having been a call-girl is a market status because it meant you were one of the most beautiful and one of the best. Blue stockings may sneer at it, but this is not a town of blue stockings, is it? This is a town of meshed stockings.'

But for those who take the sex-for-sale or casting-couch route there are many others who have worked against the odds to become famous Hollywood People.

Or infamous ones.

FORTRESS HOLLYWOOD
Chapter 12

'I am willing to go out and kill a whole bunch of people.'
Charles Manson, 1995

One of the major tragedies – and horrors – of modern Hollywood were the Manson Family murders. They changed how the rich and famous lived. Out went the easy-going lifestyle. In came the security guards, the Dobermann dogs, guns by the bedside and shotguns nearby. By 1995 Cybill Shepherd had a pearl-handled pistol next to her night-lamp. Warren Beatty, Marlon Brando and Jack Nicholson have special monitors and fences around their properties – known as Casanova Corner – on Mulholland Drive overlooking Los Angeles, the largest linear city in the world. Bruce Willis and Demi Moore often travel with their children and half a dozen bodyguards. Most celebrities have security around the clock.

Indeed, Hollywood People are as careful about security as they are about dressing for the Oscars. It is a legacy of madman Manson.

'Charles Manson is the greatest advertisement for the death penalty in the world,' says Stephen Kay with a half-smile, as he sits in his seventh-floor offices in Compton, California. Manson and his Family made society's nightmare come true with their disquieting and unforgettable killing spree which began in the Hollywood Hills shortly after midnight on 9 August 1969.

When it was over Roman Polanski's pregnant actress wife, Sharon Tate, and six others had been horrifyingly butchered.

Kay, pinstriped, a trim and bespectacled fifty, an older version of Dean Cain who starred in the television series *The New Adventures of Superman*, has performed some extraordinary feats. He has been involved with the Manson case since 1971 and turned down major political appointments always to be available to argue against parole for any of the convicted killers. It has been his crusade, his mission and, against the odds in fervently politically correct California, has not proved an impossible one.

He is certain that Manson will never be freed but he warns: 'The others will get out one day. One will be freed and the floodgates will be open. There are always people who believe prisoners must be paroled. I'm not one of them. They want to get out and rejoin society but society doesn't want them. I feel a responsibility to society to make sure that these people don't get out. I am going to struggle to keep them in as long as I can.'

He's a lifelong Republican but not a right-wing zealot. His law-and-order attitude contrasts with the bestiality of Manson and his Family, which comprised mainly middle-class girls, their minds and bodies scarred by the man they regarded as a combination of Jesus and Satan.

Kay, who runs the district attorney's office in Compton, a crime- and gang-ridden suburb forty minutes' drive from equally dangerous central Los Angeles, is also adamant that the Manson case still has an impact on society and that Manson is still wielding chilling influence: 'He gets letters every day. Many are from teenagers who want to join his Family. Other inmates act as his correspondence secretaries. His influence is enormous. Do I believe he could get someone killed? Definitely.'

In this he is supported by Manson, who, with total unpredictability, will sometimes grant interviews that range from rantings to intimidating sentences like: 'I get letters. I write people all over the country. There is no question I still run my Family.' Stephen Kay says there is still much to learn from the tragedy initiated by Manson.

Author Joan Didion believes: 'That was the end of the sixties for a lot of people in Los Angeles.' Didion, who has so often pinpointed the psyche of American society, says that in Los Angeles in 1969 there was a mystical flirtation with 'sin', a sense that it was possible to go too far and that many people were doing it. 'I recall a time when the dogs barked every night and the moon was always full.'

But Kay says Manson's acts were political not Satanic. They were not hippies. 'Manson and his Family liked to call themselves "Slippies" – they would slip underneath the fabric of society, incite a race war and then take over.'

Manson, like cult leader David Koresh of Waco, Texas, is charismatic. These fanatics have an evil appeal. 'If he walked into this room right now you wouldn't be able to take your eyes off him,' Kay told me adding: 'Manson can cast a spell – that's how he got other people to do his bidding and killing. He had these girls from nice families willing to kill for him. He had such evil control – and he still has it today.'

At the trial the girls took all the blame. They were willing to die for their maniacal messiah in the California gas chamber.

Vincent Bugliosi prosecuted Manson and his Family and later, in 1974, wrote *Helter Skelter*, his account of the crime and trial. It was a worldwide bestseller and, along with Truman Capote's *In Cold Blood* and Emlyn Williams's *Beyond Belief*, remains one of the most chilling chronicles of evil. Bugliosi continues to practise law and remains a best-selling author. When you ask him about the Manson myth he offers: 'Here's this little goon, five feet two inches tall, though he gives the sense of being taller ... Here's this little guy and his followers – ultimately killers – and they were kids from average American families. Manson sat back pulling the strings and getting other people to go and kill strangers without asking questions. When people ask me about Manson they don't ask me how many times someone was stabbed, they ask, "How did he control all these people?" When I was first assigned to the case it was called the Tate murders. Then Manson comes on the scene and he's so bizarre, so charismatic, that he upstaged the victims. It became the Charles Manson Case.'

Helter Skelter changed not just individual lives but society. And the rules. Legal and policing regulations were dramatically reorganized following the events provoked by Manson, who by 1967 had spent nineteen of his thirty-two years in one penal institution or another.

The Manson Family 'tree' has kept on growing for more than a quarter of a century. Hollywood still lives under the shadow of what became the Los Angeles Medical Examiner's Case No. 69–8796:

In the 1993 movie *Bodyguard* the Oscar-winning Kevin Costner played the title role guarding Whitney Houston's celebrity singer. The plot was not just some Tinseltown fancy but part of everyday Hollywood life. Since 1969 a protection industry worth hundreds of millions of dollars annually has been established. Gavin De Becker who works out of offices in affluent Newport Beach down the Pacific Coast from Los Angeles is credited with being the number one in the field. He has 'covered' events such as Don Johnson and Melanie Griffith's second wedding and the marriage of Michael J. Fox. Demi Moore, Bruce Willis and their children have bodyguards written into their contracts as do dozens of other stars. Warren Beatty's estate is more like Colditz than a home. His neighbours Marlon Brando and Jack Nicholson also have elaborate security. Following the suicide of his daughter Cheyenne, Marlon Brando employed guards to stop ghoulish sight-seers. He had already increased security at his home after his son Christian had killed Cheyenne's fiancé three years earlier.

Victoria Principal has automatic metal shutters in a 'security bathroom' and attack dogs. Former Israeli security man Moshe Alon has been Elizabeth Taylor's shadow for a dozen years. His past clients have included Michael Caine, the late billionaire Armand Hammer, Goldie Hawn and three cast members of *Beverly Hills 90210*, who are so paranoid they will not even admit to security needs.

Partly because of Manson the people of California and the rest of America are never free of fear. They drive home aware of police warnings about car hijackings. Children carry guns in classrooms for protection. After Manson there were many atrocities. In 1974 heiress Patty Hearst was kidnapped by the Symbionese Liberation Army and became the machine-gun wielding terrorist 'Tania'. In 1976, in Chowchilla, California, twenty-six children were kidnapped and entombed.

In San Diego there was the 1985 massacre at a McDonalds restaurant. In 1986, when 'The Night Stalker' roamed Los Angeles, people would not open a window even in the blistering summer heat. There was the Hollywood Strangler who claimed seven female victims. In New York they called him 'The Son of Sam'.

Actress Rebecca Schaefer was murdered in 1989 by a crazed 'fan' and actress Theresa Saldana was almost fatally stabbed seven years earlier. Mark Chapman killed John Lennon, having lived his life as a fantasy Beatle and even marrying his own 'Yoko Ono'. John Hinkley shot President Reagan over his obsession with actress Jodie Foster. Roger Daltrey of The Who was given a crystal ball by a Manson follower and believes it cursed him. He had a 'white witch' take it away.

Madness and mayhem and murder.

When such happenings leave the headlines they are mostly forgotten but Charles Manson and his Family remain locked in Hollywood People's consciousness.

Steven Railsback became an eerie double for Manson

in the television series *Helter Skelter* based on Bugliosi's book. At the time, in 1978, he talked of death threats, of plans to attack the film set and his own fears about playing the man he called 'the man with a thousand eyes'. During filming producer Tom Gries moved his wife and children out of Los Angeles. He received telephone calls in which voices chanted: 'Piggy, piggy, piggy.' There was talk of guard dogs for those playing major roles. Railsback saw it as his big break but he's never made it, despite the fascination with Manson and his Family which attracted 102 million viewers in America alone.

The real Manson is said to be a paranoid schizophrenic. He's locked in a cell thirteen feet by seven, in Corcoran maximum security prison fifty miles from Fresno in central California. He likes to be alone. He enjoys making model animals. A decade ago a Hare Krishna member set him ablaze, burning his hands and head but not touching the swastika cut into his forehead.

Manson granted an interview in which he said: 'I think I am a little more passive than I was. I don't have a tendency to get mad as quick. Prison has mellowed me out a little. I was pretty upset for a long time. I was really mad at a lot of people.'

Was he still mad at people? 'I'm willing to get out and kill a whole bunch of people. That's one reason I'm not really too fast on getting out. Because, if I got out, I'd feel obligated to get even. It would be an honour thing. If I'm going to jump on a convict and beat the shit out of him for beating me for a packet of cigarettes, what am I going to do for somebody that just beat me for twenty-five years of my life? I'd feel honour-bound to get even.'

He and his followers were almost executed in the California gas chamber but their sentences were commuted in 1972 when the state invalidated the death penalty. He is restless, always tapping on something. Barking mad, but with the evil energy: 'I just live in a different time zone. You call it insanity. You call it psychotic, you call it all kinds of different things because you don't function in it.'

Other Family members have vanished into the vastness of America, into militant militia groups and all manner of religious sects. Also disappeared are the children of Charles Manson's Family. After the arrest of Manson and the others they were fostered out by authorities. Court records were sealed, some destroyed. Family member Susan Atkins is still looking for the child she named Zezozoze Zadfrack.

The Manson legacy lives on ... as does violent Hollywood.

HOORAY FOR HOLLYWOOD!
Chapter 13

'Would you like to see a seventy-year-old
James Dean?'
Jay Bernstein

For all its faults and sins there will always be a Hollywood. Tinseltown is facing the future using new tech-
nology – the Steven Spielberg, Jeffrey Katzenberg and
David Geffen dream-team film studio is aimed at production for the next century – and expanding the parameters
of taste. How far will they go? Director Paul Verhoeven
and writer Joe Eszterhas – the team that gave us *Basic
Instinct* and Sharon Stone's famous flash – are aiming for
body-to-body nudity and sex in *Showgirls*. It is anticipated
as a breakthrough movie of the late 1990s.

By the turn of the century it might not be anything but
everything goes. As well as *Showgirls* there is Demi Moore
in *Striptease* – a film adaptation of Carl Hiaasen's 1993
blockbuster book – and British director Mike Figg's
Leaving Las Vegas. Martin Scorsese used the sleazy nightclubs of 1970s Las Vegas for *Casino*, which stars Robert
De Niro and Sharon Stone. Also filmed was *Melissa*, a
murder mystery featuring a topless dancer played by

Nicole Eggart, from *Baywatch*, and *Pigalle* about a peep-show stripper.

Whatever the movie trends by the millennium there will always be Hollywood People. The Hollywood sign remains on the hill only because of the people who live in its shadow.

Especially those who promote themselves, who are drawn to the glitter and glamour, who want stardom, often at any cost. They will hype themselves or, in the case, of entrepreneurial larger-than-life characters like Jay Bernstein, their clients' talents.

There will always be actresses like Pamela Anderson, who epitomize the Hollywood Dream for so many millions worldwide. She describes herself as 'a visual phenomenon' and 'a living icon' and 'the new loved goddess of the future'. It's quite a build-up – and all her own work.

Angelyne is the Billboard Queen of Hollywood. Promotional advertising has acted as her 'agent' in promoting a literally larger-than-life character. She drives the streets of Hollywood in a pink Corvette and just wants to be famous. A former rock singer, she says: 'I'm a rebel and very much into being an original. I detest clichés. When I was three I knew I would never feel right until I became famous. Fame made me feel more normal.'

She began a campaign to achieve her dream in 1985. 'I started with posters, then bus shelters. Next, we put out small billboards, then larger ones. We finally painted my picture on a ten-storey at Hollywood and Vine. After that the media were all over me – I must have gotten $10 million worth of free exposure.'

And exposure is the word. She is another Jayne

Mansfield, a platinum blonde with very vital statistics and a tough business attitude. Angelyne has parlayed her image into hundreds of personal appearances and scores of guest shots on television. She's marketed everything from Angelyne posters to Angelyne dolls. 'If you are determined enough anyone can make it in Hollywood,' she says.

Jay Bernstein would agree with her. He is a producer and personal manager who discovered – among others – Farrah Fawcett. He also managed Kate Jackson, Linda Evans and Faye Dunaway, but turned down Sharon Stone. He and his wife Cabrina staged a wedding that was, even by Hollywood standards, wacky. Jay says: 'We were married on Lifestyles of the Rich and Famous, fifty-five feet under water. I'd never been married and neither had she and we just wanted to make an event out of it. Cabrina wore an underwater wedding gown and people could not believe the guts she had to go down fifty-five feet without any fins, without any VC, without anything other than just the oxygen tank, a white one. I wore a tuxedo wetsuit and we got married four times. The first time for the law, make it legal. The second time we got married was for Lifestyles. The third time was for *Skindiver* magazine, and the fourth time was for the *Star*, which is a tabloid here in America. Cabrina's father had to do a sixty-hour certification course to give her away under water, and her sister did the same thing so she could be her maid of honour. Eddie Fisher sang a wedding song for us, "I'm Yours". Eddie and I have been friends since a long time. He sang above the water.

'I wanted to make it an event. Old-style Hollywood. A

lot of the stars today don't really know how to be stars. When I first came to this business it was the end of the studio system. They would say let's get Clark Gable and Carole Lombard and we'll get them married under water and we'll get the press here. Now Molly Ringwald would get married in a tenement somewhere and let you know how she fed four homeless people while the nuptials were going on. It would be Marie Antoinette, let them eat cake. I would imagine that some of these actresses would decide to give the cake to the homeless people.

'In other words, everything's so serious that people don't wanna have fun. I said to Cabrina, "Look, if we're gonna get married, which some people say is fun and some people say is not fun and ours has been fun so far, let's make it an event. Let's do something that no one else has ever done. I know that Dick Van Dyke was married on *Bride and Groom* forty years ago. I know Tiny Tim was married on *The Tonight Show*. I don't know anybody else that did anything with some glamour in it.

'Glamour has gone out of Hollywood because nobody will pay for it. The stars in the old days, if they were going to a première, the studio would arrange for them to have this great car and they would arrange the dates and everything would be fantastic. Now nobody arranges anything. You go to a première in Hollywood, you see people in blue jeans. There is no glamour. Everybody is driving around in as nondescript a car as possible. By the way I have an Aston Martin convertible. It's white with a red interior and I also have a Bentley Corniche. But no one does that any more. They say, "Aren't you afraid?" And I say, "I don't wanna think like that." I don't want people to make me feel that I can no longer be glamorous. I used to sit around with David Janssen and Jack Lemmon and Sean Connery and Michael Caine, but now there's really nowhere that you can go and even when you go somewhere people don't stand up and mingle. Today's stars are basically shy. There's maybe five that are not shy. Most of them don't know how to small-talk. That's why when you go to a party you can take over a room if you know how to talk 'cos everybody else is just sort of, "Gee, I don't know anybody here. How long do we have to stay?"

'They don't wanna be a moving target. If you want you can be a star and live at the beach at Malibu and never come into town and never be seen. You can live out in hidden hills where the horses are and be in that community and never be seen and it seems like the only time that somebody wants publicity is when they're in a situation like Jane Seymour, where she has a hit show, *Doctor Quinn, Medicine Woman*.

'On the other hand if you're an actress and you don't have a hit you really don't wanna go somewhere and have someone say, "Well, what are you doing now?" – "Well, I'm handling the roses, trimming them. I'm growing onions and tomatoes." But there were always people who had style and the pizazz to pull it off. Joan Collins was always good at that. Linda Evans, who I managed, was not good at that. You notice that a lot of people who I represented, once you took me away from their equation you didn't hear much about them any more, because what I tried to be is that part of their personality that stopped them from going over the top.

'Sharon Stone has always been someone who knew what she wanted. Sharon Stone asked me to manage her eight years ago. She reminded me of this at the Academy Awards a year ago and the reason that she said I turned her down was what? Her thighs were too big.

'Sharon always knew what she wanted. She used to guest-star on my series, Mickey Spillane's *Mike Hammer*, with Stacey Keach. There was a scene where Sharon played the villain and she had to land in a vat of what looked like oil. It was just black water, and she refused. She's a guest star. I said, "How can you refuse?" She said, "I'm not going to do it." Well, I found out later that evening why she wouldn't do it. I went to a dinner party after production and she was there with her hair done all nicely and she didn't want to get her hair dirty. Now Sharon is imperfectly perfect. There's no features about her that you could say, "My God, she's like when Farrah was a ten or Bo Derek was a ten. That's not Sharon Stone. Sharon Stone has guts, and she uses the left side *and* the right side of her brain. Sharon is a very bright girl. I think *Sliver* was the perfect movie to follow *Basic Instinct*. Sharon has the same qualifications that a lot of women have acting-wise but I think she was able to show even more of those qualifications by uncrossing her legs.

'The *Playboy* route to success is not a good one because already here [in Hollywood] actresses are thought of as meat. I always tell an actress that whenever someone gives them a card that says producer they're probably not a producer. Now I like Hugh Hefner. I've gone to his parties up at the Playboy mansion for years. He has a

Midsummer Night's Dream Party and a New Year's Eve Party and I hired his girls. Barbi Benton, who did an excellent job on *Mike Hammer* for me, Shannen Tweed, who did an excellent job on *Mike Hammer* for me, and Carrie Leigh, who took four hours to do two sentences, but she was very nice. Or I can have somebody like Farrah Fawcett who I started, managed, on the cover of *Playboy*. She was the second star cover. (Barbra Streisand was the first star cover on *Playboy*.) I didn't want her to do the nude thing because she was nude in bed with Raquel Welch in *Myra Breckenridge* and we didn't want people to remember that.

'When I started working in this town I was told all sorts of things and one of them was that actresses were just like everybody else. They're not, because they're governed by moods. When they are rejected this is a real put-down to them and they don't know why they're rejected except that they're wrong. So they wait for an opportunity to get power.

'I think what happens that changes stars so quickly, is the lack of privacy. I remember when I was producing a movie in Acapulco called *Sunburn* and Farrah Fawcett was in the ladies' room and a woman came in and just started clicking away while Farrah was using the lavatory. Of course I took the film away from the woman. Privacy – which we all take for granted – stars know right away they're going to lose it, that's why they say, "Okay, I'm moving to Vermont, or I'm moving to Virginia, I'm moving to Kentucky ..." But the problem is, the minute they move, all of a sudden they start missing that, "Hey,

Mary Tyler Moore, how are you? Hey, how are you? Hi . . ." Kate Jackson quit the business, and now she's back.

'But sometimes you have nowhere to turn. You can't go to the grocery store because everybody's hassling you. You can't go anywhere without having to sign autographs. I was with William Holden once in Rome. He was standing at the urinal, someone asked for his autograph and he just wet on their leg.

'Most people don't like to sign autographs. It's the new stars that are on the television series that are so thrilled to be out there to do this. Robert Wagner is one of the last of a dying breed that still enjoys glamour. Stars just don't want to go out to talk to people. I go to a psychologist and once I saw Cher, Ann-Margret, Bernadette Peters, Steve Martin and Gary Shandling there. And I'm saying, hey, if all of these people need somebody to talk to, they could run a contest saying: "I'll spend one evening with you for $100,000." And people would come running. I had somebody once spend $10,000 to come out and have dinner with me. I got so nervous the day before, thinking, you know, how am I going to live up to their $10,000, that I invited Donna Mills and her boyfriend, and Robert Culp and his wife to join us for dinner. And I told the Texans, "Just don't tell them that we haven't been friends for a long time." And we got through two-thirds of the dinner and the guy said, "I'm just so excited to be around these stars . . ." and then all hell broke loose. 'Cos the stars were talking about things that you wouldn't talk about in front of "civilians". People in showbusiness categorize people not in showbusiness as civilians. And they don't feel as comfortable with them.

'The price of fame and success can cost you a lot of loneliness, a lot of mental anguish. I read today that Kristy McNichol's working at Sears 'cos she just wants to be a "normal person". Now I started Kristy McNichol when she was on *Family*. Got her first movie. She played Burt Reynolds's daughter in *The End*. The first movie for television that I arranged for her was called *Summer of my German Soldier*. She won an Emmy. But here's somebody who just wants to live her life the way she wants to live it, but it's under a microscope. Everybody tries to stay away from that microscope.

'Hollywood's a very strange town that has become departmentalized. You have those that are forty-five years old and older, forty-five to deceased, that will go to these charity luncheons. The rest just don't show up. What it takes to survive in this town is a very thick skin. To be sensitive only when you're working. To be loyal as long as it doesn't make you bitter against the other person. And to realize that you can't stay on top all of the time. There is no one who's gonna stay on top.

'Most of the really good-looking actors in this town become alcoholics, because, as your looks start to fade with the years, you're not hired for the same parts. It's even worse for beautiful women. If they were like Roseanne Barr where she ages, she'll just mellow out and it'll be fine. But if you're Cheryl Ladd and you age, it's gonna be harder to get parts. The answer is to build for your future and be realistic about what's going to happen as you grow older. Eventually even Warren Beatty will run out of looks. And Rob Lowe. Rob Lowe in thirty years! I mean, how would you like to see a seventy-year-old James Dean? Or a sixty-year-old Montgomery Clift?'

Jay has dated some of the most famous women in Hollywood but he says: "I've never found anybody who will love me as much as I love me! Here, no matter who the woman is, she's gonna love her career fifty-five per cent and you forty-five per cent, and that's the best you're ever gonna get. And I just didn't think there was anybody around as beautiful and nice as Cabrina that I could understand, who could understand me, who didn't just want something. Someone I didn't have to wake up in the morning and tell them whether or not they're with the right agent.

'Some men bask in being the boyfriend who has gone with this star and that star and the other star. I was never like that. I just found that stars were too self-involved and I'm too self-involved too. I've been in this town thirty years, I've been fired by over six hundred stars, I just don't wanna live with it in my own house. I'd like to at least be the co-star in my own home, without having to worry that the agents didn't call and the picture fell through so she's gonna be depressed for a week.

'I'm in one of those dangerous positions where I know too much. I could sit down and tell any actress what to do about her career and sometimes I start to do it, and I say, why am I doing this? Because they just don't know, they're babies. Nobody has taught them how to be good people. My mother went to school in Switzerland where there were forty girls each learning manners in order to marry a French nobleman and my mother went on to Wellesley. They don't do that here.

'Take Angie Dickinson, she's a lovely lady, but one time, and I think she's trying to forget it, she worked in a factory in Burbank. Marilyn Monroe, the same thing. These people did not come from the kind of solidness that you need for a home going through an earthquake. And I believe that every week in Hollywood is a new personal earthquake for every actress.

'I used to manage Susan Hayward and it was interesting because people would always tell me that she was snobbish. I found out, when we became best friends and I was her manager, that she was myopic and she had to wear glasses this thick and she couldn't get contact lenses. She couldn't see people. But she was never allowed to say she was myopic, so everybody just thought she was a snob.

'Cabrina says to me, "Jay, why can't you be normal?" But it's a very hard thing for all of us to be in this town. If you're Demi Moore or Michelle Pfeiffer, things are magnified. I'm an actor and I think I'm probably more of an actor than the actors, because I've lived the glamour. I handled the rat-pack, Frank Sinatra, Dean Martin, Sammy Davis Jr, Peter Lawford, Joey Bishop. I was pinched on the ass by Noël Coward, I double-dated with John Kennedy. I was raped by Jayne Mansfield. I've done so many things, and I didn't get any training in being normal. I haven't been normal since I was in grade school but I'm working on it. I take a pill called Prozac and it's helped me for six years. It just sort of straightens me out.'

Cabrina, a soft-spoken girl from Memphis, Tennessee, says: 'Everything in my life is different with Jay. I never thought that he was going to be normal and I certainly could never change him to be normal. He's eccentric and was before he even came to Hollywood. Now it's just quadrupled. It's a totally different lifestyle here. People are different, their careers are different. You might make five million when you're on top and you might make nothing for the next five years. Our lifestyle's not normal, I don't think that it ever will be. Here, we go to charity events, we go to the Academy Awards, we do something every night. We go with the celebrities. We have a lot of luxuries that I have never had and that most people are not fortunate enough to have, so, it's not normal now and it never will be, and I think that that goes for most people in this business or around this business. It's just totally different from surburban America.

'I had maybe two or three massages in my life before I met Jay and we're not overly spoiled, I'm sure we are to a lot of people, but now I find if I haven't had a massage in a couple of weeks, it's like, gosh, my back is killing me. I used to go to the grocery and everywhere in the world with no make-up, shorts, sweatshirt, whatever . . . but I've tried to be a little more careful for Jay so that they don't say, "That's Jay's wife, running around with no make-up, hair in a ponytail . . ." There's different things that matter to Jay and to people out here and they don't react to things normally. Everything from the car breaking down to even putting gas in the car, to having work done in the house, things become major events. People here are used to having everyone else do things for them and it's hard for me to understand. They don't know normal average American things that most Americans – even from extremely wealthy families – deal with and live with. It's far from reality out here, in every area.'

In his heyday Pamela Anderson would have been a perfect candidate for Bernstein. She became the super-hyped, increasingly controversial and watched *Baywatch* babe. Her raunchy antics in 1995 upset the show's *Honk* star, David Hasselhoff. But beneath all the cascading curls and distracting figure, she is a determined lady. The one-time *Playboy* cover girl is a TV phenomenon and spoke about her beginnings: 'I'm from a very small town in Canada called Ladysmith, British Columbia, and it's on Vancouver Island with probably about two thousand people there. My father is a chimney sweep and my mother is a waitress, and they still are to this day. And that's how I grew up. I had no idea I'd be doing what I'm doing now, that's for sure. I moved to Vancouver, which is the big city. Nobody wanted me to move to Vancouver because that's off the island and nobody wants to move off the island because they think it's too dangerous. Anyway, I decided that I would do it, and that's when I went to a football game with some friends who had free tickets. When I was there a cameraman zoomed in on my face and put me up on a big screen in front of 60,000 people. They pulled me down to the fifty-yard line, did an interview with me and introduced me as Pamela Anderson the Gluvine Girl because that was what was on my T-shirt. And they gave me a promotional campaign for a year. I did a poster and that was the first thing I'd ever done. That was the first time I'd ever seen myself on television, on a big screen like that, and *Playboy* discovered me from there. And the same person that discovered Dorothy Stratten, who was Playmate of the Year in 1980, and Kimberley Conrad [Mrs Hugh Hefner] discovered me and they wanted me to do a cover for *Playboy* in October 1989. They flew me down to LA. I did the cover. And then they talked me into becoming a Playmate. They said they would help me with my immigration work papers and everything seemed too good to be true. I was twenty-two years old when I went to the football game. It was overwhelming because I was just sitting in the stands with my friends and then to be pulled down into the field of the football stadium with 60,000 people watching. I was just petrified. About three months after that I was in Los Angeles – and coming from a very small town it was a real culture shock. I was only going to come down to Los Angeles and work for as long as I could work, and it just hasn't stopped, so I'm still here! And it's working out wonderful. I'm very fortunate. The first time I came to LA was my first plane ride. And I was afraid of that, first of all. I had no idea what to expect. I thought coming to LA and – and staying at the Playboy Mansion – was too much.

'I shot the October '89 cover and I met everybody at *Playboy* and everyone just seemed so professional, so wonderful. I was never gonna get this opportunity again. "Look where I've come from. I shouldn't even be here," I said. "I'll be a grandmother, I'll be able to look back and say, 'Look at the pictures I did.'" And *Playboy* magazine has such a history. I took it as such a compliment. I talked to my parents and my mother said she would do it in a second! I thought I would do the centrefold and then possibly go back to Vancouver, but a few television series asked me to stay and do a couple of things. I did guest shots on episodes of some TV series.

'*Playboy* was a start for me: they wanted to find the girl next door. They wanted a fresh wholesome look and it's just like playing a character. I said, "What if I was Marilyn Monroe or some of these other people that have posed for *Playboy*? What if I was Kim Basinger? Or Bo Derek? Or Linda Evans?" All these people had posed for *Playboy*. I said, "I can do it. What makes them different?"

'Nudity? It's not explicit nudity. I think it's beautiful. I think the human body is beautiful and I don't see anything wrong with it. I took it as a great compliment that I could do that. And playing the different characters and everything was what really made it easier for me. If I'd thought about it too personally I don't think I could have done it. But I would not be here if it wasn't for *Playboy*. I had no intention of coming to Los Angeles and they made it easy for me. It was a wonderful opportunity, and not everybody gets handed that opportunity.

'A lot of people get handed opportunities in their life, but they're just afraid to take the risk and do something about it. And I just decided it's a short life you live and I might as well just do whatever I can. I think I've accomplished a lot since I've been here because I've taken a lot of risks, and I'm not afraid to fail.

'It's difficult living in Hollywood after you've lived in a small town, because I'm used to a normal lifestyle and in Los Angeles it seems like when you walk out of your door you're working. It just seems like such an artificial town.

And I think it's a difficult place to have a relationship or a family. I think you come to LA to work. When it's time for me to have a family I want to be on my ranch with my horses and my goats and my chickens and my dog! I shouldn't say you can't take anybody seriously in LA, but it's just such a competitive town. Everybody wants what you have. My dad taught me how to meditate when I was seven years old and that's been a big part of my life and I wrote poetry and fairy tales and I have my own fantasy world outside of Los Angeles. I think just getting to know myself and staying centred and meditating has helped me. And analysts.

'I think the majority of Los Angeles is Hollywood. I live in Malibu. I'm in the entertainment business so everything I do, everybody I know, is in the entertainment business. All of my friends are make-up artists, stylists, prop people. Everybody has something to do with movies. And from the way I look at it LA is Hollywood. I've been in LA for four years, and I'm lucky because I know it doesn't happen this way for everybody. It just happened very fast. Maybe it will stop one day and I'll just be writing fairytales. But I don't set myself up for disappointment. I think this is just a stepping stone in my life.

'It's hard for my mum and dad to understand because they don't understand the competition that there is in Los Angeles. It's very difficult to get a series or even a guest spot. They're real happy for me but I don't think they understand. I've worked really hard, things haven't just fallen in my lap. When I see a little thread of something falling in my lap I grab it and I make sure that I make the most of it.

'There's a big difference between Ladysmith, a town of two thousand people, and Los Angeles. But Hollywood is a very small town on its own. Everybody knows each other, everybody knows what's going on. It's very similar to the small town where I grew up.

'I've found some good friends and been able to keep grounded in that way, but there are a lot of traps. It's easy to get caught up in wrong parts of Hollywood. You have to just remember what your priorities are and just keep a good person. There's a lot of temptation and especially when you're struggling in Hollywood. You just have to focus to survive here, to make it. To come from nothing and be in Hollywood is real difficult.

'I've had some different people working with me, managers, agents, and everyone tries to take advantage of you, to promise you a lot of things. What I've come to believe is that you don't believe anything until you see it in front of you or you're on the set and then that way you can't be disappointed. I was very näive and gullible when I came here and everyone said, "Oh, you're gonna do this, you're gonna do this," and I said, "Oh, great, when do I start?" and then I never heard from those people again! You start realizing that a lot of what people say here is just words coming out of their mouth.

'I think nowadays the casting couch is a myth. I don't think it happens much any more. I haven't come across it at all. I think that directors or producers are not gonna give you a substantial role unless you are a good actor. They're not gonna ruin their reputation. If someone offers you a role you got the role because you deserved it. You're not getting the role because you slept with somebody. Because that is the fastest way to ruin your career in Hollywood. Women who do it don't last very long, they get chewed up and spit out fast.

'I don't compromise myself in any way. I've been in interview situations where we're meeting a director and other girls are brushing up against him or being very flirtatious and I just totally avoid that. I think that's what separated me from most girls and that's why I got the part in *Baywatch*.

'I think party networking is a big part of Hollywood but I don't like to do it. I go to the odd party. That's why I live in Malibu now, I live away from all that. It's important to do different things. I work with animal rights – there's an organization called Actors and Others for Animals. A lot of people go out to do these charity events just to get their picture taken and to be put in a magazine somewhere. But I think that's pretty obvious.

'I don't know anybody who does drugs or alcohol. I don't drink. My parents were – are – alcoholics. My brother and I drank in high school and then when I really just saw what was happening to my family and my situation I said, "No, I'm just not interested." It just doesn't do anything for me and when I do have the occasional drink it just makes me feel terrible. I don't like feeling a little off, I like being 100 per cent on. I don't know many people who drink. California's very health conscious. It seems that everybody I know is vegetarian and jogs ten miles a day, and they don't drink or do drugs.

'It's taken me a while to earn good money, I mean I can pay my rent now. It is a sense of security because I've never had money before. I don't need much so now that I have some money I'm investing into property. I'm buying a little ranch, two and half acres, little log cabin. I just feel really good because I feel like I kind of made it, you know, on my own, I've actually accomplished something that I set out to do, and I think that's the biggest reward. It's not even the money, it's just about *finishing* something.

'I don't think money means power. A friend of mine says, "Big hat, no cattle!" It just seems like everybody wears their money on them a lot of the time. In Hollywood everyone thinks that they have to look a certain way and they have to be a certain way, and so they drive a $100,000 car but they don't have a home. All their money's tied up in what they look like, what they are, how they act.

'Does glamour mean power? I don't necessarily think so. I think power is a combination of everything, and I think the number one ingredient in power is having balls! You just have to be able to take risks. You can't be concerned with failing, because – if you fail what's the worst that can happen? You really can't be any worse off than you are before you start, and you're probably gonna learn something from making a mistake.

'Does sex have power? I don't think sex is power in Hollywood, but I think the issue of sex in movies is an important thing. I don't have any problems with it and I don't see why people should have problems with it and I think it should be talked about more and then there'll be less questions. I think women use their sexuality as much as men do. There are just as many pretty men in Hollywood as there are pretty women.'

Of course, for the majority of Hollywood People the

ongoing battle is to look the part – for ever. And they are all part of the weird and wonderful world of Hollywood People.

For every Pamela Anderson success story there are tales of those whose ambition overreached their talent or luck. Hollywood glory is as much happenstance as hard work. The Jay Bernsteins are as important as acting teachers. And the 'therapists', those who massage egos and other, even more sensitive parts, all play their roles. Some are walk-on parts, others cameos. High-class call-girls and the screen's leading ladies share the same restaurants. And sometimes the same sex partners. What is real? What is false? Is that bulge in your pocket because you're glad to see me or has Dr Rosenstein been at work? And that cleavage – the surgeon's knife? An implant? Names are changed. Images are created. Reality and fantasy often blur.

Hollywood is about role-playing. That's the business.

Some play it better than others.

But wherever they are on the Tinseltown totem pole they are all Hollywood People.

INDEX

Page references in bold type indicate more than
a passsing reference